The World's Greatest Geological Wonders: 36 Spectacular Sites

Michael E. Wysession, Ph.D.

THE
GREAT
COURSES®

PUBLISHED BY:

THE GREAT COURSES
Corporate Headquarters
4840 Westfields Boulevard, Suite 500
Chantilly, Virginia 20151-2299
Phone: 1-800-832-2412
Fax: 703-378-3819
www.thegreatcourses.com

Michael E. Wysession, Ph.D.
Associate Professor of Earth
and Planetary Sciences
Washington University in St. Louis

Michael E. Wysession is Associate Professor of Earth and Planetary Sciences at Washington University in St. Louis. Professor Wysession earned his Sc.B. from Brown University and his Ph.D. from Northwestern University, both in Geophysics.

An established leader in seismology and geophysical education, Professor Wysession is noted for his development of new ways to show how seismic waves propagate through the Earth and the use of these waves to create three-dimensional images of Earth's interior. These images have provided scientists with insights into the makeup of Earth and its evolution throughout history.

Professor Wysession is an author or editor of more than 20 science textbooks, ranging from elementary to graduate school levels. He is chair of the National Science Foundation's Earth Science Literacy Initiative and has represented the earth and space sciences in the creation of the new National Science Education Standards by the National Research Council and Achieve, Inc.

Professor Wysession received a Science and Engineering Fellowship from The David and Lucile Packard Foundation, a National Science Foundation Presidential Faculty Fellowship, and fellowships from the James S. Kemper and Lilly foundations. He has received the Innovation Award given by the Academy of Science of St. Louis and the Distinguished Faculty Award given by Washington University. Professor Wysession has had distinguished lectureships with the Incorporated Research Institutions for Seismology/Seismological Society of America and the National Association of Geoscience Teachers.

Professor Wysession also has taught *How the Earth Works* for The Great Courses. ∎

Table of Contents

Table of Contents

The World's Greatest Geological Wonders: 36 Spectacular Sites

Scope:

This course takes you to the world's most spectacular geological wonders, explains the forces that have formed them, and tells you the stories that have grown up around them. Our planet remains unique in the galaxy, even after space investigations have found many hundreds of other planets around other stars. Earth is covered with a vast diversity of geological environments that have, for millennia, inspired people with their majesty, beauty, and sometimes their strangeness. Yet certain places stand out above the others and epitomize the different types of amazing geologic phenomena that are found on Earth. These are the geologic wonders of the world, and in 36 lectures, we will travel to and investigate as many of them as we can. Each of the lectures focuses on one particular geographical location but touches on other examples, as well. Some of these wonders are well known, and you may already have traveled to them. Others you may never have heard of but will likely want to visit once you have learned of them.

There is no agreed-upon list of the 30 or 40 top geological wonders of the world, the way there was once a list of the Seven Ancient Wonders of the World. There is not even a single set of criteria by which to obtain such a list. If you asked 100 different geoscientists, you would undoubtedly get 100 different lists. Each lecture in this course is devoted to a particular geologic formation or process; the lecture then explores those wonders that most epitomize that topic. For instance, in the lecture on waterfalls, we will visit the Iguazu Falls in Argentina as the most spectacular example of these formations on Earth. Each lecture also highlights the remaining wonders that might appear on a "best of" list. For waterfalls, that list would include Victoria Falls, Angel Falls, and Niagara Falls. In addition, we will dedicate one lecture to an array of unique and unusual wonders (a "rogue's gallery" of sorts) that don't warrant a full lecture but deserve mention. Some of the geologic wonders we'll explore are obvious choices because of their sheer size and spectacle, such as the Grand Canyon or the Himalayas. Others, such as the Blue Hole off the coast of Belize, are chosen because they are perfect examples of a given topic in geology (in this case, sinkholes).

The goal of this course is to heighten your sense of wonder, awe, and respect for our planet. Many people find mountains aesthetically beautiful, but when you learn about their half-billion-year history, their formation through multiple collisions of ancient continents, and their experience of powerful erosion by glaciation, you begin to see something more than just a pretty vista. You view the surface of a mountain as a great battlefield—the site of a clash between Earth's internal forces pushing up the mountain and the Sun-driven forces of erosion relentlessly tearing it down. Rather than diminish their beauty, this added knowledge makes the mountain even more beautiful. The more you know and understand the natural world, the greater will be your love and appreciation for it. As you watch these lectures, you will begin to notice countless new features of the geologic world around you, and your growing interest and fascination will add a new dimension to your appreciation for the world in which you live. ■

Antarctica—A World of Ice
Lecture 19

This lecture on Antarctica isn't completely in keeping with the rest of our course because it highlights an entire continent as a geologic wonder. But the truth is that most of the continent showcases features that can't be seen anywhere else on the planet, at least not at this time. Of course, the big story here is ice on a grand scale. The volume of ice in Antarctica is about 25 million cubic kilometers. If it were to melt, the world's sea levels would rise about 63 meters—more than 200 feet! In this lecture, we'll look at ice flow in Antarctica and how climate change on this continent affects the rest of the world.

The World's Largest Desert

- The average thickness of ice in Antarctica is about 2 kilometers, but in some places, it's as thick as about 4.7 kilometers, or about 3 miles. The thickest ice is in East Antarctica, toward the center. The ice thins toward the edges, and along the west side of West Antarctica is a much shallower region. Antarctica is about 30 percent larger than Europe, and everywhere, ice is flowing out toward the ocean. It sometimes breaks off in giant sheets that are larger than individual U.S. states.

- East and West Antarctica are separated by the Transantarctic Mountains, one of the few regions in Antarctica where rocks stick up above the ice. East and West Antarctica have very different geologic histories. East Antarctica is an ancient piece of continent; it has been around for billions of years. West Antarctica is more recent, assembled from many different pieces formed by interactions between plates. It contains two large, floating sheets of ice right at sea level: the Ross Ice Shelf and the Ronne Ice Shelf.

- Technically, Antarctica is the world's largest desert, at least as defined by the rate of precipitation. The average rainfall here is equivalent to about 16 centimeters a year, a little bit more than 6 inches, which of course, falls mostly as snow. The mean temperature in the interior of Antarctica over the course of a year is −57°C, or −70°F. The record low is almost −90°C, or −129°F.

Ice Flow

- The ice is so thick in Antarctica that it actually pushes the rock of the continent down. The average elevation of the rock surface of Antarctica is only about 153 meters above sea level, but it's as much as 2.5 kilometers below sea level in some places. Around the edges of Antarctica, the ice flows, in a sense, up and over the mountains or through mountain passes. The result is similar to rivers that flow out at a single point.

- The flow rates are not steady. In much of East Antarctica, where the ice is thickest, the ice does not flow very quickly, but it tends to flow out through narrow channels. Some of the fastest flow rates, with the greatest amount of ice, occur at the Amery Ice Shelf, fed by the Lambert Glacier—the largest glacier in the world. The Lambert Glacier drains about 8 percent of the ice of Antarctica. The ice stream here is about 60 miles wide at the mouth and extends 400 miles up into the continent; the ice it places is more than 2.5 kilometers thick.

- This massive ice sheet drains out much of Antarctica to the Amery Ice Shelf; the flow rate is more than 1 kilometer per year in some places. The presence of this giant ice stream is explained by the fact that it sits over a large rift system, the Lambert Rift, with a fairly thin crust.

- In many places, ice accumulates in large, flat ice shelves that extend out over the ocean. These ice shelves are continuously breaking up and off to form enormous icebergs that then float away. Icebergs are much less stable than ice sheets and much more susceptible to changes in climate.

Exploration and Research in Antarctica

- Antarctica has a long history of being explored. The continent was first sighted in 1820, but it wasn't mapped until 1840, by U.S. Admiral Charles Wilkes. The first human beings to reach the geographic South Pole were the Norwegian explorer Roald Amundsen and his party in December of 1911. Another group, led by Robert Scott, reached the pole 34 days later, but these men all died of starvation and cold on the way back.

- Many countries have laid claim to parts of Antarctica, but it is owned by no one. In 1959, representatives from a dozen countries met to draft the Antarctic Treaty, which has since been signed by 47 nations. This treaty prohibits military activities, mining, and nuclear blasts in Antarctica; supports scientific research; and protects the continent's ecological zones.

- Ongoing experiments are conducted in Antarctica by more than 4000 scientists from many countries and with a variety of research interests. For example, seismologists have installed equipment there to learn about the geology of Antarctica and the behavior of glaciers. Other scientists travel to Antarctica to study meteorites or to examine the thickness of the ozone hole.

  o In the 1980s, a large hole began to form in the ozone layer of the atmosphere, which protects us from ultraviolet radiation. By the mid-1990s, that hole stretched more than 25 million square kilometers— about the size of North America.

Giant calving events, where large icebergs break off, can release energy that is the equivalent of magnitude 7 earthquakes.

5

As we now know, the hole was caused by the release of chlorofluorocarbons into the atmosphere.

o By the mid-2000s, with the banning of chlorofluorocarbons, the hole showed a small decrease in size, though it probably won't heal fully until the year 2060.

Mount Erebus

- We saw Mount Erebus in Lecture 4 as the site of one of the five lava lakes in the world. This volcano dominates Ross Island, not far from McMurdo Station. Mount Erebus is huge, reaching 4 kilometers above sea level, and it is the southernmost active volcano in the world.

- The volcano has large towers entirely made of ice that extend down a ridge directly away from the summit crater. These towers are the result of gases, primarily water vapor and carbon dioxide, leaking out along the ridge; these gases melt the ice, turn it into vapor, and then redeposit it along the sides of these large ice towers. The towers can be more than 30 to 35 feet tall.

- The hot gases underneath also create a spectacular set of ice caves with unusual ice crystals. The interiors of these caves glow with a stunning aquamarine color, caused by sunlight filtering down through the ice. The caves are also very dangerous; their shapes and locations shift based on changes in the patterns of hot gases leaking out the sides of the volcano.

Climate Change

- Interestingly, deposits of coal have been found in Antarctica. As we know, coal is metamorphosed, fossilized swamp material—rich organic material from swamps that has been buried, compacted, and turned into rock. This process takes place only in tropical areas, which means that in the past, this region—now the coldest, most frozen part of the world—once contained lush, green forests.

- Given the amount of ice in Antarctica, the effects of climate change here are important to the rest of the world. Although global temperatures have been warming slightly over the past century, the regional variations in temperature change in Antarctica are unusual. In many places in the interior of East Antarctica, the temperatures have gotten colder over the past century. But the fastest warming of almost anywhere in the world has been in the Antarctica Peninsula. Some places there have warmed by more than 8 degrees in the last 40 years.

- One place of particular interest in the context of climate change is the Larsen Ice Shelf. This formation is made up of separate ice shelves at the end of the Antarctica Peninsula. Larsen A, the smallest one, broke up in January of 1995. In the winter of 2002, a piece of Larsen B broke up and disintegrated in a single season.
  o These floating ice sheets are grounded at the base, but as the temperature warms and melting occurs at the surface, the whole ice sheet lifts up a bit. Crevasses become filled with melted water during the summer, which causes calving of the ice sheet.

  o Doug MacAyeal, a glaciologist at the University of Chicago, has suggested that long-wavelength ocean swells from distant storms may aid in breaking up ice sheets.

- The instability of the ice shelf and the delicate balance of floating ice shelves mean that in warm times, the ice shelf can entirely break apart. This apparently has happened during warm interglacial periods at the end of the Pliocene Epoch, about 2 million years ago. If the West Antarctica Ice Sheet disintegrated, sea levels would rise about 20 feet, flooding parts of many major cities. This ice sheet does seem to be deteriorating, but there's no sign that it will disintegrate in the near future.

- The fact that parts of the interior of Antarctica are getting colder seems to be related to the presence of the ozone hole. The loss of ozone causes a cooling of the stratosphere, which increases a circulation of westerly winds around Antarctica called the polar vortex. These winds trap cold air in the middle of Antarctica, but they also bring warm water and cause outer regions to warm up. Repairing the ozone hole might slow the collapse of the West Antarctica Ice Sheet, but it might also warm the interior and increase the flow of ice out of the center.

• The current icecap began about 35 million years ago. It started as alpine glaciers in the Gamburtsev Mountains in East Antarctica, which are now buried under 2 kilometers of ice. As a result, Antarctica holds a record of past climate change that has advanced our understanding of the large-scale cycle of warming and cooling that occurs on our planet.

Top Ice Sheets

• Greenland is the only other giant ice sheet on Earth, and it's melting at a fairly rapid rate. If it were to melt entirely, it would contribute another 7 meters to the sea-level rise.

• The North Pole icecap is freshwater ice, like Antarctica, but it's floating on the Arctic Sea. It's a very thin layer, about 3 to 4 meters in the places that don't melt annually, with occasional ridges of up to 20 meters or so. The Arctic ice sheet becomes much larger in the winter and shrinks in the summer, but the amount it shrinks has been steadily increasing.

• During past ice ages, North America has been covered with enormous amounts of ice. Just 15,000 to 20,000 years ago, for example, Chicago was under about 2 kilometers of ice. The ice from this period left us the Great Lakes and many glacial features across North America.

Suggested Reading

McGonigal, *Antarctica*.

Myers, *Wondrous Cold*.

1. If all of the ice were suddenly removed from Antarctica, the sea level would rise instantaneously and would then continue to rise slightly for a long time. Why?

2. Sometimes, airplanes land on the ice plateaus in East Antarctica. Why is it then challenging to get them started again?

Antarctica—A World of Ice
Lecture 19—Transcript

Hello, my name is Michael Wysession, and welcome to Lecture 19 of our course on the Geologic Wonders of the World. In the last several lectures, I've talked about large rock towers at the surface of the Earth, places like Devils Tower in Wyoming. In this lecture, I'm really switching gears, and I'm going to go down to the South Pole to look at the giant ice sheets of Antarctica.

I struggled a little bit with this one because it really isn't in keeping with the rest of this course to have an entire continent be one of the Geologic Wonders. But I just couldn't figure out what particular feature of Antarctica to highlight, at the expense of so many others. I mean, the whole thing really is a wonder. For most of the continent you see things that you just can't see anywhere else on this planet, at least not at this time. I will talk briefly at the end of the lecture about the time during the Ice Ages when North America was covered by a giant sheet of ice.

And another thing about Antarctica is that it is just so unmarked and unspoiled by humans. Antarctica is big; it's really big. It's larger than Europe. In fact, it's twice the size of Australia, but the population is so small. It's about 1,000 in winter, about 4,000 in summer. This really has the lowest population density of anywhere in the world. In the wintertime, it's about one person per 13,000 square kilometers.

Antarctica is, however, really hard to get to, and unfortunately, most people will never have a chance to see it. It has a pretty big moat around it, and the southern ocean that surrounds Antarctica has some of the worst weather, the worst storms, and the largest waves of any part of the ocean. So, even if you visit it on a large ocean cruise ship, be prepared for some really large waves. However, there are tour boats that go there, and a few thousand lucky scientists and tourists get to visit it each summer.

The big story here is ice, ice on a very grand scale. The volume of ice in Antarctica is about 25-million cubic kilometers. This is so much ice, if it were to melt, the world's sea levels would rise about 63 meters; that's over 200 feet.

A lot of continental area would be flooded. Remember, about three-billion people around the world live within 60 miles of a coastline. However, it has melted in the past, and continents have been flooded. We've already seen this in previous lectures, all of the ocean-formed sedimentary rocks in places like the Grand Canyon and Bryce Canyon, so we know that this does happen.

The average thickness of ice here is about two kilometers, but it's as thick as about 4.7 kilometers. It's about three miles. And what you see is a tremendous variation in the ice, the largest, thickest ice is in East Antarctica towards the center. It thins toward the edges, and along the west side of West Antarctica we have a much shallower region.

Antarctica is about, as I said, 30 percent larger than Europe and everywhere here the ice is flowing, flowing out towards the ocean where it breaks off in giant sheets that are sometimes larger than individual U.S. states. Most of the ice is in this large region here in East Antarctica where it can be several kilometers thick, though the fastest flow rates are actually in West Antarctica. This difference between East and West Antarctica may seem a little strange to you when you are at the pole. After all, if you're down there your compass is constantly moving direction. South is always going to point to one particular location in the South Pole, but there is a difference, and it's easier to get around if you think of this side being West Antarctica because it's actually in the Western Hemisphere. In fact, the arm of the West Antarctica peninsula points in the direction of South America.

The East and West are separated by a mountain range that runs about through here. These are called the Transantarctic Mountains, and it's actually one of the few regions where you have rocks sticking up above the ice. East and West Antarctica have very different geologic histories. East Antarctica is a very old piece of continent, kind of like Australia. It's been around for billions of years. Whereas West Antarctica is more recent, geologically speaking, assembled from many different pieces over a set of interactions between the plates. West Antarctica is particularly interesting because it contains two large ice shelves, the Ross Ice Shelf, which is the largest, and the Ronne Ice Shelf, and these are large, floating sheets of ice right at sea level.

Interestingly, Antarctica has a lot less ice than you might otherwise think. Technically, Antarctica is the world's largest desert, at least defined by the rate of precipitation. Remember I talked about the global circulation pattern where you had warm air rising up at the equator; coming down roughly at 30 degrees north and south is very cold, dry air, and another band of warm air rising up at about 50 to 60 degrees north and south coming down at the poles. Well, it's that cold, dry air coming down at the South Pole that just doesn't bring any moisture with it. The average rainfall here is equivalent to about 16 centimeters of rain a year. That's a little bit more than six inches, though, of course, it falls mostly as snow, but it stays around a long time because it's just so cold there. After all, the mean temperature in the interior of Antarctica, the average temperature over the course of a year, is $-57°C$, that's $-70°F$. In fact, the record low here is almost $-90°C$, $-129°F$. This is the coldest temperature measured anywhere on Earth's surface, by far. In fact, if you're there with exposed skin, your skin will freeze in a matter of seconds. In the summertime there, which is the winter in the Northern Hemisphere, of course, and you go along the coasts, especially along the Antarctic Peninsula, the temperature can actually rise a little bit above freezing, but it doesn't happen very often.

The ice here is so thick that it actually pushes the rock of the continent down. And this is a very interesting phenomenon because the average elevation of the rock surface of Antarctica is only about 153 meters above sea level; that's about the elevation of St. Louis. But it's as much as 2.5 kilometers below sea level in places. And what you have is these large pieces of ice actually pushing down the crust, sort of like sitting down on a mattress. If you sit down, the whole mattress is going to compress down from your weight. Well, the same thing happens to the rock of the Earth, and it will flow downward under the weight of the ice on top of it. What you end up with is mountains often around the edges of Antarctica and the ice actually has to flow, in a sense, up and over these mountains or through mountain passes, and the result is kind of like rivers that flow out at a single point.

The flow rates, as I mentioned, are not at all steady, and there end up being very large ice streams where the ice flows out. In this map, blue shows very slow ice speeds, so you can see much of East Antarctica where the ice is thickest, the ice is not flowing very quickly, but it tends to flow out through some very narrow channels where the yellow colors are. Some of the fastest flow rates, with the most amount of ice, actually occur here at the Amery Ice Shelf with the Lambert Glacier, which is the world's single largest glacier in the world, by far. The Lambert Glacier, over in this area, actually drains about eight percent of the ice of Antarctica. The ice stream here is about 100-kilometers wide at the mouth, about 60 miles. It extends 400-miles up into the continent, and the ice it places is over 2.5-kilometers thick.

This massive sheet of ice flows down draining out much of Antarctica. It drains to the Amery Ice Shelf, and the flow rate is more than a kilometer per year in places, at least down near the mouth. This giant ice stream is there because it actually sits over a large rift system called the Lambert Rift, with a fairly thinned crust. This process is not uncommon; we've seen it before. It's the reason that the Mississippi River flows down the path that it does. There's actually an ancient rift in the middle of North America, the Reelfoot Rift, that runs through the New Madrid fault rift system, 750-million years ago, North America was pulling apart, and the crust was stretched and thinned, and it's a location of low elevation, and that's why the river flows down there. The same thing happens here in Antarctica with the Lambert Rift.

In many places, ice accumulates in large, flat ice shelves that extend out over the ocean. And these ice shelves are continuously breaking up and off to form enormous icebergs that then float away, much less stable than ice sheets, and much more susceptible to changes in climate.

One area that is really significant is the Ross Ice Shelf here in the part of West Antarctica that's just adjacent to McMurdo Sound here. The Ross Ice Shelf is the largest ice sheet. It's about the size of Texas, up to 750-meters thick in places. Some of the pieces that break off are huge. The largest, in fact, was about 12,000 square miles, about the size of Belgium, one single iceberg. And these things can float away and take decades to melt. Some people have actually proposed towing giant icebergs offshore of cities in dry areas as a source of water; that's how much fresh water is in them. I mean, after all, Antarctica contains about two-thirds of the world's fresh water.

We zoom in here and we see a region off McMurdo Sound where the United States base, McMurdo Station, is located. It's right adjacent to the Ross Ice

Shelf, and it's right adjacent to this large mountain that you see on the left side here. That's actually Mount Erebus, a very large volcano that I'll talk about in a moment. McMurdo Sound has to be crossed by ice-breaking ships, and you can see that's a fairly daunting challenge. But every year it will bring fresh supplies to the base, especially fuel for heating and food and other things; they have to break through this with ice breakers, and sometimes the ships get stuck and have to wait until the following summer to break free, literally frozen in place over the Antarctic winter.

Supplies are then transported by tractor or plane to other places around Antarctica, such as the South Pole base. In fact, there are now roads that will allow you—they're not really roads, they're tracks—that will take you from McMurdo to the South Pole base. In fact, some of my colleagues who are down in the South Pole this winter actually said that there was a minivan that had driven there from McMurdo, a souped-up minivan, but a minivan nonetheless.

There is a lot of science that goes on at the South Pole, including a permanent seismic station there. However, instruments that are located right at the pole have to occasionally be relocated because the ice, of course, is flowing. This isn't solid rock here, the ice is moving, actually about 10 meters a year, over 35 feet. It's a very strange place to be. It's dark half the year, and even during the summertime, the sun never rises very high, but just moves around the horizon. If you look at an animation of the sun over the course of a day, you can see something very odd. I mean, what's wrong with this picture? Usually in our perspective, the sun rises or sets. But here in Antarctica, in this sped-up image, it simply moves in a circle around the horizon, at least during the summertime. As you get towards the edge of the summer, the sun starts to dip below the horizon for extended periods. It's the world's longest sunsets, and then, of course, at nighttime, you see nothing. It's just dark for half the year.

Antarctica has a very long history of being explored, people trying to reach the South Pole. Antarctica was first sighted back in 1820, but it wasn't mapped until 1840, by the U.S. Admiral Charles Wilkes. The first human beings to be able to reach the Geographic South Pole, of course, were Norwegian Roald Amundsen and his party, which was in December of 1911, just a little more than 100 years ago. Another group, led by Robert Scott, got there 34 days later, but they all died of starvation and cold on their way back.

It is hard to imagine just how large, and stark, and bare Antarctica is. Words can't describe it. If you cross it, even in an airplane, you go for hours, hundreds or thousands of miles, seeing nothing but cold, flat ice. And sometimes this ice is very treacherous because it may look flat, but if you try to land a plane on it, there can be enormous crevasses covered by small layers of snow. In fact, work that's done down there, up on the Antarctic plateaus, is very dangerous. The pilots will often fly around a site for a long time trying to find a place to land. That's what makes crossing it so remarkable. These treks 100 years ago, or even recently. Over the 2011-2012 Antarctic summer, Felicity Aston took 59 days to cross-country ski across the whole continent, pulling a sled carrying her own supplies. It's really a remarkable feat. Of course, it's a little easier nowadays because she can be in regular contact with her family and friends via satellite phone every day.

Many countries have laid claim to parts of Antarctica, but it's actually owned by no one. There was an Antarctic Treaty signed in 1959 by a dozen countries. It's up to 47 so far. And this treaty prohibits military activities, mining, nuclear blasts, it supports scientific research, protects the continent's ecological zones. And remarkably, it's entirely self-policed by the research and the countries themselves.

There're ongoing experiments here of many different types that are conducted by more than 4,000 scientists from many different countries and a variety of research interests. Frankly, I find it very reassuring to know that there really is a place on Earth where there are never any military activities. There's no fighting, there're no nuclear tests, there're no land issues surrounding mining, where people from more than a dozen countries live together and work together harmoniously. I mean, kudos to the Antarctic science program for providing this opportunity.

One example of scientific research there is my own field of seismology, and many colleagues of mine go there every winter, at least, again, it's summer down there, to install and service a large network of seismometers. This is to understand the geology of Antarctica, but also, it's a great way to figure out

15

how the glaciers work, because as the ice flows, it creaks and cracks, and you can actually measure and monitor the glacier flow using the seismometers. In fact, these giant calving events where large icebergs break off can release so much energy, they can be the equivalent of magnitude seven earthquakes.

Another interesting phenomenon occurs when some of these large ice sheets will actually rise and fall with the tides, and they may be locked during low tide on the seabed, and then lifted off the seabed during high tide and slip a little bit, causing this periodic chirping. And other colleagues of mine have actually gone and put seismometers on these giant ice sheets and measured this chirping motion.

Other colleagues of mine go down there to find meteorites, which is a wonderful place to find a meteorite. Usually if you have a rock fall from space anywhere around the world, it can be hard to distinguish it from any other rock that might be on the ground. But if you go in the middle of a giant sheet of ice where there's no rock around, if you find rock within it, there's only one place that it came from. And so people will go to the mouth of the glacier and collect the rock when the glacier melts, and these meteorites simply get dumped at the front there.

One area of very important research is examining the thickness of the ozone hole. Ozone, which is a molecule of three oxygen atoms, naturally exists within the stratosphere. But interestingly, in Antarctica, over the Antarctica pole, during October time, due to patterns of circulation near the ozone can begin to thin. Starting in the 1980s, a very large hole in that ozone layer began to form. And this poses a danger because it's the ozone that protects us from ultraviolet radiation. And if you remove the ozone, then anyone underneath, whether it's penguins or scientists, is in danger from that radiation. By the mid-1990s, that ozone hole had reached more than 25-million square kilometers. That's about the size of North America. It turned out that the ozone hole was caused by gases that we were emitting, chlorofluorocarbons, that we were using in refrigerators, and when the global community realized this, these chlorofluorocarbons were banned in 1989. And the amount of chlorofluorocarbons released has gradually, but steadily, dropped since then, essentially as old refrigerators die off.

The hole leveled off in the mid-2000s, and there's actually a hint of decrease, though it probably won't heal fully until the year 2060. This is incredibly important because scientists at NASA projected that nearly all of the world's ozone, globally, would have been gone in a century without this ban. It's a fantastic example of countries working very well together to solve a common problem.

Another place of great interest for research is the regions called the dry valleys. And these are places that, or course, are freezing cold, but so dry that they don't have any snow or ice. There aren't a lot of other places on Earth like this, but there are other places in the solar system like this, in particular, Mars. So the dry valleys are now being visited every year by planetary scientists in preparation for work looking at Mars and its history of cold climate there.

One very fascinating place, in particular, on Antarctica is the volcano Mount Erebus that I talked about just before. We saw Erebus in Lecture 4 as one of the only five lava lakes in the world. It dominates Ross Island, not far at all from McMurdo Station, so it's very easy to get to it and study it. This volcano is huge. It reaches four-kilometers above sea level, and it is the southernmost active volcano in the world. Even more strange, it has very large towers entirely made of ice that extend down a ridge directly away from the summit crater. These are the result of hot gases, primarily water vapor and carbon dioxide, that leak out along the ridge and they melt the ice, turn it into vapor, and then redeposit it along the sides of these large ice towers when it reaches the cold air. These towers can be more than 30-, 35-feet in height. The hot gases underneath also create a spectacular set of ice caves with very unusual ice crystals that are growing on the roof of the caves. The whole caves glow this stunning aquamarine blue color, which is from the sunlight filtering down through the ice. And the caves, it's very interesting, but also very dangerous, keep shifting their shapes and locations based on the changes in the patterns of the hot gases leaking out of the side of the volcano.

One topic that's, of course, very relevant to Antarctica is climate change. If you look at the rocks in Antarctica, the few places where you can actually find them, where there isn't ice, such as in the Transantarctic Mountains, you find something very unusual. You find deposits of coal. Coal is metamorphosed, fossilized swamp material. This is rich, organic material from swamps that have been buried, and compacted, and turned into rock. This only happens in very warm areas, tropical areas, so not only have there been periods when there has been no ice in Antarctica, but there have been periods where this whole region in the past has contained lush, green forests. So clearly, the climate on our planet has changed enough over the past, that you'd go to the coldest, most frozen part of the world, and it's a lush, tropical jungle.

How climate change affects Antarctica is also important to the rest of the world, of course, given the amount of ice there. One thing that's fascinating is, even though globally temperatures have been warming slightly over the past century, the regional variations in temperature change in Antarctica are very unusual. There are many places in the interior in East Antarctica where the temperatures have gotten colder over the past century. However, the fastest warming, pretty much anywhere in the world, has been in the Antarctica Peninsula. There are places where it has warmed by more than eight degrees in the last 40 years.

One place that's of particular interest in the context of climate change, is the Larsen Ice Shelf. And these are there separate ice shelves that exist at the end of the Antarctica Peninsula. Larsen A, the smallest one, broke up in January of 1995. In the winter of 2002, a piece of the Larsen B ice shelf, the size of a U.S. state, okay it's Rhode Island, but Rhode Island is still a state, broke up and disintegrated in a single season. And it's really remarkable here. This region had been stable for about 10,000 years here, and it was gone in a couple of months, simply disintegrating and breaking away. Essentially, what happen is these ice sheets are floating. They're grounded at the base, but as the temperature warms at the surface, it melts at the surface and the whole ice sheet rises up a little bit. You get crevasses that will fill with this melted water during the summer, and this causes calving off of these sheets, and these sometimes can then suddenly break off very suddenly. In fact, some of these ice sheets can actually break up in a single day. This is what happened in another ice sheet known as the Wilkins ice sheet. There was a piece about 400 square kilometers that broke up in a single day in March of 2008. It didn't break off, it simply disintegrated. Some of the research done by a glaciologist at the University of Chicago, Doug MacAyeal, suggested that long wavelength ocean swells from distant storms came in and simply broke this thing up, and it fractured into pieces. The remaining 14,000 square kilometers is now in the process of breaking up as well, long, narrow strips of giant sheets of ice essentially working their way out into the ocean.

The West Antarctic Ice Shelf is particularly susceptible to climate change because it's actually grounded below sea level. This is the area I mentioned earlier that's up to 2.5-kilometers below sea level. The instability of the ice shelf and the delicate balance with the floating ice shelves around means that in warm times the ice shelf can entirely break apart. This apparently has happened during warm interglacial periods at the end of the Pliocene Epoch, about two-million years ago. If the West Antarctica Ice sheet did disintegrate, you'd get 3.5- to 6-meters of rise. It's up to 20 feet, again, it would flood many parts of many major cities. The West Antarctica Ice Sheet does seem to be deteriorating, but there's no sign of it disintegrating at all in the near future. No one expected, however, the Wilkins Ice Shelf to disintegrate in a single day.

It's interesting the way things are sometimes interconnected. The fact that parts of the interior of Antarctica have been getting colder actually seems to be related to the presence of the ozone hole. The loss of ozone causes a cooling of the stratosphere, which increases a circulation of westerly winds around Antarctica called the polar vortex. This actually traps cold air in the middle of Antarctica and causes the middle to stay cold, but it also brings warm water around and causes outer parts, like the Antarctica Peninsula, to warm up.

Interestingly, repairing the ozone hole might actually slow the collapse of the West Antarctica ice sheets, but it also might warm the interior and increase the flow of ice out of the center of Antarctica. If all of Antarctica melted, most major cities would be flooded, and again, because so much of the population lives near coastlines, much of the world's population would need to be moved.

The current ice cap began about 35-million years ago. It started as Alpine Glaciers in the Gamburtsev Mountains in East Antarctica, which are now totally buried under two kilometers of ice. As a result, Antarctica contains the record of past climate change. It has a continuous record of ice that has locked in the composition of gases, ices, and dust over many years. So, it's really important for us to be able to carry out research in Antarctica because it is this record here that has given us our whole history of ice ages, a large cycle of warming and cooling that's happened over the past million years.

Well it's time for my top five. First, obviously, I have to go to Greenland because it's the only other giant ice sheet out there. If Greenland were to melt, it would contribute another seven meters to the sea level rise, added to 63 meters from Antarctica. And in fact, Greenland is actually melting at a fairly rapid rate currently. Greenland is the world's largest island that isn't considered a continent. It's actually an autonomous country within the Kingdom of Denmark. It has a population of about 57,000 people and has actually the lowest population density of any actual country. By the way, Greenland has only one National Park, but it's actually most of the northern part of the island, filled with glaciers. It's almost half the total area of Greenland, the world's largest National Park.

Next, we go to the North Pole Icecap. The North Pole Icecap is freshwater ice, like Antarctica, but it's floating on the Arctic Sea. It's a very thin layer about, three to four meters, in the places that don't melt annually, and it's much thinner in places that do with occasional ridges of up to 20 meters or so. The Arctic ice sheet actually fluctuates considerably in size. It's much larger in winter, and then it shrinks in the summer. But the amount that it shrinks in the summer has been steadily increasing. In fact, the extent of the Arctic Ice is now shrinking by about four percent per decade. In addition, in the past 40 years, the thickness of the Arctic ice sheet has thinned by 40 percent

This is really significant for people because ships have never been able to cross it to take the shortest path from Europe to the Pacific, what's known as the Northwest Passage. It's 6,000 miles shorter than going down around through the Panama Canal. Annual shrinking finally opened up the Northwest Passage in the year 2004, starting with a few ships, and the U.S. Navy projects that it could be a viable international shipping route in just a few years if the shrinking of the ice sheet continues.

Last, I want to take us to the North American and Scandinavian ice sheets during the last Ice Age. I showed this briefly during the lecture on the Blue Hole, the animation of the ice sheet in North America shrinking. Antarctica, it turns out, the ice sheet there can't get much larger. The strong ocean currents in the southern ocean there would simply break it up. But the top part of North America can have an ice sheet, and it can be huge. And during Ice Ages, North America gets covered with enormous amounts of ice. During the last ice age, just 15-, 20,000-years ago, Chicago was under about two kilometers of ice. In fact, in Missouri, the ice came down as far as Route 70, essentially the extension of the Mason-Dixon Line. It left a few remnants, like the Great Lakes or the thousands of lakes in Minnesota, Minnesota after all is called the land of 10,000 lakes, and all sorts of glacial features all over North America.

In the next lecture, I'm going to continue with this theme of ice, and I'm going to go to the world's most studied glacier with a very strange and unusual way of behaving, the Columbia Glacier in Alaska.

Columbia Glacier—Unusual Glacier Cycles
Lecture 20

In Antarctica and Greenland, which are covered with ice that flows out in all directions, the glaciers are simply massive, both in length and width. These are continental-style glaciers. In these regions, ice flows down to the coasts whether mountains are present or not. In the rest of the world, glaciers operate differently. They snake between and around tall mountain peaks, eroding away the mountains themselves in the process. In this lecture, we'll discuss alpine glaciers and visit one of the most remarkable glaciers in the world: the Columbia Glacier in Alaska.

Formation of Glaciers

- Glaciers start from snow, which as we know, is light and fluffy. The density can be only about 8 percent of water. In the formation of glaciers, snow gets compacted, largely by the process of melting and refreezing during the summer. Eventually, the snow becomes névé, a form of snow made from small, round ice crystals that is about half as dense as ice.

- On a glacier, the névé survives the summer; it becomes a new layer of ice on top of the glacier called the firn. Year after year, multiple layers of firn accumulate and continue to compact. The final density of the ice of glaciers is, therefore, much higher than that of snow. It's about 85 percent of the density of water.

- The ice of glaciers tends to have a blue color to it; contrary to popular belief, this coloring is not due to the scattering of light off of air bubbles within the ice. Glaciers appear blue for the same reason that ocean water appears blue. Water slightly absorbs red light, removing it from white light that passes through it, which gives the remaining light a slightly blue color.

Slow-Moving Rivers

- Alpine glaciers are much like rivers of liquid water, although they move much more slowly. Still, glaciers may move even more rock than rivers do. Essentially, we can think of them as giant conveyor belts, tearing down whole mountain ranges over time.

- A glacier gains its mass through accumulation—snowfall in the higher parts. The glacier then runs downhill, eventually losing ice, either by direct melting or through a calving off of pieces at the front, a process called sublimation.

- Glaciers tend to start small at higher locations and become larger as they flow downhill, ending up with a system of tributaries, much as rivers do. Technically, ice is a mineral, one with a very low melting point. Like basalt, it can flow, and it flows faster down the middle than it does along the bottom or the sides. That's also similar to how a river behaves.

- The process called glacial plucking involves the ice ripping up large chunks of rock as it slides along. The rock is then embedded into the bottom of the glacier, which accelerates the process of grinding out the rock underneath. In some places, after a glacier is gone, you can see long streaks, called glacial striations, carved out by rocks embedded in the glacier.

- A glacier doesn't move constantly at the same speed, and anytime it goes down over a slope, it tends to speed up. That's when it forms crevasses: Essentially, the glacier starts to flow too fast for the ice to remain flowing in a fluid manner; it then cracks and opens up crevasses. As soon as the glacier levels out again, the crevasses close.

- Though glaciers are made of ice, they're often not white because of all the rock that gets torn off along the sides or falls down onto the glacier. In fact, an enormous amount of rock can pile up at the bottom of a glacier.
  - As the rock gets torn off the sides of mountains, it creates long lines that run through the middle called medial moraines. At

the edge of the glacier, all the rock that is deposited is called the terminal moraine.

o The front of a glacier can be stationary, advancing, or retreating, but at all times, ice is still flowing downhill, depositing any rock within it at the front. If temperatures are warming, the front of the glacier might retreat uphill, but the ice is still flowing downhill. If temperatures are gradually cooling, the front of the glacier advances. If the glacier front is sitting still, all the rock gets deposited in one place, similar to what we see in a river delta.

o Once glacial sediment is deposited, melted ice water carries that sediment downstream in sediment-clogged braided rivers. We saw this in the lecture on the Ganges Delta. A network of streams also carries sediment under the glacier.

Types of Glaciers

- A wide variety of factors, including snowfall, elevation, temperature, humidity, and topography, can make glaciers behave in different ways and take different forms.

- A surging glacier, for example, can suddenly flow 100 times faster than normal. In Alaska, these glaciers tend to start and stop suddenly and may experience up to 100 surge events per year. In Norway, surging glaciers tend to start and stop gradually, sometimes over a period of years. This process is often controlled by a buildup of water underneath the glacier.

- In the case of a debris-covered glacier, so much rock has fallen on top of the glacier from surrounding slopes that a significant fraction of its mass is rock. This greatly affects the rate at which the snow melts because rock tends to absorb sunlight much more efficiently than ice.

- The Columbia Glacier in Alaska is a tidewater glacier, meaning that it dumps its ice directly into the ocean, where icebergs break off and float away. This glacier is one of the most studied in the world.

Recession of the Columbia Glacier

- The first map of the Columbia Glacier was made in 1899 by a team led by George Harriman. At the time, the Columbia Glacier was 66 kilometers long from its end up to the top, making it one of the longest in the world. The glacier has been revisited regularly in the time since, and for 80 years, not much changed. Starting just before 1980, however, the glacier started to recede upstream at a remarkable pace.

- By 1995, the Columbia Glacier was only about 57 kilometers long; by 2010, it was 49 kilometers long, with no indication that the retreat would stop anytime soon. In this process, the whole glacier has thinned by about 400 meters, as well.

The recession of the Columbia and other glaciers in Alaska has had a significant impact on plants and animals there, moving their habitats northward at the rate of about 12 meters a decade.

- Alpine glaciers around the world have been melting and receding at a rapid rate in response to globally increasing temperatures. Over the last couple of decades, glaciers have lost an average of about 1 meter of ice and thickness each year. Over the past 50 years, the total loss has been about 14 meters, or 50 feet. But the Columbia Glacier has lost 400 meters, which tells us that something more complicated is going on here.

- The behavior of tidewater glaciers—and other types of glaciers—is not a direct response to climate change or other factors on the ground, such as sea level, humidity, and so on.
  - o Instead, tidewater glaciers are part of a complex feedback system that involves the amount of snowfall, the area of accumulation, the level of water into which the ice flows, and the construction of the terminal moraine. As a result of these factors, tidewater glaciers advance and retreat in a particular cycle.

  - o At the beginning of the cycle, very little of the glacier is exposed across the water. The glacier then goes through a period of advancing; the front begins to move outward, pushing the terminal moraine. It reaches some final point, with the terminal moraine growing quite large and essentially blocking up a large amount of ice.

  - o Then, some trigger goes off, and after moving forward at rates of 10 to 50 meters a year, the glacier will suddenly move back and its speed will increase. An enormous amount of ice is dumped into the water. It's likely that recent rising temperatures have provided the trigger that started the Columbia's rapid recession.

- This unusual process of tidewater glaciers advancing slowly over decades or centuries and then receding rapidly over a much shorter time makes them fascinating geologic oddities. They also have an important relevance on a larger scale. When a tidewater glacier recedes, it dumps an enormous amount of ice into the ocean, which directly affects sea level. By the end of this century, global sea level may rise 1 to 2 meters with an increased flow of glaciers, particularly the tidewater glaciers in Greenland, playing a major role.

Top Alpine Glaciers

- On the west end of the Tibetan Plateau the world's greatest concentration of 8000-foot mountains sits amid the Karakoram, Kunlun, Pamir, and Tien Shan mountain ranges. The world's longest alpine glaciers are also found here, and the largest among them is the Fedchenko Glacier, at 77 kilometers long. It's in Tajikistan in the Pamir Mountains.

  o The Fedchenko Glacier starts at an elevation of more than 20,000 feet and drops more than 10,000 feet, ending at the Balandkiik River. The Fedchenko is only about 3 kilometers at its widest, and the maximum thickness of the ice is about 1 kilometer.

  o Still, with all the tributaries that flow into it, the Fedchenko contains about 35 cubic miles of ice. From the many medial moraines, we know that many different tributaries combine to flow down into this one stream. Some of these tributaries used to be separate glaciers, with separate termination points, but they have been encompassed by the Fedchenko into a large tree-shaped pattern.

  o The moraine at the end of the Fedchenko also shows that the front of that glacier has been rapidly receding over the past century.

- The Siachen Glacier in the Karakoram Mountains of India is the world's second longest glacier, at 70 kilometers. It sits along the border of Pakistan and India and has the dubious distinction of being the world's highest military battleground. India and Pakistan have fought over this border intermittently since 1984, and both countries still maintain costly military bases there at elevations of more than 6 kilometers.

- The Biafo Glacier is also in the Karakoram Mountains. It is the world's fourth longest glacier, at 63 kilometers. At the very top of the Biafo Glacier is another long glacier, the Hispar Glacier, which is 49 kilometers long. The two create the longest continuous glacial system anywhere outside of Antarctica.

- The world's third largest glacier is the Brüggen Glacier, at 64 kilometers, in southern Chile. This glacier empties into the vast Southern Patagonian Ice Field. Note that we don't find glaciers only in Alaska or on the Tibetan Plateau; anywhere that tall mountains exist, we will find snow, ice, and glaciers.

Suggested Reading

Hambrey, *Glaciers*.

Sharp, *Living Ice*.

Questions to Consider

1. How are the Pamir Mountains related to the Himalayas?

2. Long Island, New York, is a glacial moraine that formed during the ice ages as ice flowed down from Canada, carrying rock within it. Why do you think Long Island sits south of the Connecticut coast?

Columbia Glacier—Unusual Glacier Cycles
Lecture 20—Transcript

Hello. My name is Michael Wysession, and welcome to Lecture 20 of our course on the Geologic Wonders of the World. In the last lecture on Antarctica, we saw a strange world filled with ice. During that lecture, we visited the world's longest glacier, the Lambert Glacier, a massive ice stream that's more than 400-kilometers long and 100-kilometers wide in places.

In this lecture, I will continue to look at the process of glaciation by visiting one of the most remarkable glaciers in the world, the Columbia Glacier in Alaska. We're also going to visit other glaciers that are found around the world, mostly in mountainous areas, typically called Alpine glaciers. I should say a word about the difference between Alpine-type glaciers and glaciers in Antarctica. The Lambert glacier in Antarctica is a massive ice stream. For Antarctica and Greenland, which are covered with ice that flows out in all directions, the glaciers are simply massive, both in length and width. These are continental-style glaciers. Because the whole land is covered with ice, there ice is going to flow down to the coasts whether there are mountains there or not. For the rest of the world, glaciers operate differently. They end up snaking in between and around tall mountain peaks, and in the process, they erode away the mountains themselves over time. Most of these are called alpine glaciers, though there are other kinds, as I will discuss in a moment. They have less ice, but they're more varied and more unusual in how they behave.

If you sail up the coast of Alaska, you will find a lot of glaciers, a huge number, in fact, over 100,000 separate, individual glaciers. About 5 percent of all of Alaska is presently covered with the ice of glaciers; that's about 75,000 square kilometers. This includes 11 different mountain ranges, one very large island, Kodiak Island, and large numbers of islands, the Aleutians and the Fox Islands.

Glaciers are made of ice, obviously, but, how do they form? This may sound like a silly question, but obviously solid blocks of ice aren't falling from the sky; snow does. So, I guess the question really is, how does snow turn into the ice of glaciers? Well, glaciers start with this stuff, snow. And it tends to be fairly light, and what they end up with is this stuff, ice. So, how does this process happen? Actually, it happens very slowly, over about 30 to 100 years or so.

The snow starts out very light and fluffy; you know that yourself from your own experience. The density can be only about 8 percent of water. That snow eventually gets compacted, largely by melting and refreezing during summer days. Eventually it becomes a snow that's made from small, round ice crystals. It's called névé. And this is about half as dense as ice. This was actually made from an ice shaver, so this is a good example of névé. It's been a little warm around here recently. If you go to a glacier, you will see that the névé survives the summer, it becomes a new layer of ice on top of the glacier—we call that firn. And year after year, multiple layers of firn accumulate and continue to compact. The final density of ice of glaciers is therefore much higher than the snow. It's about 85 percent of the density of water. That's different than the ice cubes that you make in your freezer, which tend to be about 92 percent of the density of water. Why is this different? It turns out, even with all the compaction that happens in the glacier, you can't get all the air bubbles out.

The ice of glaciers tends to have a blue color to it, and contrary to popular belief, this is not due to the scattering of light off of the air bubbles within the ice. It's actually because of the same reason that ocean water appears blue. Remember back in the lecture on the Blue Hole? I talked about how water slightly absorbs red light, removing it from white light that passes through it, and therefore it gives the remaining light a slightly blue color. Well the same thing happens here. The blue wavelengths of light are not absorbed, so they are what gets left over.

Alpine glaciers are very much like rivers of liquid water, only they move a lot more slowly, but they may end up moving even more rock than rivers do. Essentially you can think of them as giant conveyor belts, tearing down whole mountain ranges over time. We can look at a diagram for how this process occurs. Essentially, the glacier gains its mass through accumulation, that snowfall in the higher upper parts, and that glacier then runs downhill, eventually losing its ice, either in terms of direct melting to water or a calving off of pieces at the front or a process called sublimation; that's where you go directly from the ice phase to water vapor phase.

You know, nature just hates mountains, and glaciers are the primary mechanism that it uses to demonstrate that. Glaciers tend to start small at the higher locations and become larger as they flow downhill. You end up with a system of tributaries much like rivers do. The ice is entirely solid. Actually, ice is technically a mineral, just one with a very low melting point. We've already talked about minerals melting. We looked at basalt, which melts at $1,100°C$, water melts at $0°C$; it's still a mineral, but it can flow, and it flows faster down the middle than it does along the bottom or the sides, and that's also very similar to how a river behaves.

The glacier does something, however, that's very important. It also slides right along the bottom, and this causes a process called glacial plucking. The ice can literally rip up large chunks of rock, which then get embedded into the bottom of the glacier, which then help accelerate that process of grinding out the rock underneath. In fact, if you go to some places after a glacier is gone, you will see long streaks gouged out in the bed of the valley. These are called glacial striations, where rocks embedded in the glacier have just carved out long passageways.

But the glacier doesn't go constantly at the same speed downhill, like a river. And anytime it goes down over a slope, it will tend to speed up., and you can tell that simply by looking at a photograph, because that's when it tends to form a set of crevasses. Essentially, the glacier starts to flow too fast for the ice to remain flowing in a fluid manner, and it cracks and opens up these crevasses. However, as soon as the glacier levels out again, those crevasses will close up again. Though the glaciers are made of ice, they're often not white, and that's because all of the rock that gets torn off either along the sides or that falls down onto it. In fact, by the time you get to the bottom of a glacier there can be an enormous amount of rock piled up in the front.

As the rock gets torn off the sides of the mountains, it creates long lines that run through the middle, and these are called medial moraines. So for instance, if I have one ice stream coming through here, as it carves by, it's going to gouge the rock off here. If I have another arm of the glacier that comes by here, it's going to gouge them together. And then when they come together you'll see the black line running right down the middle. That's a symbol that two separate ice streams have come together, so we can see this medial moraine run down the middle here.

When you get to the end of the glacier, all of that rock gets dumped, and that's called a terminal moraine. And so essentially, you're taking all the sediment from up here and you're dumping it down here. The front of that glacier can either be stationary, advancing, or retreating, but at all times, ice is still flowing downhill, dumping any rock within it right at the front. If your temperatures are warming, that front of the glacier might retreat uphill, but the ice is still flowing downhill. If temperatures are gradually cooling, the front of the glacier advances. If the glacier front is sitting still, however, all of the rock gets dumped in one place, and that's very similar to a river delta as well.

Once the glacial sediment is deposited, melted ice water carries that sediment downstream in sediment-clogged, braided rivers. We saw this in the lecture on the Ganges Delta. There is so much sediment given the water there that it just sort of moves the sediment around, and you get this braided, interconnected stream. There's actually a whole network of streams that goes on under the glacier as well, carrying sediment down.

It's a mistake to think, based on the simple picture I just showed, that all glaciers behave in the same way. Actually, there's a wide variety of factors, snowfall, elevation, temperature, humidity, the topography, that can make the glaciers behave in very different manners and actually take a variety of different forms. One type of form is called a surging glacier. These are very variable in the speeds at which they flow. They can have episodes where they will suddenly flow 100-times faster than normal. In Alaska, they tend to start and stop very suddenly, and there might be a dozen or a hundred surge events per year. This is very different from how the glaciers in Norway work, where you also have surging glaciers, but they tend to start and stop surging gradually, sometimes over years. And this process is often controlled by a buildup of water under the glacier that will suddenly allow it to start moving more quickly.

You can also get debris-covered glaciers. In this case, you have so much rock that has fallen down on top of them from the surrounding rocky slopes, that they actually contain a significant fraction of their mass as rock. This greatly affects the rate at which the snow melts because the rock tends to absorb sunlight much more efficiently than the ice, which tends to reflect most of it.

The Columbia Glacier in Alaska is another special kind of glacier. It's something we call a Tidewater Glacier, meaning that it dumps its ice directly into the ocean, where icebergs break off—we call that process calving—and float away. There are about 50 Tidewater Glaciers in Alaska. That sounds like a lot, but remember, given the number of glaciers there, that's less than one tenth of one percent of Alaskan glaciers, so they're fairly infrequent.

However, the Columbia Glacier is one of the most studied glaciers in the world, for more than a century, fortunately, and that allows us to understand the unusual behaviors of these kinds of glaciers. Some of the work has been done here by a glaciologist at the University of Colorado, Tad Pfeffer, who's fortunately also a professional photographer, and has taken some incredible photos of the glacier. I know Tad from a small town in Northern New Hampshire, where we both spent part of our childhoods clearing mountain trails up in the Presidential Range of the White Mountains.

How do we know what the Columbia Glacier was like so far back in the past? Well, our first map comes from 1899, and this was down by a team led by Edward Harriman. Harriman was a very rich and powerful railroad magnate, and his doctors told him he'd been working too hard and needed a vacation. He decided to go hunt grizzly bears in Alaska. But not one to do anything in a small way, he bought a boat, outfitted it with an elite group of scientists, artists, photographers, and naturalists, and spent the next two months sailing from Seattle to Siberia and back, mapping and documenting everything in between.

What they found was the Columbia Glacier, back at that time, was 66-kilometers long from its end all the way up to the top, making it one of the longest in the world. Today, that would make it the third longest alpine glacier anywhere in the world. For reference, the longest, Fedchenko Glacier in Tajikistan, is 77-kilometers long.

The Columbia Glacier has been revisited regularly in the time since, and for 80 years, not much changed. It was still about 66-kilometers long. But starting just before 1980, a very strange thing happened. It was almost as if a gun went off at the start of a race. The glacier started receding back upstream suddenly, at a remarkable pace. By 1995, it was only about 57-kilometers long; by late 2000 it was 54-kilometers long; by the year 2010, it was 49-kilometers long, with no indication that the retreat would stop anytime soon. It this process, the whole glacier had thinned by about 400 meters as well. If you look at the pictures of this, it's really stunning. Here's a picture of the Columbia Glacier winding its way down here and ending out in Prince William Sound here, dumping its ice right into the water. What I want you to do is take a look at the peak of this mountain here as a reference for where the mouth of this glacier is. So let's go from 1965 to 1980, by this point the ice was still well past this mountain, but it had already begun that process of breaking away and retreating back. If we go to 1996, we see that the end of the glacier is right at the same level with that peak. If we move on to 2004, the glacier has now moved back up. All this white stuff in here is all the mass of icebergs that are now slowly floating away out across the sound.

If you look at the level of that retreat, you can see how year after year, ending with this line here for 2010, the glacier is very rapidly moving backwards. The front has receded more than 20 kilometers since 1980. It would be really easy to say that this was a direct result of globally warming temperatures, but actually, something much more complicated is going on here. After all, it is true that alpine glaciers around the world have been melting and receding at a rapid rate in response to globally increasing temperatures, so glaciers are a wonderful sort of measuring stick for global temperatures in that sense. So, for example, if you were to look at a graph at the average glacier thickness change over the last 50 years or so, you can see that things weren't changing much 50 years ago. But certainly over the last couple of decades, every year, on average, a glacier has lost now up to about a meter of ice and thickness. Over this 50-year span, the total loss has been about 14 meters or about 50 feet.

The Columbia Glacier lost 400 meters, and so, something very different is going on here. The result is that this whole process of melting the glaciers in the Columbia area and other places in Alaska, all of Alaska's glaciers, in fact, have been receding during the last few decades. It's had a significant impact on plants and animals, as well as the geology. As temperatures have been warming, the habitats of plants and animals have been moving northward, because it's just been more mild at northern latitudes. They've been moving northward, in fact, on a globally average rate of about 18 kilometers a decade; it's about a mile a year. At the same time, plants and animals are now moving uphill into the mountainous areas at an average rate of about 12 meters a decade. Essentially, what used to be ice, is now being covered with vegetation.

The tidewater glaciers are not so simple. They don't fit the model of these other Alaskan glaciers, in fact, neither are surge glaciers or debris-covered glaciers. Not one of these behaves in a way that directly responds to climate change. They behave in a way that we refer to as a non-linear response, meaning there isn't a direct one-to-one correlation between the behavior of the glacier and any ground, whether it's sea level, or temperature, or humidity, or anything.

Tidewater glaciers involve a complex feedback between the amount of ice that enters the bay, and that's a result of how much snow falls on the mountains, therefore how much humidity is, and how large that area of accumulation is, and also the level of the water, and the construction of a terminal moraine, which I just talked about with the Alpine glaciers, where all the sediment gets dumped, because this impedes the process of calving, essentially it's like a cork in a bottle that stops that ice from leaving. The Tidewater glaciers end up, as a result, advancing and retreating in a very particular repeating cycle. They begin far back in this cycle with very little of the glacier actually exposed out across the water. And then they go through a period of advancing here and, of course, the glacier is always flowing, but the front begins to move outward, and it begins to push this terminal moraine across. At some point, it will reach a final point. It will extend out as far as it can, and this terminal moraine can end up growing quite large, essentially blocking up a large amount of ice here. Then, some trigger goes off, it's not really clear what happens, but after moving forward on the rates of maybe 10 to 50 meters a year, the front will move backward, but the speed will suddenly increase, and the ice that had been flowing 10 meters a year, may now flow as much as a kilometer a year. So now, you begin dumping an enormous amount of ice into the water. The Columbia Glacier is in one of those retreating periods where the whole front is receding quickly, and ice is being massively dumped into the Prince William Sound.

Interestingly, the Chugach Mountains here in Alaska, where Columbia is, have five separate tidewater glaciers. They all empty into Prince William Sound, and they span all of the stages of the tidewater glacier cycle. Columbia, as I mentioned, is rapidly receding. The Meares and Harvard glaciers are slowly and stably advancing. They are getting longer; and the Yale and Shoup glaciers, are in a stable position after having already rapidly receded all the way back to their starting positions. It is likely that the recent rising temperatures have provided the trigger, the "gun," that's caused the start of this period of rapid recession of the Columbia. After all, during the little Ice Age, back in the 17th to 19th centuries, all of the tidewater glaciers advanced and had became unstable in how long they were. With the rise in temperatures that began in the mid 1800s, all of these tidewater glaciers had already reached their critical tipping points and receded back, except for the Columbia. It's the last one to do so.

This unusual process of tidewater glaciers, rivers of ice, advancing slowly over decades or centuries, and then receding rapidly over a much shorter time period, makes them very fascinating geologic oddities. They also have an important relevance on a larger scale. As I said, when a tidewater glacier recedes, it allows an enormous amount of the ice of that glacier to flow into the ocean, and that directly affects sea level. In fact, it's predicted that the global sea level may rise one to two meters by the end of this century, with an increased flow of glaciers, particularly the tidewater glaciers in Greenland, playing a major role.

For example, during 1996 to 2007, a little more than 10 years, the Columbia Glacier alone—I mean this one glacier out of 100,000 in Alaska, and hundreds of thousands around the globe, even including all the melting in Greenland and West Antarctica—was responsible for one percent of the global sea level rise. I'm going to come back to the topic of sea levels and how they change over geologic time in a couple of more places in the course, particularly when we visit the Maldive Islands later on.

Well, it's time for my top-five list, and let me visit some other spectacular Alpine Glaciers around the world. First, let me return to the most impressive mountains in the world, in the Tibetan Plateau, which we saw back in Lecture 8. The Himalayas get most of the attention in this part of the world, but if you travel around to the west end of the Tibetan plateau, there are some other mountain ranges there that would be the star of any other planet. These are the Karakoram, the Kunlun, Pamir, and Tien Shan mountains in a land-locked part of the world that most people, frankly, don't know very much about. This is the region that sits at the intersection of China, India, Pakistan, Afghanistan, Kazakhstan, Kyrgyzstan, Uzbekistan, and Tajikistan.

The greatest concentration of 8,000-foot mountains is not in the Himalayas, it's here. In fact, K2, in the Karakoram Mountains, is only 237 meters lower in elevation than Mount Everest. I mean, that's just a couple of football fields. The world's longest alpine glaciers are also found here, and the prince among them, as I mentioned before, is the Fedchenko Glacier, 77-kilometers long. It's in Tajikistan in the Pamir Mountains.

The Pamirs have a long history. Pamir means a broad flat valley, carved by a large ice sheet, surrounded by mountains. And if you go to this region, this is what you see in a very impressive way. The Fedchenko Glacier starts very high up. It actually starts at an elevation of over 20,000 feet, and drops more than 10,000 feet, ending at the Balandkiik River. Unlike things like the Lambert Ice Stream, which can be 100-kilometers wide, the Fedchenko is very narrow, snaking its way through the mountains. At its widest it's only about three-kilometers wide, and the maximum of ice is about a kilometer thick.

Still, with all the tributaries that flow into it, it contains about 35 cubic miles of ice. That's about a third of the size of Lake Erie. When you look, you can see many stripes running down the length of it, and so now we know that's a clue. That means, because these are the medial moraines I talked about, there must be many different tributaries combining together to flow down into this one stream. A lot of these, actually, used to be their own separate glaciers, with their own separate termination points, but the Fedchenko pirated them and took on a large sort of tree-shaped pattern, all these separate arms coming together. The moraine at the end of the Fedchenko also shows that the front of that glacier has been rapidly receding back over the past century.

However, interestingly, in this case, it's largely associated with a change to a drier climate in this region. There's actually been much less precipitation.

Next, let me go to the Siachen Glacier in Karakoram Mountains of India. This is the world's second longest glacier, at 70 kilometers. It sits along the border of Pakistan and India, and it has the dubious distinction of being the world's highest military battleground. India and Pakistan have fought over the border up here intermittently since 1984, and both countries still maintain costly military bases at elevations of over six kilometers here.

Next, let me go nearby to the Karakoram Mountains in Pakistan for the Biafo Glacier. This is the world's fourth longest glacier at 63 kilometers. At the very top of Biafo Glacier, you actually meet the top of another long glacier, the Hispar Glacier that's 49-kilometers long, that's no small amount on its own, carving away the other side of the mountain. In fact, you can go directly from one up over the top down the other, and that creates the longest, continuous glacial system anywhere outside of Antarctica. It's 100-kilometers long. This highway of ice actually used to connect two independent, separate ancient mountain kingdoms—the kingdoms of Baltistan and Nagar. This is the way that the two would communicate with each other.

There are many other glaciers that I could mention, like Baltoro Glacier, also in the Karakoram Mountains of Pakistan; or Inylchek Glacier; it's in the Tien Shan Mountains in Kyrgyzstan. Both of these are just a little bit shorter at 62 kilometers in length.

But, last I want to take you to Southern Chile to the Bruggen Glacier. And this is actually the world's third longest by length at 64 kilometers. It doesn't empty out into the ocean here; it actually empties out into the vast Southern Patagonian Ice Field, and I mention this last because I didn't want to give the impression that you only find big glaciers in Alaska or up in the Tibetan Plateau. I mean, anywhere you have tall mountains, you're going to have snow, you're going to have ice, and you'll have glaciers. Remember, there were even glaciers up on the top of the slopes of Mount Kilimanjaro sitting at the equator.

Climate change has been the rule on this planet, long before people were around. There have been times when nearly our whole planet has been covered with ice. Remember back in the lecture on the Burgess Shale I talked about the Snowball Earth scenario where almost the whole planet was covered with ice. And there have also been times when there was hardly any ice at all, times like the Cretaceous, when the dinosaurs ruled. So clearly our planet has undergone a huge variety of climates, and this has tremendously shaped, not only the geology of our planet, but the very course that evolution has taken as well.

It was during a very recent warming period, just 2.5 thousand years ago, that the mountain passes in places like the Pamir Range up in the Tibetan Plateau opened up. The ice melted, and trade started between the eastern cultures in China and the western cultures in the Middle East and Europe. I mean, this was very beneficial for cultures both in the East and West. Well, we're in another such warming trend. And people up in the mountains of the Himalayas are going to find it a slightly nicer place to live, but people down in arid regions may have a rougher time of it.

In the next lecture, we're going to look at the spectacular sights of what is left over once the glaciers are done carving away the mountains, and we're going to look at what's left over and visit the beautiful fiords of Fiordland National Park, in southern New Zealand.

Fiordland National Park—Majestic Fjords
Lecture 21

In the last lecture, we discussed the power of glaciers, carrying a continuous stream of ice and rock from the tops of mountain ranges down to the base, often the sea, as at Columbia Glacier in Alaska. In this lecture, we'll look at what's left over when the ice is gone. For this, we'll visit Fiordland National Park, on the South Island of New Zealand, a classic and spectacular example of glacial erosion. The park covers a large region with many fjords, lakes, mountains, and tall cliffs that rise up out of the sea. The fjords here are called sounds, and in this lecture, we'll look at three famous ones, Dusky Sound, Doubtful Sound, and Milford Sound.

Three Famous Sounds

- Dusky Sound is the largest of the fjords in Fiordland National Park. It's 40 kilometers long—that's a 40-kilometer arm of the ocean reaching up into the mountains—and 8 kilometers wide at the mouth. Dusky Sound has many different islands and inlets. During an active rainy season, this whole region breaks into hundreds of waterfalls, cascading beautifully down the steep slopes of the fjords.

- Doubtful Sound was originally named Doubtful Harbor by the famous British explorer Captain Cook because he wasn't sure if it was navigable by boat. The sound here heads up into three large fjords, which also break out into hundreds of waterfalls in the rainy season. Two of the waterfalls, Browne Falls and Sutherland Falls, are permanent and are among the tallest in the world.

- Milford Sound is much smaller than Dusky or Doubtful Sound, but it's the real attraction for visitors to this area. Within Milford Sound, massive rocks reach out of the water to heights of almost a mile. Mitre Peak, the most striking of the rocks here, is the tallest continuous sea cliff anywhere in the world. There are also two permanent waterfalls here: Lady Bowen Falls and Stirling Falls. Milford Sound receives about a million visitors a year.

Features of Alpine Glaciation

- Milford Sound and the surrounding fjords contain excellent examples of many of the features we find where alpine glaciation has occurred. For instance, we see many examples of the classic U-shaped glacial valleys. Many glacial valleys begin as V-shaped stream valleys, but as the ice flows throughout the valley, it carves the land into a wide U shape.

- Often at the back end of one of these glacial valleys, we find a cirque, a half-bowl–shaped formation, that represents the far area of ice carving. Cirques often contain large boulders that have fallen down from the surrounding hills, and they often block the water to form lakes that are known as glacial tarns.

Doubtful Sound breaks into hundreds of waterfalls in the rainy season and has a rare abundance of sea mammals, including seals, dolphins, and whales.

- An unusual structure found in alpine regions is the hanging valley. Here, one arm of a glacier has cut off another arm, resulting in a sudden drop, where one glacial valley ends and plunges downward to the floor of another glacial valley. These tend to be the locations of some of the most spectacular waterfalls, such as Sutherland Falls in Fiordland National Park.

- Mitre Peak in Milford Sound is a perfect example of a horn. This feature forms by the action of glaciers carving a mountain away on all sides until all that's left is a tall, narrow, razor-sharp peak in the middle. The Matterhorn in the European Alps is a classic horn.

Formation of Fiordland

- If these valleys were once filled with ice, why is there now ocean extending great distances through them? We've seen the answer to this question in previous lectures. The sea level rose 400 feet at the end of the last ice age. When these valleys were being carved out by ice, they were above sea level, but as the sea level rose, the ocean wove its way in between these peaks.

- The mountains at Fiordland are at the edge of the Southern Alps. The mountains rise quickly here to more than 10,000 feet—about 2 miles—but they are not the result of continental collision.

   o The island of New Zealand lies right along the boundary between the Pacific Plate and the Australian Plate. North of New Zealand, the Pacific Plate is plunging underneath the Australian Plate at the large Tonga and Kermadec subduction zones. South of New Zealand, the subduction goes in the other direction. The rock of the Australian Plate plunges underneath the Pacific Plate.

   o This situation isn't stable; in fact, the process is tearing the island apart at what's called the Alpine Fault, one of only three transform faults in the world. There is motion across this fault of several centimeters per year that has been taking place for more than 20 million years. In fact, the rock on the north part of the South Island is actually the same as the rock in the southwestern part of New Zealand. It has been dragged to the northeast by the motion along this fault.

   o As a result of this fault and many others in New Zealand, the island is seismically active. The Alpine Fault has had four large earthquakes in the past 1000 years and seems to be overdue for a fifth.

   o Compression along the Alpine Fault is pushing up the Southern Alps at a rate of about 7 centimeters a year.

- The stunning cliffs and peaks of Milford Sound are made of granite. This composition is a typical one for the cores of continents but not for the rocks at the top of continents. Granite has large interlocking crystals and is very hard; thus, it can maintain steep vertical slopes for long periods of time.
  - This granite forms deep underground. Both the Appalachian Mountains in the United States and the Southern Alps were once much taller than they are today. Much of the rock has eroded away, exposing rock that was once deep within the cores of the mountains. In the case of the Southern Alps, there may have been as much as 20,000 feet of sedimentary rock that has eroded away from the top.

  - The rock that is pushed downward in a subduction zone, forming the "roots" of mountains, heats up, and some of the minerals melt, eventually becoming granite. Because magma is lighter than the surrounding rock, it begins to move upward, but if the mountains are tall, it can't reach the surface to erupt. It cools underground as large granite plutons or batholiths.

  - As the mountains begin to erode, the plutons are exposed. Not only do the mountains erode down, but the weight is lifted off of the crust, which rebounds upward. This uplift brings the granite that was once miles beneath the surface up to the top.

- Metamorphism is another geologic process that occurs when plates collide and mountains form. Here, the mountain-building process causes metamorphic reactions that create other rocks from preexisting rocks, through temperature, pressure, or the action of hot fluids flowing through.
  - At the Fiordland National Park, one of the most culturally important metamorphic rocks is a particular type of jade called greenstone. This rock is made from fibrous minerals, such as asbestos.

  - Greenstone is used by the Maori culture to make jewelry, weapons, tools, and religious talismans.

Top Glacial Erosion Sites

- Yosemite in California is the classical example of a glacial valley and of the exposure at the surface of a giant granite pluton—the Sierra Nevada Batholith. This region formed 200 to 150 million years ago, when the Farallon Plate was subducting beneath the western United States. Uplift in the region began about 10 million years ago, exposing the granite, which was then exposed even more by glacial erosion that began in the region starting about 3 million years ago.

  o Most people visit only the small Yosemite Valley at the west end of the park, but the east side shows fantastic examples of a process called exfoliation. Essentially, as layers of rock erode, the release of pressure enables the rock behind to expand, causing cracks and a new layer of rock to peel off.

  o One of the most recognizable features of Yosemite is El Capitan, a stunning vertical face of granite, about 1 kilometer high. In fact, El Capitan is actually post-vertical in places, which makes it a favorite of rock climbers.

  o Another famous site in Yosemite is Half Dome, again, created by the activity of glaciers. Yosemite also has some spectacular waterfalls, including Yosemite Falls, the highest waterfall in North America at almost 1 kilometer high. Bridalveil Falls in Yosemite is a classic hanging valley fall, similar to what we saw with Sutherland Falls in New Zealand.

  o Those who visit Yosemite in the spring may see frazil ice. As the snowpack of Yosemite starts to thaw, the streams begin to overrun their banks and flood through the whole valley, turning all of the snow into a giant, slowly moving wall of slush.

- In Norway, we find Geirangerfjord and Sognefjord. Geirangerfjord is the most visited fjord in Norway, and Sognefjord is the longest fjord in Europe, stretching more than 200 kilometers inland. Surrounding cliffs rise a kilometer above the water, but they are actually much steeper because they extend beneath the surface of the water almost another mile down.

- The only fjord in the world that's longer than Sognefjord is Scoresby Sound in Greenland. Scoresby Sound is 350 kilometers long. It branches out like a huge tree into many other fjords that cover a total area of Greenland of almost 40,000 square kilometers. Scoresby Sound is often filled with a variety of large icebergs of many unusual shapes.

- Gimmelwald and Grindelwald are two small, beautiful glacial valleys in the Swiss Alps. The valleys are very narrow, with pine forests and green fields along the floor. The cliffs rise up incredibly high on one side to the spectacular peaks of the mountains Eiger, Munch, and Jungfrau.

Suggested Reading

De Roy and Jones, *New Zealand.*

Patrick and Peat, *Wild Fiordland.*

Questions to Consider

1. Why is the granite rock of the cliffs of Milford Sound stronger and more resistant to weathering than sedimentary rocks?

2. What do you think will happen to New Zealand if earthquakes continue to occur along the Alpine Fault?

Fiordland National Park—Majestic Fjords
Lecture 21—Transcript

Hello. My name is Michael Wysession, and welcome to Lecture 21 of our course on the Geologic Wonders of the World. In the last lecture, I looked at the power of glaciers, carrying a continuous stream of ice and rock from the tops of mountain ranges down to the base, often the sea, such as at Columbia Glacier, in Alaska. In this lecture, we're going to look at what is left over when the ice is gone, and we're going to visit Fiordland National Park, on the South Island of New Zealand.

This region is a classic and spectacular example of glacial erosion, of what's left over after the ice has carved away a set of mountains. Fiordland National Park covers a broad expanse, a huge region, with many separate fjords, lakes, mountains, tall cliffs that rise right up out of the sea. The fjords here are called sounds, but it's the same thing as a fjord, and though there are many of them, there are three famous ones, three very large ones, Dusky Sound, Doubtful Sound, and Milford Sound.

Dusky Sound here is the largest of the fjords. It's 40-kilometers long; that's 40 kilometers of an arm of the ocean, or arms reaching up into the mountains, eight-kilometers wide, huge at the mouth. Dusky Sound is the most complex of them. It has many different islands and inlets. In fact, the largest island in the middle of the sound, Resolution Island, contains a region called the Five Fingers Peninsula, which kind of gives you a feel for what this land looks like.

The sides of the fjords here are so tall and steep that there is no way to get here from the mainland, except either by sailing by boat or by flying into a very small airport. In other words, the walls are so steep no roads get down there. There is an interesting change in the appearance of this whole region over the course of a year, and during a very active rainy season, the whole area breaks out into hundreds of waterfalls that cascade beautifully down the steep slopes of the fjords. This region was first visited by the famous British explorer Captain Cook, back in 1770, and it was frequently visited over the next 50 years or so by many boats that were hunting seals, which are still very plentiful and can be seen playing in the waters here.

Next, if we move up along the coast we move to the next large sound, Doubtful Sound. It was named Doubtful Harbor also by Captain Cook, and that was because he wasn't sure if it was navigable by boat. He thought that because of the narrow conditions and the complex winds within the harbor, it was doubtful that if he sailed inside the fjord he'd ever be able to sail back out again. Whalers and sealers in the region felt the same way, and the name stuck; it changed only to Doubtful Sound. The sound here heads up into three large fjords, which also break out into hundreds of waterfalls in the rainy season. Two of the waterfalls are permanent year round, and they are some of the tallest in the world. Browne Falls cascades almost a kilometer down a 45-degree slope, and Sutherland Falls, which is about a half a kilometer, comes down a slope that's a little bit steeper. These aren't true waterfalls in the sense that we've seen previously with Iguazu Falls or Victoria Falls. The water doesn't fall straight down, but nonetheless, they're spectacular as large amounts of water come down the sides of these cliffs.

For Doubtful Sound, there is a road that reaches the sound from the mainland. It heads over a narrow pass, and this place has a rare abundance of sea mammals in the water, seals, bottlenose dolphins, orcas. It's also visited by a wide variety of whales, such as right whales, humpbacks, mink whales, sperm whales, and giant-beaked whales. There's a really nice quote from a former Governor-General of New Zealand, Charles John Lyttelton who wrote,

There are just a few areas left in the world where no human has ever set foot. The westerly arms of the two great lakes Manapouri and Te Anau seem to reach out to meet the deeply etched easterly indentations of Doubtful and Dusky Sounds, and yet between the lakes and the coast jagged razor-backed mountains rear their heads into the sky. This is big country.

A country, moreover, as capricious as a prima donna, one day peaceful, a study in green and blue, the next melancholy and misty, with low cloud veiling the tops, and only a few days later perhaps a turbulent welter of wind and water, wind moreover that seems to blow almost hourly from a different direction, and water that cascades down the valleys in a rushing torrent.

It's really very nicely put.

One place that's not untouched by human feet is Milford Sound, a little bit farther up the coast. And Milford Sound is much smaller than Dusky or Doubtful Sounds, but it's really the real attraction for visitors here. In fact, in the 2008 Traveler's Choice Destinations Awards by TripAdvisor, this region was judged the world's top travel destination. Many famous people have visited it. The writer Rudyard Kipling once came and declared it the 8th wonder of the world. Currently about a million people actually come to this very remote region every year to see the incredible sites there.

Within Milford Sound you have massive rocks that reach right up out the water, up to a mile high. Mitre Peak, the most striking of the rocks here, is actually the tallest, continuous sea cliff anywhere in the world. It rises 1.7 kilometers—that's over a mile straight up from Milford Sound.

Other huge peaks in the area include The Elephant, a kilometer and a half high peak that resembles the elephant's head, and also the Lion, which bears the resemblance to the shape of a crouching lion. There are two permanent waterfalls here, Lady Bowen Falls and Stirling Falls, that are absolutely spectacular; though, like the other sounds in the region, it can have many hundreds when it rains, which it does a lot. The mean rainfall in this part of the world is up to seven meters per year. It's one of the wettest places in the world. In fact, it can rain up to 10 inches a day at times. Seeing how narrow Milford Sound was, Captain Cook didn't even try to enter it, and, in fact, it wasn't even explored until 40 years later when a Welsh Captain, John Grono, entered and named it Milford Haven after his home in Wales.

Though the whole Fiordland area has remained largely unexplored due to its geographical inaccessibility—it's just so hard to get here—Milford Sound very quickly attracted international attention. A low pass into the Sound was found called the Mackinnon Pass, back in 1888, and very soon this was part of the Milford Track, a walking path used by visitors from around the world. New Zealand is famous for its tracks. These are very rugged hikes, but there are often very nice hotels around, so you can stay in luxurious conditions at night.

About 1950, a tunnel was finally built through another low pass, and a road finally was built into Milford Sound. And nowadays, there are, as I said, about a million people who visit each year, and most of these tourists will take a four-hour bus ride from Queenstown, the closest large city, about a one- to two-hour boat ride around the sound, and then take the bus back. As a result, Milford Sound is very quiet for most of the day, there are only about 100 people who live there fulltime, but it's incredibly busy for a couple of hours right in the middle of the day.

Milford Sound and the surrounding fjords contain great examples of all of the features that you would typically find where alpine glaciation has occurred. For instance, you see many examples of the classic U-shaped glacial valleys. Now, we've seen before when you have a river, it tends to cut a V shape down into the rock to form a V-shaped canyon; the water just flows at the bottom, and as the water flows down, the canyon will tend to widen out to keep that V shape. Many glacial valleys begin as V-shaped stream valleys, but the ice flows throughout the valley, and it carves the whole thing out into this large, wide U shape.

Often at the far back end of one of these glacial valleys, you'll find something called a cirque, which is like a half-bowl shaped circular formation, which represents as far back as the ice was carving. In fact, if you go skiing out on the Western U.S., many of the best skiing is in some of these large cirques up at the tops of mountains. The cirques often contain large boulders—house-sized rocks that have fallen down from the surrounding hills—and they often block the water to form lakes that are known as glacial tarns.

One very unusual structure that you find in alpine regions is something called a hanging valley, and this is where one arm of a glacier has actually cut off another arm, and so you have a sudden drop where one glacial valley just ends and plunges down, sometimes huge distances, to the floor below of another glacial valley. And these tend to be the locations of some of the most spectacular waterfalls, such as Sutherland Falls, there in Fiordland National Park.

All of these features are found around the world, but the thing about Milford Sound is everything is just so large; the size of them is staggering. You can take this cruise boat to the base of some of these waterfalls and look up enormous distances to see water plunging down on top of it. Mitre Peak, as I mentioned, which is the tallest continuous sea cliff in the world, is the perfect example of a horn. The classic horn is the Matterhorn in the European Alps. But this formed exactly the same way by the action of glaciers carving away a mountain on all sides until all that's left is a tall, narrow, razor-sharp peak in the middle.

If these are glacial valleys, why are they now flooded? If these were filled with ice, why is there ocean extending great distances up through them? In other words, how does a fjord form? We already know the answer to this. We've seen it in previous lectures. The sea level rose 400 feet at the end of the last Ice Age. So, when these valleys were being carved out by ice, they were all above sea level. The sea was way off the coast here, but as the sea level rose, as ice around the world melted, the ocean reached up and wove its way in between these peaks.

But if you are asking how the Fiordlands, in particular, formed, that's another question all together. In other words, why are these mountains even there? And why do they drop off so sharply right down into the ocean? A very rare thing. It turns out the Fiordlands are at the edge of the Southern Alps. New Zealand isn't all that far south. It's about 45-degrees south in latitude. That's as far south as Maine is north, but the mountains of Southern Alps here rise very quickly to over 10,000 feet, about two miles. And as you can see, the whole area is covered with snow and ice. There're over 3,000 glaciers here. The longest is Tasman glacier, which is almost 30 kilometers. This whole area was first identified by the Dutch explorer Abel Tasman, back in 1642. It's after Tasman that Tasmania and the Tasman Sea was named. This area wasn't explored more fully and named, in fact, until Captain Cook came in 1770.

Why are the Southern Alps even here though? Because we've looked at mountains before, but they've always been places where you've had collisions of continents, and there are no other continents in sight here. Well, it turns out there is a plate boundary that runs right through New Zealand, though it's a really strange one. If you look at the island of New Zealand, it lies right along the plate boundary between the Pacific plate and the Australian plate. Only, here's the strange thing about it. North of New

Zealand the Pacific plate is plunging down underneath the Australian plate at the very large Tonga and Kermadec subduction zones. South of New Zealand there's still subduction, but it goes the other direction. The rock of the Australian plate, which was recently formed in a spreading ridge with Antarctica, turns around and plunges down underneath the Pacific plate. This doesn't sound like a very stable situation to have subduction going like this, and indeed, it isn't. In fact, if you zoom in on here you can see this process is actually tearing the island apart. There's a very large fault called the Alpine Fault, in fact, if you look closely, you can see a line stretching right across here, and that fault is in the process of tearing New Zealand into two pieces.

There are only a couple of large, we would call these transform faults, on continents in the world. One of them is the San Andreas Fault, in California, and the other is the Anatolian Fault in Turkey. The Alpine Fault here makes three. These are the three largest in the world. And what's happening is, there's motion across this fault of several centimeters per year, and this has been happening for more than 20-million years, to the point that the rock that's over here on the north part of the south island is actually the same rock that's down in the southwestern part of New Zealand. It's been dragged to the northeast over 20-million years by motion along this fault.

New Zealand, as a result, is very seismically active. It has earthquakes all the time. There were some very deadly and damaging earthquakes that happened in the Christchurch area in 2011 and 2012. And this wasn't even the Alpine fault. There are lots of other faults in New Zealand as well. The Alpine Fault, in particular, has had four very big earthquakes over the past 1,000 years. We know their dates, 1100, 1450, 1620 and 1717. We don't know how big they were because seismometers weren't invented until the end of the 1800s, but we know that they were large by the damage they did. And, if you look at those four dates, we're overdue. I mean, the average interval between those is about 200 years, and that would've meant the last one should've occurred in the early 1900s, so we're about a century overdue.

Compression along the Alpine fault is pushing up the Southern Alps, fast, in fact, about seven centimeters a year. In fact, the Southern Alps are rising faster than almost any other mountains in the world. If you think about this, this might seem a little odd, because normally, if you have a transform fault where two plates are sliding past each other, there shouldn't be anything going up. However, if the plate boundary is not a straight line, if it has any kinks in it then when one of these kinks meets and the two plates are pushing against each other, the rocks have to go somewhere, and it goes up.

Now, we've seen this in Southern California, the San Gabriel mountains that are just adjacent to Los Angeles, they are there because the San Andreas fault at that point takes a little bend, and as the Pacific plate crashes into a little corner of the North American plate there, the rock gets pushed upwards. The same thing happens here. The fact that this Alpine fault is not a straight line has pushed up, and it continues to push up the Southern Alps at a very rapid rate.

This also explains the very steep drop off at the Fiordland coast, because the fault runs right along it, and on the north side are rocks that very recently were in the sea to the south. In other words, if you go right off the coast of Milford Sound, the rock there used to be far to the south in the middle of the ocean seafloor, and it's now been dragged right up adjacent to the tall rock of the Southern Alps.

There is one more important component, however, in making the stunning cliffs and peaks of Milford Sound. The rocks of these cliffs are made of a composition called granite. We've seen a lot of volcanic rocks already in this course, so a lot of basalt erupting at volcanoes. Granite is a more typical composition for continents, but not the rocks at the top of the continents, not the sedimentary rocks like limestone and shale and sandstone, but the rock that forms the cores of continents. This formed directly out of magma as well. It's a volcanic rock, but deep underground. It has very large, interlocking crystals, and it's a very hard rock. Remember the Grand Canyon? There were all these weak rocks there like shales and mudstones that weathered very easily and crumbled and gave you very shallow slopes at times? Well, that's not granite. Granite is a very hard rock, and so it can maintain very steep, vertical slopes for long periods of time.

There are plenty of different kinds of rocks in the Fiordlands area. I mean this area has a long history of deposition of sedimentary rocks, like anywhere else on the Earth's surface. In fact, if you go up the coast a little bit from

Milford Sound, you find one of the more fascinating-looking outcrops of rocks. It's in Punakaiki, and here you have limestone along the shore that has eroded to look like giant stacks of pancakes. But it's the granite along the coast that's tough and strong and can form very steep slopes.

I spent a good part of my childhood in the mountains of New Hampshire. There's lots of granite there, like the Old Man of the Mountain, the state symbol of New Hampshire. I mean, it's not there anymore, it fell down in 2003. But, it wasn't actually a face that stuck out. If you actually go and look at that region, you'll see, in fact, that there's a steep cliff of granite that's quite vertical, and if you viewed it from just the right side, you would see the appearance of a face.

But where does all this granite come from? We don't see it forming anywhere at the surface. It turns out it only forms very deep underground. Both the Appalachian Mountains in New Hampshire and the Southern Alps were once much taller than they are today, and much of the rock has eroded away, and that's exposed rock that was once deep within the cores of the mountains. In fact, in the case of the Southern Alps there may have been as much as 20,000 feet, that's six kilometers, of sedimentary rock that has eroded away from the top.

We can figure out how this happens by looking at the process of the subduction zone. So let's say you have a situation where you have some sort of a collision of plates. You have rock pushed together, some of the rocks have to go up, some of the rock goes down to form sort of roots of the mountains underneath. That rock that gets pushed down ends up heating, and some of the minerals begin to melt, and those minerals that melt will eventually form the rock granite. The magma is lighter than the surrounding rock, so it begins to move upward, and it would like to erupt out the surfaces of volcanoes, however, it can't make it there because the mountains are quite tall. So these will cool underground as large, granite plutons or batholiths.

If we roll the picture ahead and see what happens next, as these mountains begin to erode down, these plutons become exposed, but there're actually two parts to this. Not only do the mountains erode down, but the weight is lifted off of the crust here, that's sort of like sitting up off of a mattress, and the whole crust rebounds upward. This whole uplift brings this granite that was once miles beneath the surface suddenly up at the surface, and you see it in places like New Hampshire or in the Southern Alps.

Another geologic process occurs when plates collide and mountains form, and that's the process of metamorphism. Here, the mountain-building process causes metamorphic reactions that create a whole variety of other rocks that form out of preexisting rocks either through temperature, or pressure, or hot fluids that flow through. In the case of the Southern New Zealand region, the Fiordlands National Park, one of the most culturally important is a particular type of jade, called greenstone. And this is actually a metamorphosed rock that is made from fibrous minerals, like asbestos. You may be familiar with another form of metamorphosed asbestos, the shimmering rock called Tiger's Eye. In this case, the more iron that you have in it, the greener the jade appears, but at any case, you have these compressed fibers that end up having this shimmering optical appearance.

This material is very important in the local Maori culture, very highly prized, and it's used to make jewelry, weapons, tools, and religious talismans as well. This rock, this greenstone, is very closely connected with the legends and creation myths of the Maori. And if you actually go to New Zealand today all the craft and tourist shops will contain many of these examples carved into a variety of sculptures. But this rock is only found in this one region along the coast of Fiordland National Park.

Incidentally, you actually might have had the opportunity to see some of the spectacular geology of Fiordland National Park, and the Southern Alps as well, if you've watched any of the *Lord of the Rings* movies that came out a few years back. The giant battles in these movies were done with computer graphics, but not the scenery. New Zealand really looks like that. Fangorn Forest, with all the moss-covered trees, was filmed right down in Milford Sound. And the scenes of the Great River Anduin with tall cliffs rising up on either side, those were also filmed directly in Fiordland National Park. The giant snow-covered mountains that the Fellowship crosses, the Misty Mountains, these are the Southern Alps. And even the last scenes of the movies, where Frodo climbs Mount Doom in the land of Mordor, that was filmed on the North Island of New Zealand on the Giant Taupo volcano that takes up much of the island.

Well, it's time for my top-five list. And first, let me go to Yosemite in California. To many people, Yosemite is the classic example of a glacial valley, though many valleys around the world are larger. This is largely due to the spectacular photography of Ansel Adams whose stunning black-and-white images really inspire the country. The reason Yosemite even exists as a national park is because of Teddy Roosevelt, like so many of the other national parks in America. Teddy Roosevelt visited in 1903, and it's a wonderful story. He came with a huge entourage of advisors and others, and he ditched them all and went out camping in the wilderness for three days with the naturalist John Muir. And it was after this period and seeing Yosemite from the eyes of John Muir that Roosevelt decided to make this a national park.

Yosemite is also a classic example of the exposure at the surface of a giant granite pluton. It's called the Sierra Nevada Batholith. This region formed about 200- to 150-million years ago when the Farallon plate was subducting beneath the Western United States. Uplift in the region began about 10-million years, exposing the granite. It was exposed even more by the huge amounts of glacial erosion that began in the region starting about three-million years ago.

Yosemite is actually very large, though most people, and again, there're about 3.5 million a year who visit Yosemite. Most people just visit the small Yosemite valley at the west end. But the whole rest, the east side, shows fantastic examples of a process called exfoliation, which is a process that caused the Old Man of the Mountain in New Hampshire to fall down. Essentially, as layers of rock erode, the rock behind is suddenly able to expand with the release of the pressure, and it causes cracks that allow that new layer of rock to peel off and fall, like the layers of an onion.

One of the most recognizable features of Yosemite is El Capitan. It is a stunning kilometer high, vertical face of granite. In fact, it's actually post-vertical in places. It's more than 90 degrees, which makes it a great favorite of rock climbers. A college roommate of mine actually climbed it over a period of two days. He slept in a hammock on the rock face suspended half a mile above the ground. When I hear stories like that, I think that maybe the dangers of crawling around in caves don't seem so bad.

Another famous place in Yosemite is Half Dome, which looks like a perfect dome, sliced in half, and in a sense it was, by the activity of the glaciers there. You can go climb Half Dome without technical climbing, you don't need ropes, though I have to say it's a grueling 8.5-mile hike, and you have to pull yourself up through a pair of steel cables in the final ascent, but it's really a spectacular climb. Yosemite also has some spectacular waterfalls. The highest waterfall in North America, Yosemite Falls, is almost a kilometer high, though the most recognizable waterfall is Bridalveil Falls, which is a classic hanging valley fall like we saw with Sutherland Falls in New Zealand.

Most people end up visiting Yosemite in the summer, but in fact, in the spring, if you go, you might catch one of the most strange sights you will ever see, and that is frazil ice. It turns out that as the snowpack of Yosemite starts to thaw, the streams begin to overrun their banks, and they flood through the whole valley, turning all of the snow into a giant, slowly moving wall of slush. It's like a giant flowing slushy.

Next, let me take you to Norway for fjords like Geirangerfjord and Sognefjord, which is where the word "fjord" came from originally. Geirangerfjord is the most visited fjord in Norway. And at the end of this long, snaking fjord is a small village, Geiranger, which frankly is about as scenic a place to live as you could ever imagine, surrounded by these massive, tall mountains on all sides. Sognefjord is the longest fjord in Europe. It stretches over 200-kilometers inland. Surrounding cliffs here rise a kilometer above the water, but they actually are much steeper because they extend beneath the surface of the water almost another mile down.

Next, we'll go to Greenland for the only fjord in the world that's longer than Sognefjord in Norway, and that's Scoresby Sound. Scoresby Sound is 350-kilometers long. It branches out like a huge tree into many other fjords that cover a total area of Greenland of almost 40,000 square kilometers. In fact, the sound is so large, it's more than 30-kilometers across at its widest point. The Scoresby Sound is often filled with a huge variety of very large icebergs of many unusual shapes that are constantly floating out to the sea.

Last, I want to take you to Switzerland for Gimmelwald and Grindelwald. These are two small, beautiful glacial valleys within the Swiss Alps. They're not large by comparison to other glacial valleys, but they are some of the most scenic in the world. The valleys are very narrow, with beautiful pine forests and green fields along the floor. But the cliffs rise up incredibly high on one side, in fact, almost three kilometers, that's two miles, nearly vertically from the valley up to the spectacular peaks of the Mounts Eiger, Munch, and Jungfrau. I mean I have stood at the bottom of Mount Eiger and looked up at this two-mile-high wall of rock, and it is truly an inspiring event that totally shapes my perception of what the Earth is capable of.

In the next lecture, we're going to return to the Mediterranean Sea where we started this course, with Santorini, but this time I'm going to look at the Rock of Gibraltar and the Bosphorus Strait, which have controlled a fascinating history of flooding within the Mediterranean and Black Seas.

Rock of Gibraltar—Catastrophic Floods
Lecture 22

In the last lecture, we looked at tall rocks that rise up out of the sea at the stunning fjords of Fiordland National Park in New Zealand. In this lecture, we'll visit another rock that rises out of the sea; it's not as tall, but perhaps it's more well known: the Rock of Gibraltar. Primarily limestone and shale, this rock is connected to Spain by a long, flat stretch of land called a tombolo. The Rock of Gibraltar is not large by the scale of some of the places we've visited—say, the giant mountains in the Himalayas or the Andes—but it's distinctive, and it plays an important role in the history of early humans.

Description and History of Gibraltar

- The Rock of Gibraltar is oddly shaped. It is gently sloping on the west side—where most people live in this small British territory—and quite steep on the east side. The rock rises about 1400 feet out of the water and is a popular tourist destination.

- The rock contains limestone, shale, and interbedded layers of dolomite and sandstone. Limestone, as we've seen, tends to form caves, and in fact, more than 100 caves are accessible from the surface of the rock.
  - Gorham's Cave, on the steep eastern side, holds the remains of Neanderthals who lived here as recently as 24,000 years ago.

  - The caves here also played a role in the Great Siege of Gibraltar by the Spanish in 1779–1783 and were used in the British Operation Tracer during World War II.

- The Rock of Gibraltar has a counterpart called Jebel Musa on the African side of the Strait of Gibraltar. Gibraltar itself was originally called Jebel Tariq. These rocks form what the early Greeks called the Pillars of Hercules.

- According to one Greek myth, Hercules split open the Atlas Mountains to make the two sides of the strait, but in another myth, he closed up the strait, making it narrow to prevent sea monsters from entering the Mediterranean. The existence of these two opposing stories is telling.

- Satellite images show the Mediterranean closing into this narrow spot at the straits. It's just a short distance across from Jebel Musa to Gibraltar. In fact, this separation hasn't even been present at various times in the past.

- The early Phoenicians sailed through the Pillars of Hercules to explore the Atlantic coast of Africa. In 711, the African general Tāriq ibn Ziyād brought his Muslim forces across the Mediterranean from Africa and captured what is now Spain. The Moors were removed from the Iberian Peninsula by the Spanish in 1492, although the Islamic presence in the region is still strong.

- Spain had control of Gibraltar until 1704, when a combined English and Dutch force captured it. The English took control, and Gibraltar has been a British territory ever since, though Spain tried to reclaim it in the late 1700s and again in the 1950s.

Geologic History of Gibraltar

- The Iberian Peninsula was part of Africa for hundreds of millions of years, even during the time that the supercontinent Pangaea formed. At that time, Spain was adjacent to Newfoundland. Spain broke away from Africa about 170 million years ago and has jostled against North Africa ever since as a separate microcontinent. The jostling of these pieces of continent has caused the rock there to be highly deformed. Some of the blocks of rock have rotated relative to others.

- Two interesting clues here give us a sense of the extreme tectonic history of the region. First, the layers of rock in Gibraltar are highly folded and deformed; thus, we know they have been caught up in tectonic plate collisions.

The sedimentary rocks that make up the Rock of Gibraltar formed about 200 million years ago, during the Late Jurassic.

- Even more interesting is the fact that these rocks are actually upside down. The oldest rocks of Gibraltar are on the top, and the rock gets younger as it goes down into the Earth. This inversion may even explain why the Rock of Gibraltar still exists. The weathering-resistant capstone has allowed it to survive while rocks around it have eroded away.

Unusual Ocean Currents

- The competing myths of Hercules opening and closing the Strait of Gibraltar are not too far off the mark. In fact, the strait has opened and closed at various times in its history.

- Fifty million years ago, there was no Mediterranean Sea. Africa was still far enough away from Europe that there was an open ocean from the Indian Ocean to the Atlantic. A strong equatorial ocean current ran westward between the two continents that would have changed global climates tremendously, allowing warm equatorial water to circulate around the globe.

- But by 30 million years ago, Africa had rotated counterclockwise enough that the Mediterranean closed in the east. We saw this in our first lecture on Santorini; in fact, this is the reason that Santorini and similar volcanoes exist. This was also the start of an unusual ocean circulation pattern.

- A map of the bathymetry of the Mediterranean and Black Seas shows a shallow section by Gibraltar in a region called the Camarinal Sill; the maximum water depth there is just 290 meters.
  - The water is even shallower—just 250 meters deep—in the Strait of Messina, between Sicily and Italy. In fact, Sicily is actually a continuation of the African land.

  - There are really two separate Mediterraneans here—a deep basin in the east and one in the west. Any water that flows between them must cross the shallow straits on either side of Sicily.

- The patterns of water circulation throughout the Mediterranean are unusual. In the region of Gibraltar, the surface ocean currents seem to indicate that water flows only into the Mediterranean, but the Mediterranean isn't filling up. Where does this water go?
  - If we look at the Mediterranean in a cross section, we see water coming in from the Atlantic at the surface at Gibraltar, but we see it heading back out into the Atlantic just beneath Gibraltar.

  - Water coming in from the Atlantic evaporates away quickly in the Mediterranean, but it leaves salts behind. When the heavier water flows back out to the Atlantic, it has to move up over the Camarinal Sill at Gibraltar, and it then flows down into the Atlantic.

- At certain times in the past, the Mediterranean has been entirely cut off from the Atlantic and has actually dried up. This was caused by a combination of tectonic collisions between Spain and Africa, narrowing the strait, and the occurrence of ice ages, lowering sea levels. The evidence for the drying up of the Mediterranean is found in large layers of gypsum and salt on the Mediterranean seafloor.

o The bottom of the Mediterranean Sea is as much as 5 kilometers below sea level, 3 miles down. Early hominids in this environment would have experienced air pressures of 1.7 atmospheres, almost twice the pressure at the surface. Further, the temperatures at this depth would have been about 170°F.

o The Atlantic finally broke through for the last time about 5.3 million years ago. The Mediterranean probably would have filled up in a matter of years, and the channel that we now see just east of Gibraltar would have been carved out on the Mediterranean seafloor.

• But the story doesn't end there. At the northeast end of the Mediterranean is the narrow, shallow channel that connects the Mediterranean through the Dardanelles, the Marmara Sea, and the Bosporus. During the ice ages, when sea levels were 400 feet lower, the Bosporus, which is only about 118 feet deep, would not have existed; the Black Sea was not connected with the Mediterranean.

o As the ice ages ended and the ice thawed, melting ice water would have flowed into a depression that is now the Black Sea and made a large freshwater lake. Over time, the lake would have begun to dry out, and the level of the Black Sea would have dropped.

o At some point, about 7600 years ago, the sea rose high enough in the Mediterranean that it broke through the Dardanelles, the Bosporus, and flooded into the Black Sea. Some scientists believe that it flooded catastrophically, in a fairly short period; others think the flooding happened gradually.

o The interesting point here is that some anthropologists place the homeland of the earliest speakers of the proto-Indo-European languages to be in the area just north of the Black Sea. It was from these people that came all the major languages spoken by peoples from India and westward. Perhaps the flooding here played a role in shaping the lives and cultures of these early

Lecture 22: Rock of Gibraltar—Catastrophic Floods

people and, therefore, the lives of those who spread throughout Europe and Asia.

Top Straits and Catastrophic Flood Sites

- The Bering Strait, between Alaska and Siberia, is another artificial divider of continents. The Bering Strait is fairly wide—about 85 kilometers at its narrowest—and incredibly shallow—only about 30 to 50 meters deep. This whole region was about 240 feet above sea level during the peak of the last ice age. About 14,000 years ago, some people and other large mammals came across from Siberia and settled into the northern parts of North America.

- In eastern Oregon and Washington, we find the Channeled Scablands, ancient ripples on the ground formed from the catastrophic flooding of Glacial Lake Missoula. This flooding took place in about 40 separate flows some 15,000 to 13,000 years ago. The ice lake here could fill up as much as 2000 feet and burst out in a volume of water equivalent to 10 times the amount of water in all the world's rivers combined. Such flooding carved out enormous canyons and spillways and dramatically shaped the land.

- Similar flooding occurred at the juncture of Russia, Mongolia, China, and Kazakhstan, as we see in the spillway of the Altai flood. The ripple marks on the ground here are larger than those in Oregon and Washington—as much as 50 feet high and 650 feet apart. The flood that took place here may be the largest one for which we have geologic evidence.

- The Dover Strait and English Channel were also carved out by catastrophic floods. About 425,000 years ago, an ice-dammed lake in the North Sea overflowed and rushed southward, carving out the weak chalk layer and beginning to separate England from France. About 225,000 years ago, another giant lake overflowed and finished the job of carving out the Dover Strait and English Channel and creating the beautiful cliffs of Dover.

Questions to Consider

1. What do you think the climate might have been like when the Mediterranean was open at both ends and a warm equatorial current flowed freely through it?

2. Many cultures have a story of being expelled from their place of origin, never to return again (such as the Sumerian/Babylonian/Judeo-Christian story of being expelled from an Eden). What might be the geologic origin of these stories?

Rock of Gibraltar—Catastrophic Floods
Lecture 22—Transcript

Hello, my name is Michael Wysession and welcome to Lecture 22 of our course on the Geologic Wonders of the World. In the last lecture, I looked at the tall rocks that rose right up out of the sea at the stunning fjords of Fiordland National Park, in New Zealand. In this lecture, I'm going to visit another rock that rises right up out of the sea. It's not as tall, but perhaps, a lot more well-known. It's the Rock of Gibraltar.

I want to start and end this lecture, however, at another part of the Mediterranean, and I'm going to start this lecture, actually, at the eastern end.

Just a couple months ago, I sailed into and out of the Black Sea. We wound our way from the Mediterranean, up through the Dardanelles, past Istanbul, and through the narrow Bosporus strait before opening out onto the Black Sea. These two big bodies of water, the Black Sea and the Mediterranean, are connected with just a narrow strait. Here's a video I took, in fact, from the front of the boat. On the left side is Europe, in front of you here is the Black Sea, and on the right side here is Asia. They're really that close to each other. North of the Black Sea, there's no easily observed dividing line between Europe and Asia; one just blends right into the other. And to geologists, there really isn't one. We just call it all Eurasia, in fact. But here, just north of Istanbul, it's very different. This is a very sharp line, the Bosporus, that separates the two. I mean, it's very clear. This side is Europe; this side is Asia. It turns out that this line has totally shaped the history of the people here. Just for reference here, this is the Bosporus, and this is the point right here where I took that video. Ancient armies were stopped by this water, or not, building pontoon bridges, enormous bridges that cross the Bosporus, like the great Persian Emperor Darius did, crossing the Bosporus here, or his son Xerxes did, crossing farther to the south, the Dardanelles, both of them on their way to battling the Greeks.

But here's the thing, if you look at this important continental division with the eyes of a geologist, then you realize that this line doesn't exist either. After all, there's land right under the shallow water of the Bosporus that connects Europe and Asia. And what's more, as we know now, it was just during the last Ice Age that sea levels were 400-feet lower than today, and because the Bosporus is incredibly shallow—it's only 118 feet deep—that means that it wasn't so long ago that there was no such thing as the Bosporus. The land went continuously around the southern end of the Black Sea, just like it does around the northern end. And the Black Sea was entirely land-locked. It knew nothing about the ocean that lay just over a narrow isthmus of land.

But I'm getting a little bit ahead of myself now. Let me get back to one of the most famous rocks in the world, the Rock of Gibraltar. This is a huge piece of limestone and shale, primarily, that's connected to the mainland of Spain, by a fairly long flat stretch of land that we call a Tombolo; it connects a land that sticks out into a body of water. The long Tombolo there is only a few feet above sea level. That's where the Gibraltar airport is.

The Rock of Gibraltar is not very big by the scale of some of the places that we've recently visited during this course—the giant mountains in the Himalayas or the Andes. But it's very distinctive, and it actually plays an important role in a very interesting story that involves the history of early humans, but not in the way that you might think. The Rock of Gibraltar is an odd-shaped rock. It's gently sloping on the west side, and this is where most people live in this small British territory, and very steep on the east side. It drops straight down. In fact, there's a large catchment for water on the steep side there. It's too steep to live on, but they collect rainwater down here. There's not a lot of access to freshwater here.

The rock rises about 1,400 feet up, out of the water, and it's a very popular tourist destination, especially for cruise ships in the Mediterranean, which is how Margaret and I visited it some years back. People will go up to the top of the rock there, they'll take beautiful pictures, stunning views of the Mediterranean, and also a lot of pictures of the Barbary macaques, the monkeys that are all over the top there.

The rock itself, as I mentioned, contains limestone and shale and also interbedded layers of dolomite and sandstone. Limestone, as we've previously seen several other times in this course, tends to form caves, and there are a large number of caves here, more than 100 that are accessible from the surface. The largest of these, St. Michael's, is a very popular tourist site.

These caves have played important roles over time, in a variety of different ways. There's one particular cave on the steep eastern side called Gorham's Cave, and it holds the remains of Neanderthals that lived here as recently as 24,000-years ago. I mean, that's really recent. Neanderthals had been in the region starting about 125,000-years ago. Our species of humans, Homo sapiens, didn't arrive here until maybe 40,000-years ago. And this is really a very remarkably puzzling question about our own history as a species. There was another species of human, in direct competition with us, living here for over 10,000 years, as recently as 24,000 years ago. What happened to them?

These caves have also played an important role in more modern times, especially for the use of cannons during wars. During the four years of the Great Siege of Gibraltar, which happened from 1779 to 1783, this is a time when the Spanish fleet was attacking the British-held Gibraltar, the caves began to be expanded into a set of tunnels, and when completed, there were about 1,000 feet of interconnected tunnels with many holes carved into the outside walls for mounting cannons.

These tunnels actually were expanded by the British in 1942 during WWII. They were afraid that the Germans might capture Gibraltar, which they never did, but they had a team of six men hide in the caves for 2.5 years, called Operation Tracer, so that if the Germans did take it, these men could spy on them. Nowadays the caves are filled with scenes from the various battles that entertain the tourists, complete with mannequin soldiers. And there's a certain theme here that runs through a lot of the lectures I've talked about. We often take geologic wonders and alter them to make them into tourist attractions, like putting spotlights with gaudy rainbow colors into caves, often to the detriment of the attractions.

For many of the Geologic Wonders I've visited, it's really easy to get caught up in all the tourist stuff, whether it's Mount Fuji, or Devils Tower, Niagara Falls, these places are all filled with gift shops and tacky hotels, theme parks for kids, and so on. If you are part of a tour there, maybe you arrive on a bus, you get 45 minutes to look at something spectacular, and then you get carted off to somewhere else. Here at Gibraltar, when they take you up to the top of the rock in tour buses, there are even tour guides dumping food into bins to attract the Barbary macaques to give the tourists something to take pictures of. But if you know the background of the place that you're visiting, if you know its story, then even that 45 minutes can be inspirational. The Rock of Gibraltar has several interesting stories involved with it. To begin with, the Strait of Gibraltar has long played a very important role for the cultures in the area. The Rock of Gibraltar has a counterpart on the other side, on the African side, the other side of the Strait of Gibraltar. It's called Jebel Musa, to go with Jebel Tariq, which is what Gibraltar used to be called, in fact, that's where the name Gibraltar comes from.

If you look on either side of the strait there, the Rock of Gibraltar and Jebel Musa, on either side, form two pillars. In fact, they were called the Pillars of Hercules by the early Greeks. According to Greek myth, Hercules split open the Atlas Mountains, that are a little bit farther to the south in Morocco, and he made the two sides here of the strait. What's interesting is in another myth, Hercules also closed up the strait, making it narrow to prevent giant sea monsters from entering the Mediterranean from the Atlantic. And actually, the coexistence of these two totally opposite stories is very telling, as we will soon see.

If you look at satellite images, you can really get a sense of how the Mediterranean closes in to this one narrow spot. And in fact, if you zoom in even farther, you can see it's a very short distance across from Jebel Musa over to Gibraltar. And this, in fact, this separation at various times in the past hasn't even been there. The early Phoenicians sailed through these pillars to explore the Atlantic coast of Africa. Back in 711, the African Tāriq ibn Ziyād came across the Mediterranean from Africa, and the African Muslims captured what is now Spain. They built the famous Moorish Castle. It was a very large stone fortress up on Gibraltar, which was held by the Moors from 711 to 1309, about 600 years, and then again for about a century, from 1350 to 1462; they controlled the strait during these long periods of time. The Moors were removed from the Iberian Peninsula by the Spanish, in 1492, the same year that Columbus sailed to the Americas. But there is still a strong Islamic presence in the region.

Spain had control until 1704, when a combined English and Dutch force captured it from the Spanish. The English took control, and Gibraltar has been a British territory ever since, though Spain actually tried to take it back in the late 1700s and again in the 1950s, under Generalissimo Francisco Franco.

The story of the geology of the Rock of Gibraltar has been a bit more complicated. The sedimentary rocks that make it up formed about 200-million years ago, during the Late Jurassic. And these are shallow marine sediments, muds, and sands, and coral reefs. The Iberian Peninsula though, what is now Spain, has a very unusual history. It had been part of Africa for hundreds of millions of years. In fact, during the time that the supercontinent Pangea formed, when all the continents came together, at that time, Spain was actually adjacent to Newfoundland. But Spain broke away from Africa about 170-million years ago and has jostled against North Africa ever since as a separate microcontinent. These jostlings of these separate pieces of continent have caused the rock there to be very deformed. Some of the blocks have actually rotated relative to others. And there are two very interesting clues here that give you a sense of the extreme tectonic history of the region. First of all, the layers of the rock in Gibraltar are highly folded and deformed, so you know these have been caught up in tectonic plate collisions. A more interesting fact is these rocks are actually upside down. The oldest rocks of Gibraltar are on the top, and the rock gets younger as you go down into the Earth. This likely played a significant role and the reason that the Rock of Gibraltar is even there, the fact that it has eroded more slowly than surrounding rocks. And again, this is a theme that we've seen before in the course, having a more resistant capstone allowing one rock to survive erosion while the rocks around it have weathered away.

And the myths of Hercules, both opening and closing the Gibraltar Strait, as I said, might not be too far off. The Strait, in fact, has opened and closed at various times in its history. And this is very important, because the Strait is the only connection between the Mediterranean and the Atlantic. At least, it is now. If you go back in time, 50-million years ago, there was no Mediterranean. Africa, at that time, was still far enough away from Europe that there was open ocean from the Indian Ocean all the way over to the Atlantic. In fact, there was a very strong equatorial ocean current that ran westward right between the two continents, flowing continuously, would've changed global climates tremendously to allow this warm equatorial water to circulate around the globe. But by 30 million years, Africa had rotated counterclockwise enough that the Mediterranean closed in the east. And we saw this in the very first lecture, on Santorini. And after all, this is the reason that volcanoes like Santorini even exist. And this was the start of a very unusual ocean circulation pattern.

If we look at a map of the bisymmetry of the Mediterranean, so this is the map of the Mediterranean and Black Seas with the water removed. We see a very interesting feature. First of all, the shallowest section over by Gibraltar here is a region called the Camarinal Sill, and the maximum water depth there is now just 290-meters below the surface. However, there's another location where the water is even shallower, and that's the Strait of Messina, between Sicily and Italy. The water here is only 250-meters deep, and in fact, you can see that Sicily is actually a continuation of the African land. It's shallow all the way across from Africa to Sicily.

There are really two separate Mediterraneans here. There is a deep basin in the east and then a deep basin in the west, and any water that flows between them has to go across the shallow straits on either side of Sicily. If you look at this pattern of water circulation throughout the Mediterranean, you see some very unusual patterns. Because of the arm of Italy that sticks out and of Greece, the water follows a fairly unusual pattern, but there's something odd about this picture if you look at the left side of it. The arrows only point to the right at Gibraltar.

How can this possibly be? If you are in the region of Gibraltar and look at the surface ocean currents, it appears as if water only flows into the Mediterranean. This is odd because the Mediterranean isn't filling up, and after all, there are other rivers, like the Nile and the Danube, that flow into it as well. So where does this water go? Well, two places, really. First of all, if you were to look at the Mediterranean in a cross section, so you were to cut down into it, you'd see a very interesting pattern. You'd see water coming into the Mediterranean from the Atlantic at the surface at Gibraltar, but you'd see water heading back out into the Atlantic just beneath it, and the reason for this is very simple. The Mediterranean is a really warm place. The sun shines a lot, evaporation rates are high, and so water comes in from the Atlantic, the water evaporates away, but it leaves the salts behind, so the water becomes saltier over time so that the water of the Mediterranean is significantly saltier than the water of the Atlantic Ocean. That heavy water, as a result, flows back out to the Atlantic, it has to come up over the Camarinal Sill at Gibraltar, and then flows down along the slopes, down into the Atlantic.

However, at certain times in the past, the Mediterranean has been entirely cut off from the Atlantic, and it has actually dried up. This has occurred due to two different factors, some combination of the tectonic collisions between Spain and Africa, so the straits have narrowed a little bit in terms of the geology of the rock there, and the occurrences of Ice Ages, which we have already seen, cause sea levels to be very low. The relative amounts of these are somewhat debated still, but we know that there have been periods where the Mediterranean gets entirely cut off from the Atlantic, and the evaporation rates are so high, that the Mediterranean would have, if not entirely dried up, mostly dried up, leaving a few extremely salty lakes at the bottom.

The evidence for this is in large layers of gypsum and salt that lie underneath the Mediterranean seafloor. If you've ever flown across the Western U.S. you've seen this type of a phenomenon. If you fly across places like Nevada or Utah you'll often see sort of white, bright areas at the bottom of valleys in between hills. These are called playas, and they're a type of geologic formation called an evaporite. Essentially, when it rains the rain falls in the hills, washes salts out of the hills, they form shallow lakes down in the bottom of the valleys, but then when that water evaporates away, it leaves a new layer of salt, and it grows into this white salt layer. In the Mediterranean, we see many layers of this down underneath the normal stream sediments flowing into the Mediterranean. In fact, this probably happened at least eight different times, each time followed again by a refilling of the Mediterranean. The sea level is always going up and down; as we know, and between six-million years ago and 5.3-million years ago the Mediterranean got cut off many times.

This would've been a very unusual situation because if you take the water away from the Mediterranean, the bottom of the Mediterranean Sea would have been as much as five kilometers below sea level. We're talking about three miles down. And of course, as you know, if you go up the air pressure gets less and less, well, if you go down, the air pressure increases to the point that if you had been, and of course there were early humans around at this time, early ancestors of the humans, early hominids, if they were down here, they would've experienced air pressures 1.7 atmospheres, almost twice the pressure at the surface. It would've been like being under 25 feet of water. And of course, the added air pressure makes the temperatures go up, so the temperatures down here would've been about 170°F, far hotter than any place on the surface of the Earth. I mean, truly unbearable conditions. Even more so, rivers like the Nile that would've entered in, would've suddenly plunged down miles, and in the process they would've cut out deep channels, like new Grand Canyons, cutting miles down into the rock. In fact, beneath the current Nile River those giant canyons exist today. They have since been filled in with sediment, but they're there.

The Atlantic finally broke through for the last time, about 5.3-million years ago. It's estimated that this would've happened very quickly, perhaps filling up the Mediterranean in a matter of years, and this time, it would've carved out the big channel that we now see just east of Gibraltar on the Mediterranean seafloor. But the layer of salt pokes up in a few places, most notably, in Messina, Sicily, and in fact, this period of time is called the Messinian Salinity Crisis because of this. This whole region there has been uplifted by tectonics, a result of that collision in between Africa and Eurasia, and it's a reminder of the extreme conditions that existed here not too long ago, geologically speaking, at least.

But the story doesn't end there. At the northeast end of the Mediterranean, is the very narrow, shallow channel that connects the Mediterranean through the Dardanelles, the Marmara Sea, and the Bosporus. As I started out the lecture, the Bosporus is only about 118-feet deep, so during the past Ice Age, when sea levels were 400 feet lower, the Black Sea was not even connected with the Mediterranean. As the Ice Ages ended and the ice thawed, melting ice water, it would've flowed into a large depression that is now the Black Sea, and would've made a large freshwater lake. But over time it would've begun to dry out, and the level of the Black Sea would have dropped. As humans began to develop communities in the Middle Eastern region, many tribes settled along the shores of the Black Sea. At some point, about 7,600 years ago, based on radiometric dates of fossils, the sea rose high enough in the Mediterranean that it actually broke through the Dardanelles, the Bosporus, and flooded down into the Black Sea.

Some scientists believe that it flooded catastrophically, in a fairly short period. Others think that it happened gradually. And in fact, there're even some supporters for the idea that the Black Sea filled up so much from the runoff of melting glaciers that it was the one to overflow its borders and to burst into the Mediterranean. But this view isn't supported by the majority of scientists who study it. In any case, there are archaeological remains of early towns, things like tool-worked timbers, parts of early houses, and shells of freshwater clams that had been used for food that are now more than 100-meters below sea level, that's more than 330 feet. So the Black Sea got filled in over a fairly short amount of time.

The interesting point here is that some anthropologists place the homeland of the earliest speakers of the Proto-Indo-European languages to be in the area just north of the Black Sea. And it was from these people that came all of the major languages spoken by peoples from India, like Sanskrit, and westward, or most of the languages, languages including Latin, Greek, Slavic, Celtic, etc. Perhaps the events of the flooding here played a role in shaping the lives of these early people, and therefore, the future of the peoples that first started speaking the earliest ancestor of the language that I'm speaking right now. Perhaps, the spread of these languages throughout Europe and Asia was a direct result of this single geologic flood. It's also likely that the numerous flood stories that existed in so many cultures throughout Central Eurasian regions, as civilization was just starting, were influenced, or even inspired, by the giant flood of the Black Sea 7.5-thousand years ago.

Well it's time for my top five. And I really have two different themes going on here. I have straits, you know, connections of water between two larger bodies of water, and the remnants of catastrophic floods. So my top five are going to represent a combination of those. First, let me go to the Bering Strait, between Alaska and Siberia. This is another artificial divider of continents. After all, it's all continental rock between it. Remember, the north island of Japan is actually part of North America, as is Eastern Siberia. The Bering Strait is pretty wide. It is currently about 85 kilometers at their narrowest, but it's incredibly shallow. It's only about 30- to 50-meters deep;

that's about 160 feet. So, this whole region was about 240-feet above sea level during the peak of the last Ice Age. This was actually a huge problem during the Cold War because the Bering Strait is so shallow that Soviet subs from the Arctic Sea had to come right up to the surface if they wanted to go directly into the Pacific Ocean and were easily identified. At this time, during the Ice Age, some of the Native Americans were able to come across as the ice pack began to thaw about 14,000 years ago, and they came across from Siberia, as well as large mammals, like mammoths, settling into the northern parts of North America.

Next, let me go to Eastern Oregon and Washington for a very strange sedimentary feature that mystified geologists for years. Ripples naturally form on stream beds or sea beds from flowing water. You've walked across the bed of a stream and felt the little ripples of the sand. The spacing of these ripples is typically centimeters to meters. In Eastern Oregon and Washington, there are ancient ripples on the ground here, only they're 20- to 30-feet high, and they're 200- to 300-feet apart, and individual ripples can be two-miles long. Obviously, an enormous amount of water flowed across here at some point in time.

These are called the Channeled Scablands, and these form from the catastrophic flooding from Glacial Lake Missoula. This is a time when at the last Ice Age, that large ice sheets were melting, and the water would sometimes get dammed up by ice and burst out catastrophically across the land. These particular floods happened 15- to 13,000-years ago, and there were about 40 or so separate flows over this 2,000-year period. The ice lake could fill up as much as 2,000 feet and burst out in a volume of water that could be 10 times the amount of water of all of the world's rivers combined. This carved out enormous canyons and spillways and dramatically shaped the land.

Next, I want to go Russia for a very similar event. This is at the juncture of Russia, Mongolia, China, and Kazakhstan, for the spillway of the Altai flood, which also happened in the same period about 14- to 11,000-years ago. The ripple marks on the ground here are much larger than the Missoula floods, by a lot. The ripple marks here can be 650-feet apart, and as much as 50-feet high. This is, possibly, the largest flood ever recorded that we have any geologic evidence of. The water would have greatly overflowed; rivers flowed across land into the Caspian Sea. It would've filled up the Caspian Sea, flowed out and down into the Black Sea, and been part of that process of filling up the Black Sea that I just spoke about earlier in the lecture.

Last, I want to go to the Dover Strait and English Channel, the land between England and France. Half a million years ago, England was connected to continental Europe as part of a continuous, single land mass. But there were two separate, catastrophic floods from the bursting of ice dams that actually carved out the channel forever separating England from France. The depth of the Dover Strait is only about 45 meters, so it was all above land during the past severe Ice Ages. Well, 425,000 years ago, and ice-dammed lake in the North Sea overflowed, burst out, and rushed southward, carving out the weak chalk layer there that exists beginning to separate England from France. This happened again, about 225,000-years ago. The French rivers Meuse and Rhine, which flowed north at that time, got dammed up into a giant lake, and when that dam broke, it finished the job of carving out the chalk of the Dover Strait and English Channel, creating the beautiful cliffs of Dover and forever separating England from the rest of Europe. I like this example at the end of the lecture because it really ties together the two themes that I've been talking about, ocean straits and catastrophic floods.

In the next lecture, I'm going to talk about rising sea levels of a very different kind, the kind that happens twice a day due to tides, and I will take us to the Bay of Fundy, in Eastern Canada.

Bay of Fundy—Inexorable Cycle of Tides
Lecture 23

In the last lecture, we visited the Rock of Gibraltar, with its unusual history of ocean currents and catastrophic floods. In this lecture, we'll visit a place where the sea level can rise or fall an enormous amount in a matter of hours: the Bay of Fundy in eastern Canada. This area is stark and largely low-lying; it's peaceful and undeveloped, but it's renowned for having the largest ocean tides anywhere in the world. At the Bay of Fundy, the water can rise and fall more than 50 feet two times a day.

Tidal Range at the Bay of Fundy
- More than 200 million years ago, the supercontinent Pangaea was starting to break up, and several rifts began forming in various places. The Bay of Fundy was one of these early rifts. It started opening about 220 million years ago, but then it stopped, as many rifts did.

- The largest tidal range anywhere in this region—with a variance of 17 meters—is measured in a place called Burntcoat Head. The highest water level ever recorded in the Bay of Fundy occurred during a tropical cyclone, Saxby Gale, that hit on October 4, 1869. In one location of the head of the Minas Basin, the water level reached a record of 71 feet.

- During the 12.4 hours that varies between high tides, 115 billion tons of water flow in and out of the Bay of Fundy. How and why does this happen?

Why Do Tides Occur?
- The force of the Moon pulls on the Earth, although not the same amount everywhere. Gravity falls off as $1/\text{distance}^2$; thus, as we get farther from the Moon, the effect of gravity becomes less and less. This means that the Moon pulls more on one side of Earth than in the middle; it stretches the Earth into a prolate ellipsoid—a football

shape. The effect of the Moon pulling on the Earth is very small; the Moon stretches the Earth about 2 feet on either side, although for the oceans, this can be several meters.

- The Sun does the same thing, but Earth is much farther away from the Sun; thus, the relative effect on either side of Earth is much less. As a result, even though the Sun pulls on Earth much more strongly than the Moon, the effect of the lunar tides from the Moon is twice as great as the solar tides. Of course, both the Sun and the Moon create tides on Earth, and the effects can either add together, creating a spring tide, or subtract from each other, creating a neap tide.

- The bulge of the Earth adjusts as our planet rotates. This effect causes a good deal of tidal friction inside the Earth, which affects the tides on the Moon. In fact, this friction causes moonquakes.

© Design Pics/Thinkstock.

The tidal range is not the same everywhere at the Bay of Fundy; at the mouth, the effect of the tides may be only 6 to 10 meters, but farther in, the tides may reach up to 15 meters or more.

More Questions about Tides

- The Earth rotates once every 24 hours, and in that time, there are two high tides and two low tides, but they're not at the same height. In other words, each day there is a higher high tide and a lower high tide—why? This phenomenon is due to the tilt of the Earth's axis of rotation, which is not exactly perpendicular to the direction that the Earth moves around the Sun or the direction that the Moon moves around the Earth. Our axis is tilted 23.5 degrees.

- Why is the time between high tides about 12.4 hours rather than exactly 12 hours? The Earth makes one full rotation in 24 hours, but in that time, the Moon has moved a little bit in its orbit around the Earth. That "little bit" means that the high tides are spread apart by 12.4 hours, not 12 hours.

- Why is the Bay of Fundy so unusual? As the tidal bulge moves westward, with particular geometries of inlets or bays, the water can take a long time to work its way around the land, and the tide can become much larger. For the Bay of Fundy, there's also a tidal resonance due to a coincidence of timing. The time it takes the water to move up the bay and down is about the same as the time from one high tide to the next; thus, the tides begin to amplify. Very quickly, the result is a huge amount of water in the bay, draining out and back in each period of 12.4 hours.

Saxby Gale

- Several factors came together to yield the record high tide of 71 feet in the Bay of Fundy during the Saxby Gale of 1869. One of these factors was air pressure.
  - Right now, a column of air hundreds of kilometers high is pressing down on top of you. You don't notice it because you're used to it and because it presses around you on all sides equally, but you do notice when it changes, as when your ears pop when you're landing in an airplane.

  - The air pressure also changes when the weather changes; that change is what a barometer measures. Bad weather is usually associated with areas of low air pressure. With an impending storm, the warm, lighter air rises, creating a low-pressure region over the land. The hot air cools, water vapor condenses into water droplets, ice crystals make clouds, and then it rains or snows.

o During a hurricane, a cell of extremely low pressure can sit right in the center eye of the storm. Less air pressure means that the whole surface can rise up, creating a storm surge that can topple levees.

o Remember that sea level is never constant in any one place. As low-pressure or high-pressure air cells move over water, the sea level goes up and down in response. This is part of the reason why hurricanes and typhoons are so dangerous for flooding along coastlines, as we saw in the lecture on the Ganges delta. The elevation of the water can change and rise up over levees.

• In addition to air pressure, two other factors came together to create the high tide during the Saxby Gale. The storm took place during a time of spring tide, when the Earth, Moon, and Sun were all aligned, and very strong winds from the hurricane essentially helped push water up into the Bay of Fundy.

Life in the Bay of Fundy
• The area of the Bay of Fundy in Newfoundland is a strikingly beautiful place but not in the dramatic way that we've seen in other lectures—there are no tall mountains or steep fjords here. Instead, it has a beautiful weathered appearance, the result of countless winter storms blowing off the North Atlantic and scraping away at the land.

• The rhythm of life here is controlled by the tides to a degree that most of us don't experience in our lives. Fishing has been the major industry along the coast of Newfoundland for centuries, but the fishing boats must wait for high tide. People here are acutely aware of the tidal schedule, and they plan their lives accordingly; they also pay close attention to the weather report because of the ability of storms to amplify the effects of the tides.

- An unusual feature of the incoming tide is a phenomenon called a tidal bore—a wave as the incoming tide rushes into the bay. You can sometimes see the front of the advancing tide moving upstream, against the flow of the river. Sometimes these tidal bores are large enough that people can actually surf the wave as it comes in—surfing upstream in a river!

- In a couple of locations around the Bay of Fundy, you can also see another strange phenomenon: reversing waterfalls. These are rapids that form as the stream goes downhill, but rapids also form as the tide comes in and the water goes upstream. In other words, the rapids form in either direction. This effect can be seen in Maher Point, near Eastport, Maine, and in Saint John, in New Brunswick. Saint John is also the location of the Stonehammer Geopark, which features interesting rock outcrops and a fascinating array of fossils.

- Recent research has shown that not very long ago, tides in many places of the world were much more extreme than they are today. It is also the case that millions and billions of years ago, the Moon was much closer to the Earth. It would have filled a much greater area in the sky and caused much larger tides.

Top Sites for Tidal Phenomena
- Ungava Bay in northern Quebec encompasses an area called Leaf Basin that has a maximum tidal range of 16.8 meters, almost equal to that of the Bay of Fundy.

- The largest tidal bore in the world is the Qiantang tidal bore on China's Fuchun River. This wave can be up to 30 feet high and can move at about 25 miles an hour.

- Along the west coast of England, the Severn estuary, which empties into the Bristol Channel, has a 15-meter tidal range. Although the tidal bore isn't large here, the Severn estuary is famous for surfing. The wave can carry surfers up to 10 kilometers inland.

- The Pororoca in Brazil is the tidal bore on the Amazon River and its estuaries. Tidal bores here can run 13 kilometers inland. The record for surfing is an amazing 36-minute-long ride.

- Whirlpools or maelstroms are among the more unusual effects of tidal currents, and one of the most famous of these is the Lofoten maelstrom in Norway. This whirlpool develops as the tide comes in along the Norwegian coast and goes past a promontory.

- The largest maelstrom is the Saltstraumen, also along the coast of Norway, where strong tidal currents are forced through a narrow strait. Whirlpools here can be more than 30 feet across and make a depression in the water surface, a cone, as much as 15 feet deep.

- The Corryvreckan whirlpool, along the coast of Scotland, is the third largest in the world. A Scottish TV documentary crew once threw a human mannequin with a depth gauge attached to into this whirlpool; the gauge showed that the mannequin had been sucked down to a depth of more than 850 feet.

Suggested Reading

Leslie, *Bay of Fundy*.

Thurston and Homer, *Tidal Life*.

Questions to Consider

1. If the Moon had an ocean, what would the ocean tides there be like?

2. Inlets with large tidal ranges are often proposed as sites for hydroelectric power plants, but the power from them would not be continuous. Explain why.

Bay of Fundy—Inexorable Cycle of Tides
Lecture 23—Transcript

Hello. My name is Michael Wysession, and welcome to Lecture 23 of our course on the Geologic Wonders of the World. In the last lecture, I visited the Rock of Gibraltar, with its unusual history of ocean currents and catastrophic floods, as sea levels have historically gone up and down there. In this lecture, I'm going to visit a place where the sea level can go up or down an enormous amount in a matter of hours and that's the Bay of Fundy, in eastern Canada.

It's one of the basic tenets of geology that streams flow downhill, carrying water across the land to the ocean, except when they don't. There are a small number of rivers in the world, about a hundred or so, where the water can actually flow upstream some of the time, as a result of ocean tides. I grew up in New Jersey; I used to go to the Jersey Shore as a kid, and the largest tides there are about 1.5 meters, that's 4 or 5 feet, not very much, but it's enough to make you have to move your beach towel if you're there for more than a couple of hours.

I've also been other places where the tide rises and falls a lot more than this, and it's just wonderful for exploring. When the tide goes out, it can expose, for a few hours at least, a cascade of small tidal pools with all kinds of fascinating creatures inside, sea anemones, starfish, urchins, barnacles, crabs, and eels. But I've been to one place where the tides can rise and fall a huge amount over 15 meters—that's more than 50 feet in a single day, actually twice a day, in fact. And this is the Bay of Fundy, between Newfoundland and Nova Scotia, in eastern Canada, and a little bit of Maine.

This is a stark, largely low-lying area. It's very peaceful and undeveloped, but it's renowned for having the largest ocean tides anywhere in the world. The scale of this is really remarkable. Following the end of the last Ice Age, as I've talked about before, most of the 400 feet of sea level rise occurred over about a 10,000-year period, from about 16,000-years ago to about 6,000-years ago, so this is 400 feet in 10,000 years. That's really fast. That's about half an inch a year, and geologically speaking, that's really rapid. Here at the Bay of Fundy, the water can rise over 50 feet two times a day and go back down.

Some sources believe that the word Fundy, from Bay of Fundy, is a corruption of a French word, Fendu, meaning split. Others believe it comes from a Portuguese word, fondo, meaning funnel. And I actually think the latter makes a lot more sense, because the Bay has a funnel shape, and it certainly has that effect on the water, which I'll show you soon—of funneling that water into a particular shape.

Incidentally, the reason that the Bay of Fundy is even there in the first place is an interesting story of its own. More than 200-million years ago, the supercontinent Pangaea, remember when all the continents were together as one large land mass, was starting to break up, it was stretching out in a variety of places, and several rifts began forming in various places in Pangaea, the Bay of Fundy was one of these early rifts. It started opening about 220-million years ago, but it stopped as many of them did. A lot of times the rifting in continents doesn't open up into an ocean. The rifting that would become the Atlantic Ocean happened farther to the east in what is now the Mid-Atlantic Ridge. But the rift there remains, but that's not why you would go visit the Bay of Fundy today.

I've been there as a kid, and it is truly a bizarre experience to return back and forth from the water, and sometimes you go there and you see boats floating up high, attached to the docks. And you come back at another time of day and there's no water; it's all gone. And you look for the boats and they're down low, resting on the mud with no water in sight. Come back at a later point, and the water has come back in, and the tides have risen up. The largest tidal range anywhere within this region is measured in a particular place called Burntcoat Head, and the tidal range here can vary by 17 meters, that's almost 56 feet. The highest water level ever recorded in the Bay of Fundy actually occurred at one particular time during a very bad tropical cyclone that was called the Saxby Gale, which hit this region on October 4, 1869. And in one location of the head of the Minus Basin the water level reached a record of 71 feet, resulting from three factors, a combination of high winds, unusually low atmospheric pressure, and the presence of something called a spring tide, and I'll explain these factors in just a moment.

During the 12.4 hours that varies between high tides, 115-billion tons of water flow in and out of the Bay of Fundy, each time. And we have a lot of questions here. How does this happen? How do the tides even work in the first place? Why do they occur? Why are there close to two high and two low tides each day, but not exactly two? And why is it that the few places in the world that are like the Bay of Fundy are just so unique? Why doesn't this happen more often? These are a lot of questions.

First of all, why do the tides occur at all? Well, to do this, let me use a football to demonstrate here. Imagine that this is the Earth and to do that, because the Earth is fairly round, I'm going to point it to you in this direction so it looks to you like a circle. The Earth has two neighbors, the moon and the sun, that cause significant tides on it. So let's say I have a moon nearby, and it's going to pull on the Earth, only it's not going to pull the same amount everywhere on Earth. Why is this? Well, gravity falls off as one over the distance squared, so as I go farther from the moon, the effect of gravity gets less and less. So that means the moon is going to pull more on this side of the Earth than the middle. It's also going to pull less on this side, so the effect is going to pull this side towards the moon, and let this side go out. And it's going to stretch the Earth out into what we call an ellipsoid. It's actually a particular type of ellipsoid called a prolate ellipsoid; that's what a football is. It's a sphere that's been stretched out in two directions.

I have to be careful here because I don't want to confuse things. The Earth actually does have an ellipsoidal shape, but it's in the other direction. And this is due to the fact that the Earth is rotating. As the Earth is spinning around its axis, the Earth gets, essentially, thrown outward away from the rotation along its axis. If you've ever ridden on a merry-go-round you've had that experience of being thrown away from the center. Well, that rotation of the Earth is enough to send the equator 21-kilometers farther from the center of the Earth than the poles. You're significantly farther from the center of the earth along the equator; I've mentioned this earlier in the class, so that's an enormous effect, 21 kilometers.

The effect of the moon pulling on the earth here in this direction is very small. It stretches the side out about two feet on either side. That's the solid earth, so when we talk about tides, we're not just talking about the ocean, we're talking about the solid earth as well. It can be several meters for the ocean.

We not only have the moon, we also have the sun. The sun does the same thing. In the case of the sun, you have a situation where you have the sun pulling on one side and letting go on the other, and it stretches the Earth, but the difference is we're a lot farther away from the sun, so the relative effect on either side of the Earth is much less. As a result, even though the sun pulls on us much more strongly than the moon, the effect of gravity of the sun is much greater; after all, we orbit around the sun; we don't orbit around the moon, the effect of the lunar tides from the moon are twice as large as the solar tides. Of course, both the sun and the moon create tides on Earth, and the effects can either add together or subtract from each other. And we can show you this with a small animation here.

Suppose you have an alignment of the Earth, the sun, and the moon, so that they're all in one line. The dark blue here shows the effect of the solar tide, and as I said, it's about half the size of the moon. The light blue shows the effect of the lunar tide, and because both the sun and the moon are on the same side here, they end up adding, and you get what's known as the spring tides. These are the highest high tides that you get. If we go to a later point in time, a week later, the moon has rotated around to its first quarter position, now you have the high tides from the moon and from the sun fighting each other. So, now the moon is causing the tides to stretch the Earth out in this direction, but the sun is causing the tides to stretch out in this direction. You still get a high tide because the moon's effects are stronger than the sun's, but they're much dampened. We call this a neap tide. If you go a week later, the moon now has rotated into its full-moon position, and here's something that's very unusual because you might think that the sun and the moon would cancel each other out, but in fact, because each one of these is stretching the Earth out into this prolate ellipsoid, they end up adding together. Go a week later, into the third-quarter position, we're back from the spring tide to another neap tide, and then go a week later, and we go back into the new moon position. They're all lined up and that's our monthly cycle of the tides.

The interesting fact here, the Earth keeps rotating, so the bulge has to keep moving to keep up, so the Earth rotates a little, the bulge readjusts, the Earth rotates, the bulge readjusts. The effect is actually the cause a lot of tidal friction inside the Earth. It's not a big deal for the Earth. It's not like this affects plate tectonics or anything, but the effect of the Earth's tides on the moon is huge. And in fact, that's responsible for all the moonquakes that happen. The NASA Apollo mission put out a set of seismometers on the moon, and it detected all these moonquakes in the interior, thousands of them. The reason for them is not plate tectonics; it's the tidal stretching due to the presence of these large tidal effects.

Another question, the Earth rotates once every 24 hours, and so, as I said, there're two bulges, two high tides, two low tides, but they're not at the same height. In other words, each day there'll be a high high tide and a lower high tide. Why does this happen? This is due to the tilt of the Earth's axis of rotation, which is not exactly perpendicular to the direction that the Earth moves around the sun or the direction that the moon moves around the Earth. Our axis, of course, is tilted 23.5 degrees. Imagine I'm at the Jersey Shore, let's say, and the Earth is rotating, and if I'm at this location over here, then I'm very close to that maximum bulge made from the moon, the maximum high tide. But 12 hours later I'm up over here. It's still a high tide, but in this case I'm missing most of that bulge, so the high tide is not as large.

Here's another question, I said that the time between high tides is about 12.4 hours, and not exactly 12 hours. Why is this? After all, Earth makes one full rotation in 24 hours. Twenty four divided by two, you should get 12. What changes during this time so that the tides are not exactly 12 hours apart? The moon has moved a little bit in its orbit around the Earth. The moon takes 28 days to go around the Earth. Each day, the moon moves a little bit more, so the Earth rotates, but the moon has moved over here and the Earth has to rotate a little bit more. One more rotation of the Earth, the moon has moved a little bit more; it has to go a little bit more. That little bit more means that the high tides are spread apart by 12.4 hours and not 12 hours.

The last question I asked was why are places like the Bay of Fundy so unusual? As the tidal bulge goes westward, if there are particular geometries of inlets or bays, the water can take a long time to work its way around the land, so the tide can become much larger. For the Bay of Fundy, there's actually a tidal resonance due to a coincidence of the timing. The time it takes the water to go up the bay and down is about the same as the time from one high tide to the next, so they begin to amplify. It's sort of like if you're pushing your kid on a swing, and the swing is rocking, if you're pushing at the wrong time the swing just comes to a stop, but if you push at just the right time, even a little bit each time, that creates a resonant effect that pretty soon your kid is flying high on the swing, very similar to the effect of the water flowing in and out of the Bay of Fundy. Very quickly, you get a huge amount of water in the bay draining out and back in each 12.4 hours. But here's an interesting point; it's not the same everywhere. You really need to go all the way up the bay to see this effect. If you're at the mouth, the effect of the tides may only be six meters or 10 meters or whatever, but by the time you get far up you can get 15 or more than 15 meters.

I mentioned that the record high tide was 71 feet. How did it get so high during that storm back in 1869? There are several factors that come to play here. One of them is air pressure. Right now, though you don't know it, there's a column of air, hundreds of kilometers high that's pressing down on top of you. You don't notice it because you're used to it and because it presses around you on all side equally, but you notice it when it changes. Have your ears ever popped going up or down an elevator, or when you're landing in an airplane? During a long flight, actually, the cabin pressure is not set at sea level, it's set to be about three-fourths that of sea level. Here's an interesting experiment, next time you fly in an airplane take an empty water bottle and seal it tight while you're up high, and then watch it as it gets crushed as you land by the increasing of the air pressure within the cabin. At sea level, the pressure of the air is just under about 15 pounds per square inch. And you probably have some sense of this from putting air in tires. A typical car tire pressure is about 30 pounds per square inch. For a bicycle, it's on the order of about 60 or 100 pounds per square inch; 15 pounds per square inch is like having a column of water 35 feet high on top of your head or like walking around with a stack of rocks 10 feet high on your head. Only, again, because it squeezes you all over, you don't ever notice it. When weather changes; however, the air pressure changes, and that's what a barometer measures. Some people claim they can even sense the change in pressure—their joints or something.

Bad weather is usually associated with areas of low air pressure; that's why people pay attention to barometer readings. In the case of a storm, the warm, lighter air rises, and that creates a low pressure region right over the land. The hot air cools, water vapor condenses into water droplets, ice crystals make clouds, and then it rains or snows out. That's why we have bad weather, rain and snow. During a hurricane, there can be an extremely low-pressure cell right in the center eye of the storm, the eye of the hurricane. Less air pressure means that the whole surface can rise up, creating a storm surge that can topple levees. This is a really interesting thought. Sea level is never constant in any one place. As low-pressure or high-pressure air cells move over water, the sea level goes up and down in response, but this is of the reason, or part of the reason, why hurricanes and typhoons are so dangerous for flooding along coastlines, as we saw in the lecture on the Ganges delta. The whole elevation of the water can change and rise up over your levees.

There is supposedly a very clever trick using this principle that the Vikings used to do when they were in a storm and the ocean waves were high. Supposedly they could build a fire on deck. The rising hot air creates a low-pressure zone, and it actually pulls the surrounding water up, and the boat with it, at least, that's the story. I'm not really sure if it's true, but it makes a lot of sense to me. I can actually try to demonstrate this using a very simple model for a Viking ship here. Pretend that this walnut here is the Viking ship and the candle on here is the fire on the deck. Now, if I light this, then I'm going to have a situation where I'm going to have hot air rising up above this. It's not exactly the same, but if I now capture this hot air using this glass here I'm going to fill up this glass eventually with a lot of hot air. If I suddenly then close this off, that hot air is going to begin to contract, making a low-pressure zone. So if I now drop this down here, I've now cut off entirely my boat. Over time now, as this air eventually is going to end up cooling, as soon as my fire goes out, the sudden contraction of this hot air will cause the air to shrink, and the result will be that the water inside the glass will actually rise upward, lifting the boat up with it.

So now we see the three factors that came together to make that very high tide during the Saxby Gale in 1869. You had a storm with very low atmospheric pressure, like I just demonstrated, causing the water to be elevated. It was a time of spring tide when the Earth, moon, and sun were all aligned together, and you also had very strong winds from the hurricane that essentially helped push water up into the Bay of Fundy. And the three came together to create these incredibly high tides.

This area of Newfoundland is a strikingly beautiful place, but not in the dramatic way that we've seen in other lectures, there're no tall mountains or steep fjords here. But it has a beautiful weathered appearance to it, like the land has been scraped away by countless winter storms blowing off of the North Atlantic, which it has. There is also, however, a rhythm to the place that's controlled by the tides that most of us don't get to experience in our lives anymore. I've spent much of my life in or around large cities, like New York City, you know, the city that never sleeps. With all of the lights there, it's easy to forget that the sun is below the horizon half the time. If you want to go out to eat, it doesn't matter what time it is, something is going to be open. But here, along the coast of Newfoundland, where fishing has been the major industry for centuries, you have to abide by the rhythm of the Earth. You have no choice. If you go down to your dock, and your boat is sitting in mud, and there's no water in sight because the tide is out, you're just out of luck. You simply have to wait. So people here are acutely aware of the tidal schedule, and they plan their lives out accordingly, and they pay very close attention to the weather report, because of the way that storms can amplify the effects of the tides.

A particularly unusual feature of the incoming tide is a phenomenon called a tidal bore. And this is a wave as the incoming tide rushes into the bay. You can sometimes see the front of the advancing tide moving upstream against the flow of the river. Sometimes these tidal bores are large enough that people can actually surf the wave as it comes in. That's a remarkable thought, surfing upstream in a river. In a couple of locations around the Bay of Fundy, there's also another very strange phenomenon, it's called reversing waterfalls. And these are rapids that form as the stream goes downhill, but you also get rapids that form as the tide comes in and the water goes upstream. They form either direction.

In one particular place in Maher Point, near Eastport, Maine, which, by the way, is the east-most part of the United States, you see this effect. Another is in St. John, in New Brunswick. Incidentally, St. John has a very unique location in the northern hemisphere, or at least in North America. It has a fantastic park for seeing the geology of the region that's called a Geopark, the Stonehammer Geopark. UNESCO, the United Nations Educational, Scientific, and Cultural Organization, has started a global network of

Geoparks. There are 77 of them so far, and there's only one of them in North America, and this is the one. You can see fantastic rock outcrops here, and a fascinating array of fossils.

Recent research has shown something very interesting, and that's that not very long ago tides in many places of the world were actually much more extreme than today. I'm not talking about the far distant past; it is also the case that hundreds of millions and billions of years ago, the moon was much closer to the Earth. It would've filled a much greater volume, area in the sky. There were much larger tides at that point. And actually, here's a very interesting thought. If you ever get sent in a time machine, but you're not sure if you're sent into the past or the future, you could use the size of the moon to tell. The moon is currently, entirely by chance, far enough from the Earth that it appears to be about the same size as the sun. But if you go back in time, the moon would've been much closer, and would've appeared larger. The moon currently is moving away from us, and the amplitudes of the tides are slowly decreasing, so if you go into the future, the moon will appear smaller than the sun. What I'm talking about is the very recent past, just 9- or 10,000-years ago.

The ranges between high tides and low tides were as much as four times greater than today in many places. The sea level was lower then, remember the Ice Ages had just ended, so most of the continental shelves were not yet flooded and were exposed, places like the Blue Hole in Belize. And this meant that bays and channels were deeper and more steeply walled, and this would have accentuated the geometrical effects of these funnels of amplifying these tides. Can you imagine a 200-foot variation in tides at the Bay of Fundy? I mean, Native Americans were living there at the time, and they would've experienced this.

Well, it's time for my top fivr. Let me first got to a region just north of the Bay of Fundy, Ungava Bay in Northern Quebec. It's off of the Hudson Strait, on the way to Hudson Bay, and in an area called Leaf Basin here, the maximum tidal range is almost that of the Bay of Fundy. It's 16.8 meters, just barely slightly less than the maximum observed in the Bay of Fundy.

Next, let me go all the way over to China for the Qiantang tidal bore on China's Fuchun River, which is, by far, the largest tidal bore in the world. This wave moving upstream can be up to 30-feet high, a single wave that propagates 22 kilometers inland and moving really quickly at about 25 miles an hour. It makes for some spectacular surfing, though it's really difficult, because the record for staying on your surf board at the maximum height of the wave here is just a little more than 10 seconds.

For surfing though, you want to go to the Severn Estuary, along the west coast of England, which empties into the Bristol Channel. Here you get a 15-meter tidal range, so this is also one of the largest tides anywhere in the world. But the Severn Estuary is famous for surfing. The tidal bore here isn't very large. The wave is only a couple of meters, six, seven feet, but it can carry surfers up 10 kilometers inland, so it's an amazing ride, going all the way up.

Next let's go to Pororoca, in Brazil, which is named for the tidal bore on the Amazon River and its estuaries. Tidal bores here can run 13-kilometers inland. The record for surfing is actually an amazing 36-minute-long ride.

And last, let me go to Norway and Scotland for one of the more unusual affects of tidal currents, and these are whirlpools or maelstroms. The most famous of these is the Lofoten maelstrom in Norway, and it's a whirlpool that develops as the tide comes in along the Norwegian Coast, and goes past a promontory, and develops into this large, swirling cone of water. This was actually described famously by Edgar Allan Poe in his story *Descent into the Maelstrom*. The largest maelstrom, however, is the Saltstraumen, also along coast of Norway, where strong tidal currents are forced through a very narrow strait. Whirlpools here can be more than 30-feet across and make a depression in the water surface, a cone, as much as 15 feet deep. A Scottish TV documentary company once threw a human mannequin with a depth gauge attached to it down into one of these whirlpools, the Corryvreckan whirlpool. It's actually the third largest in the world, along the western coast of Scotland. The mannequin got sucked down into the water, and finally came back a long ways away, showing signs of having been dragged along the bottom a significant distance. The depth gauge showed that it had been sucked down to a depth of over 850 feet.

The last point I want to make is, we take it for granted in our lives that the things we see around us on the Earth were the same in the past as they are today. But as I've already shown you, this is not necessarily the case. Certainly, in terms of location and geography, I've shown you that the continents themselves have moved around great distances.

But it's not only that space has changed; time has changed as well. We take for granted that our day is a 24-hour day. We rely upon it. But if you went back in time, even not that long ago, simply when the earliest creatures of the Cambrian were alive, 500-million years ago, the moon was much closer to the Earth, and at the same time the Earth was actually spinning much faster, so your day would've been only 18 hours. As it is now, with the moon constantly drifting away from us, we are, as a result, despinning tidally, and the Earth is slowing down. The good thing is you're going to get a few more hours per day, but there're going to be fewer days per year, so there's no free lunch here. But in any case, I hope you get a sense from this course that as you go back over geologic time everything that we take for granted changes.

In the next lecture, I'm going to visit a place that has lots of surfing, and that's the islands of Hawaii.

Hawaii—Volcanic Island Beauty
Lecture 24

We've already looked at a spectacular volcano at a subduction zone, Mount Fuji, and the bizarre volcanic environment at the Galapagos Rift, but in any discussion of volcanoes, nowhere else on Earth compares to Hawaii. The Big Island of Hawaii is not only the biggest volcano on Earth, but it's the biggest mountain on Earth of any kind. The highest point on the Big Island, Mauna Kea, is 13,796 feet above sea level. However, Hawaii actually rises a significant distance from the base of the seafloor, which makes it about 33,500 feet, or more than 6.3 miles, tall, and it's about 100 kilometers across.

A Classic Hotspot

- The state of Hawaii is actually 8 main islands, but the Hawaiian Islands are part of a much larger set of about 130 islands, smaller islets, and rocks that stick up above sea level, spanning 1500 miles. The Hawaiian Islands are the easternmost part of a long chain of islands and underwater islands (seamounts) that extend all the way off to the West Pacific. The chain heads into the subduction zone at Kamchatka, in eastern Siberia.

- This chain is almost 3600 miles long; there were even more seamounts at one point, but they have since subducted back into the mantle at Kamchatka and are gone. Altogether, the amount of volcanic rock on the Pacific seafloor is incredible. Over the past 65 million years, more than 1 million cubic kilometers of lava has erupted. This would have made a single massive volcano, except that the Pacific Plate has been steadily moving westward during this time.
  - The key to understanding how this works comes from dating the rocks taken either from the tops of seamounts or off islands. As we follow the chain, the rocks get progressively older. The seamounts that are now subducting into the trench at the top are about 85 million years old.

o Hawaii is the classic example of a hotspot. There is a large amount of hot rock underneath Hawaii—solid rock, not a plume of magma. As it moves up through the mantle, this hot, solid rock begins to melt as it reaches the surface. At the same time, the Pacific Plate is moving westward, pushing volcanoes out on the surface that are constantly being dragged away. As you go from one island to the next, the ages get progressively older. This explains why all the lava hasn't come out in just one location.

• The idea of hotspots was vital in the early days of the science of plate tectonics to explain volcanoes that didn't occur along plate boundaries. But we have since learned that volcanoes can occur in the middle of a tectonic plate for a number of other reasons. Recent seismic tomography has shown, however, some locations where plumes of hot rock rise up to the surface from deep within the mantle. Hawaii is the quintessential example of this.

• Still not fully understood is the connection between the Hawaiian hotspot at the surface and the giant lower-mantle Pacific Megapile. This is a massive region of hot rock in the lower mantle that seems to rise up as a large cone, occupying much of the lower mantle beneath it. Current research is trying to determine whether this material is rising upward all the way from the core-mantle boundary or whether it represents a hot, dense region of iron-rich rock spawning hotspots.

• An interesting aspect of the Hawaiian hotspot is that the volcanism there seems to be relatively fixed in relation to the mantle of the whole planet. Together with Yellowstone, another fixed hotspot, Hawaii provides a reference frame for measuring the motions of the tectonic plates at the surface.

• The cause of the bend in the Hawaiian-Emperor hotspot chain presents another intriguing question.
  o Perhaps 20 years ago, the bend would have been explained by a change in direction of the Pacific Plate 43 million years ago in response to the subduction of the Kula Plate (a piece

of the Pacific Ocean seafloor) beneath North America. This subduction was thought to have rearranged the motions of the Pacific Plate.

○ More recent work has shown that the Pacific Plate may not have changed direction; instead, it may have been the case that the Hawaiian hotspot within the mantle was moving and didn't stabilize until 43 million years ago.

• Another complication comes from recent work done by seismologists at MIT, who have shown that the hotspot plume may not go continuously from the lower mantle to the surface. In fact, it may reach resistance at the boundary between the upper and lower mantles, spread out at that boundary, and then rise up to the surface just through the upper mantle.

○ The mantle isn't a single layer of rock; there are separate layers depending on the minerals found within the rocks.

○ At a depth of 660 kilometers from the surface is an especially important boundary. At this location, the mineral olivine, the primary mineral in the upper mantle, is squeezed by intense pressure to convert to a rock called perovskite, which determines the boundary between the upper and lower mantles.

○ The hotspot plume for Hawaii at the surface is not necessarily connected to its location in the lower mantle.

Visiting the Hawaiian Islands

• The Hawaiian Islands are at different stages of development; we can get a picture of how an island changes over millions of years just by visiting each island. The island of Maui, for example, is a little more than 1 million years old; Molokai is about 2 million years old; Oahu, about 3; and so on.

• The Big Island is young; it has active volcanoes and lots of lava. As you move west, the amount of lava decreases; erosion increases; the sea cliffs become steeper; deep valleys are carved out by rain; and weathering creates thicker soil, allowing lusher vegetation.

- Some of the most popular beaches in the Hawaii Islands are on Oahu or Maui, while the island of Kauai offers a bit more wilderness. Kauai also has the famous rugged Na Pali coast, a spectacular 17-mile stretch of dramatic cliffs and waterfalls, and Waimea Canyon, known as the Grand Canyon of the Pacific.

- Beaches on the different islands can even have different colors. Some of the islands tend to have a greenish color from the mineral olivine; others can be dark black from the mineral pyroxene. Plivine and pyroxene are the major minerals of the volcanic rock—basalt—that makes up most of the islands.

- As you go farther west, the islands become smaller, and the landscape features are less pronounced. Signs of active volcanoes disappear. Eventually, you reach small, flat islands and then no islands at all. The islands become seamounts.

The Big Island
- The Big Island is a composite of recent volcanoes. The most active are on the southeast side, Mauna Loa and Kilauea. In fact, Kilauea has been erupting continuously since 1980. The lava here is hot (2000°F) and low in silica; thus, it's very fluid. You can stand right next to the lava as it's flowing, pull out pieces with a stick, and watch as they quickly cool into obsidian. The lava usually looks black because it's cooling on top, but underneath, you can see that it glows red.

- Lava can flow all the way to the sea and often does, extending the island outward. Again, because the top of the lava forms a crust, it doesn't seem to be moving, but underneath may be a rapidly flowing river of lava heading toward the ocean. When the lava hits the water, it can explode and steam as it instantly cools, forming lava tubes. At 41 miles, Kazumura is the longest lava tube in the world; it's also the deepest.

The lava from Kilauea is fluid because it's low in silica; it can slowly ooze great distances horizontally.

- The lava here flows primarily in two forms, either as a sort of ropy texture, called pahoehoe, or as a blocky form, called aa. The difference between the two is largely related to the differing composition of the gases in them.

- The crater called Kilauea Iki is a former lava lake, with steep walls, a strong sulfur smell, and almost no surrounding vegetation.

Earthquakes and Tsunamis
- Hawaii experiences numerous small earthquakes because, as the magma cracks its way up to the surface, it breaks open the rock. The earthquakes may be stronger when large pieces of the edges of the island break off and slide downward. Earthquake activity is closely monitored in Hawaii as an indication of when a volcano might erupt.

- On rare occasions, Hawaii experiences strong earthquakes. The Pacific Ocean seafloor was covered with ocean sediments long before the islands developed. Lava later spread out across this layer of sediment, but the sediment is weaker rock; thus, the Hawaiian Islands are decoupled from the crust. Occasionally, a whole island can suddenly slide down across the seafloor. Destructive earthquakes occurred in 1868, 1951, and 1975 from this phenomenon.

- Tsunamis also represent a hazard in Hawaii. Tsunamis begin in the Ring of Fire, travel great distances across the Pacific, and become focused when they hit shallow regions, such as the broad underwater islands of Hawaii. The Big Island has been severely hit by tsunamis many times in the past century.

- Because of the trade winds that blow from the northeast, the Big Island has an incredible diversity of microclimates, making the surface geology fascinating. The north side, near Hilo, has some beautiful, lush, tropical areas, but to the south is the Ka'ū Desert, and Mauna Kea is so high that it often has snow.

Top Hotspots

- The Louisville hotspot chain in the southern Pacific Ocean is a track of about 70 underwater seamounts that stretches more than 4000 kilometers, from the mid-ocean ridge into the Tonga-Kermadec Trench, where the Pacific Plate is subducting beneath the Australian Plate.

- At the Great Meteor hotspot track in the North Atlantic, magma has been rising to the surface for more than 200 million years. This makes it the longest continuous hotspot on Earth, in both time and distance. The length of this hotspot chain is almost 6000 kilometers, stretching from northern Canada to the African Plate on the other side of the Mid-Atlantic Ridge.

- The Ninety East Ridge is a line of underwater seamounts that extends about 5000 kilometers across the Indian Ocean in a north-south line at a longitude of 90 degrees. It stretches from the coast of Sumatra southward into the Antarctic plates.

- The Chagos-Laccadive Ridge is exactly parallel to the Ninety East Ridge. This ridge began 65 million years ago as the large outflow of lava known as the Deccan Traps in India. Eventually, it jumped across the mid-ocean ridge and is now located beneath the island of Réunion just off the coast of Madagascar.

Suggested Reading

Hazlett and Hyndman, *Roadside Geology of Hawai'i*.

Lillie, *Parks and Plates*.

Questions to Consider

1. Look at a map of the bathymetry of the Pacific Ocean. Notice the shape of the subduction zone where the Emperor seamount chain enters it. Propose a hypothesis to explain the shape of the subduction zone there.

2. Why is it that volcanic eruption on Hawaii rarely causes the loss of any human lives?

Hawaii—Volcanic Island Beauty
Lecture 24—Transcript

Hello. My name is Michael Wysession, and welcome to Lecture 24 of our course on the Geologic Wonders of the World. In the last lecture, I looked at ocean tides and visited the Bay of Fundy, in Eastern Canada. In this lecture I'm going to head out to the middle of the ocean and visit the beautiful Hawaiian Islands.

We've already looked at a spectacular volcano at a subduction zone, Mount Fuji, and the bizarre volcanic environment at the Galapagos Rift, but if you want to talk about volcanoes, nothing else on Earth compares to Hawaii. Hawaii is a long way away from any land. It isn't the farthest island from any continental land mass; that distinction actually goes to Pitcairn Island, in French Polynesia, to the south of Hawaii. But Hawaii is still a far distance from any land, and as a result, it actually took a long time to be discovered, first visited by Polynesians starting sometime around the year 300.

Recent research suggests that the Polynesians originated in Southeast China in the Fuzhou Basin, which was flooded at that time, due to rising sea levels following the melting of ice at the end of the last Ice Age. This turned this agricultural community into a seafaring one. And starting about 5,500 years ago, these Chinese began sailing out to the outer islands, first to Taiwan, then the Philippines, then Indonesia, the Solomon Islands, Vanuatu, Samoa, Tonga, French Polynesia, and then, eventually, to Hawaii.

A quick word about the word Hawaii, to people on the mainland, the word Hawaii often refers to the state, and therefore, the whole set of Hawaiian Islands. To a native, Hawaii is just the Big Island, distinct from the other islands. And to avoid confusion, some people will refer to the island Hawaii as the Big Island, and I will do that as well. The big island of Hawaii is not only the biggest volcano on Earth; it's the biggest mountain on Earth of any kind at all. The highest point on the Big Island, Mauna Kea, is 13,796 feet, that's about 4.2 kilometers above sea level. However, Hawaii actually rises from the base of the seafloor, a significant distance, which makes it about 33,500-feet tall or 10.2 kilometers; this is over 6.3 miles. For comparison, Mount McKinley, the tallest land mountain, when measured from the surrounding land, is only about 18,000 feet tall, about half as tall as Mauna Kea. And the Big Island is about 100-kilometers across. It's shaped like a giant shield on the ground. In fact, it's often referred to as a shield volcano. We saw that previously in the lecture on Erta Ale.

But the Big Island is only one of many islands. There are eight main islands here: Hawaii, Maui, Oahu, Kahoolawe, Lanai, Molokai, Kauai and Niihau. However, these are part of a much larger set of about 130 islands and smaller islets and rocks that actually stick up far above sea level, spanning 1,500 miles. But here it gets even more interesting, and is the key to understanding what Hawaii is, what it's doing here, and how it formed in the middle of the ocean. If you look at the Hawaiian Islands, they are the easternmost part of a long chain of islands and underwater islands that we call seamounts that extend all the way off to the West Pacific. They take a bend at one point. They have a different name, but it's part of the same chain, the Emperor Seamount chain, in fact, it heads then right into the subduction zone at Kamchatka, in Eastern Siberia. This is almost 6,000 kilometers in length, or 3,600 miles, which means that there were even more seamounts at one point, but they have since subducted back into the mantle at that subduction zone, and they're entirely gone. Altogether, the amount of volcanic rock on the Pacific seafloor is incredible. Over the past 65 million years, over a million cubic kilometers of lava have erupted. This would've made a single, massive volcano, except that the Pacific Plate has been steadily moving westward during this time.

The key to understanding how this works comes when you put ages on the rocks dredged either from the tops of these seamounts or taken off the islands themselves. And you can see that these are not randomly placed. The lava is coming out today at the Big Island of Hawaii, so its age is now, it's zero. As you go to the older islands, though, they can be as old as five-million years. Go back farther, eventually you get to the bend, and the rock there is 43-million years old. As then as you go up the Emperor Seamount chain it gets progressively older, and the seamounts that are now subducting into the trench up at the top are at most about 85-million years old.

So, how does this form? There's a clue here, and that is that they follow a straight line, and that straight line is the same direction that the Pacific plate moves. Hawaii is the classic example of a hotspot. And what we mean by that is there's a large amount of hot rock underneath Hawaii, and I want to stress this is solid rock; this is not a plume of magma rising up. As it comes up through the solid mantle this hot, solid rock rises up, begins to melt a small amount as it reaches the surface, and, of course, the Pacific plate is moving westward during this time, so as it punches volcanoes out on the surface, they are constantly being dragged away, one after the other. So as you go from one island to the next, the ages get progressively older. This is the classic example of how a hotspot works. And it explains why all the lava hasn't come out in just one location.

For the first scientists who put together this whole idea of plate tectonics, back in the 1960s, the presence of hotspots was really a vital part to this. And later on modeling, either on computers, such as some of the images that I will show you, or done in the lab; there are places where there're giant tanks of corn syrup that model how these plumes operate. They showed how the mantle plumes could be generated from the very base of the mantle, the region that we call the core-mantle boundary. And the idea here is that hot rock is heated by the heat coming out of the core. The core is liquid iron, and that iron doesn't come up into the mantle, so the heat has to conduct across that boundary. And it means that the temperature changes very rapidly over the bottom couple of hundred kilometers of the mantle. It may be 1,000 degrees cooler by the time you just go up a couple hundred kilometers.

The result is, if you were to have some of that hot rock suddenly begin to rise upward in sort of a mushroom-shaped plume, it suddenly finds itself 1,000 degrees warmer than rock on either side, which means it's much more buoyant and will continue to rise upward. This was the idea that we had. It's the same principle by which a lava lamp works, and soon after, any volcano that didn't occur along the plate boundary, that occurred in the middle of a continent, was called a hotspot. And soon geologists had catalogued more than 400 different hotspots.

It ended up there was a large backlash against this because, of course, there are all sorts of other geologic reasons why you can have volcanoes occurring in the middle of a tectonic plate. In fact, soon, there were some people who were even saying that there was no such thing as a mantle hotspot plume.

Recent seismic tomography, this is imaging the Earth using the seismic waves from earthquakes, however, has shown that there are, indeed, some plumes of hot rock that do rise up to the surface from deep within the mantle, and Hawaii is the quintessential example of this. It's the largest amount of lava coming out of a single place for an enormous amount of time.

One thing that certainly is still uncertain, however, is the connection between the Hawaiian hotspot at the surface and the giant, lower-mantle Pacific Megapile. These are these features in the lower mantle that I've talked about previously. Remember in the lecture on the African Rift Valley I said that there was a massive region in the lower mantle beneath Africa that seemed to rise up as a large cone, occupying much of the lower mantle beneath it. There's another one beneath the Pacific. And we now can take images of this. This is work done by a seismologist Jeroen Ritsema, and these are slices, think of these as like CAT scan slices through a human body, only in this case our body is the Earth here, and it's cutting through at different angles, but this orange feature that you see here in all of these images, the orange represents regions where the seismic waves are traveling more slowly, and this occurs because the rock down there is hot. This is this massive pile of hot rock at the base of the mantle. And what we don't know, and current research is working on, is if this is, itself, the hotspot that is rising from the core-mantle boundary. That's represented by the boundary here at the bottom of the colored region. The center part here would be the core, the iron of the core, whether this material is rising upward all the way from the core mantle boundary, or if this represents a hot, dense region of iron-rich rock, and the hotspots are coming off the surface of this, spawning off with this large megapile heating up the base of the rock and the mantle that creates, not only Hawaii, but places like Easter Island and French Polynesia and Samoa and all of these other hotspots that are in the Pacific.

There's another interesting aspect of the Hawaiian hotspot, and that is the volcanism down there seems to be relatively fixed in relation to the rest of the Earth, in relation to the mantle of the whole planet. In other words, if you have Hawaii here and you have Yellowstone here, they seem to be fixed relative to each other. And this is really good because it provides a reference frame by which we can measure the motions of all the tectonic plates at the surface. So on top of Yellowstone you have North America moving, and on top of Hawaii you have the Pacific plate moving, and if we consider these hotspots to be anchored within the Earth, we now have a reference frame that lets us quantify the speeds of all these plates. It turns out the hotspots aren't exactly fixed with respect to each other. In other words, the locations of Hawaii, and Yellowstone, and Iceland, and other hotspots, they do move relative to each other, but very slowly, on the order of about millimeters a year, whereas the tectonic plates are moving an order of magnitude faster on the order of centimeters a year. So, we can still use those hotspots as a reference frame for all of plate tectonics.

There are still a lot of questions that remain. One very significant one actually has to do with that bend in the Hawaiian-Emperor hotspot chain. If you had asked me 20-years ago why this bend is there, I would've said, well, this is a very easy question, 43-million years ago the Pacific plate changed its direction. Before 43-million years ago, it would've been moving primarily north-northwest, and then 43-million years ago it started going west-northwest. What happened in between? Well, we thought that this was due to the fact that there was a piece of the Pacific Ocean seafloor, its own plate, called the Kula plate, that totally finished subducting beneath North America. In fact, the word Kula in the language of the Native Americans from the Pacific Northwest actually means all gone. So this plate entirely disappeared at that point. It rearranged all the motions in the Pacific, and the Pacific plates started moving in a different direction.

Unfortunately it's not quite so simple because more recent work has shown that the Pacific plate may not have changed direction, and in fact, before 43-million years ago, it may have been the case that the Hawaiian hotspot within the mantle was actually moving itself. And it didn't actually stabilize until 43-million years ago. This is a problem that's still being worked on, and hopefully, sometime when a future course like this is done, we'll know the answer.

Another complication comes from recent work done by seismologists at MIT who have shown that the hotspot plume may not go continuously from the lower mantle to the surface. In fact, it may reach resistance at the boundary between the upper and lower mantles, spread out at that boundary, and then rise up to the surface just through the upper mantle. Yes, the mantle isn't a single layer of rock; there are actually separate layers depending upon the minerals found within the rocks. At a depth of 660-kilometers down from the surface is an especially important boundary. This is the location where the mineral olivine, which is the primary mineral in the upper mantle, gets squeezed so much from the intense pressures of all the rocks sitting on top of that it converts into a totally new atomic structure and makes a rock called Perovskite. This is actually what determines the boundary between the upper and lower mantles. So what happens is the location of the hotspot plume for Hawaii at the surface is not necessarily connected to its location in the lower mantle. The two might be entirely disconnected.

When you visit the Hawaiian Islands, you see, as a result of their progression in ages, a set of islands that are in different stages of development. It's kind of like looking back in time at any one island. It's sort of seeing how an island would change over millions of years, only you get to do it at one time by just going to different islands. The island of Maui is a little bit more than a million-years old. For Molokai, it's about two-million years old; Oahu is about three, Kauai is about five. And in terms of tourism, what you get is a wide range of sceneries. Go to the Big Island, it's big, it's young, there're active volcanoes, there's lots of lava. As you go west, the lava becomes less; the erosion becomes greater; you get steeper sea cliffs; deep valleys that are carved out by all the rain; weathering creates thicker soil, so the vegetation becomes increasingly lush. These are some of the top tourist destinations because one thing you also get is spectacular beaches from all that eroded, weathered rock that now becomes sand around the island. These beaches are surrounded by huge coral reefs so there's great snorkeling and scuba diving. I've gone snorkeling in the islands there, and it's just fantastic, these large reefs, multicolored fish; you can go swimming with giant sea turtles, and it's really a remarkable time.

I don't think I need to spend too much time actually describing the different islands. There is a lot of tourist information available on them. Some of the most popular beaches are on Oahu or Maui. If you go to the island of Kauai, it gives you a bit more wilderness; roads only reach about 10 percent of the island there. Kauai also has the famous rugged Na Pali coast, is a spectacular 17-mile stretch of dramatic cliffs and waterfalls. And it also contains the

Waimea Canyon, which is called the Grand Canyon of the Pacific. It cuts about a half-mile down into the lava flows.

A lot of movies, in fact, that want to show wild scenery with primitive jungles have been filmed on Kauai, movies like *Jurassic Park*. Beaches on different islands can even have different colors. Some of the islands tend to have a greenish color from a lot of the mineral olivine there; some can be dark black from the mineral pyroxene. These two minerals olivine and pyroxene are the major minerals of the volcanic rock, basalt, that makes up most of the islands.

As you go farther west, the islands become increasingly smaller, the features are less pronounced, there are no more signs of active volcanoes, and eventually you just get, small flat islands and then no islands at all. They're below sea level. They're seamounts. Why do islands disappear as they get older? One reason is obvious, erosion. There's a lot of rain here, and the rock basalt weathers fairly easily. There's another reason that I'm actually not going to get to until Lecture 28, when I talk about the Maldive Islands, and that is the seafloor here is actually sinking as it gets older.

If you want active geology, really the gem of all of these is the Big Island. The whole island is a composite of very recent volcanoes. The most active are on the southeast side, and these are Mauna Loa and Kilauea. In fact, you can see from the black streaks here, these are where the most recent lava flows have occurred. In fact, Kilauea has been erupting continuously since 1980. The lava here is hot and low in silica, so it's very, very fluid. Silica is what makes up quartz—a combination of oxygen and silicon—and it's very gummy. The bonds between the atoms are strong, so lava that has a lot of silica tends to be very thick. This is low in silica, so it's much more fluid. You can stand right next to it as it's flowing, you can even stand on it in certain cases.

I've had the pleasure of visiting Kilauea on a couple of occasions and actually watching the lava flow, and it's a remarkable site. I've stood there, I've poked sticks into the lava flow, pulled out pieces that cool nearly instantly. In fact, they cool so quickly they quench into black glass; we call that obsidian. The lava's really hot; it's about 2,000 degrees Fahrenheit, that's about 1,100 degrees Celsius. So you feel the radiant heat coming off it. It's like getting a sunburn in a matter of minutes. But even though it becomes thick as it starts to harden, because the lava is so fluid, it just can slowly ooze great distances horizontally. It usually looks black because it's cooling on the top, but anytime it goes even over the slightest ridge it stretches out and you see this glowing red, hot lava underneath.

One time I even hiked there at night. At first I couldn't tell if I was near the lava at all, but it was raining slightly, and as I got close to the lava, I began to hear this sizzling noise as the raindrops were landing on the hot rock. As I got close to the lava flow, I could actually begin to see the glow of the rocks around me. Large areas that would've appeared black during the day were now glowing various shades of red and orange, warning me that they were 2,000 degrees Fahrenheit. It's really a spectacular experience.

The lava can flow all the way to the sea, and does often, making new land, growing the island out. Though often it flows in a very interesting way; it will begin to form a crust over the top of the river of lava, and so from the surface you don't see anything, but underneath you can have this rapidly flowing river of red, hot lava sort of making a beeline right from the top of the volcano out to the ocean. When it breaks out, out into the sea, and hits the water, it can explode, and erupt, and steam as it instantly cools. These are called lava tubes and the longest in the world are here. There's one, Kazumura, that's actually 41-miles long. It's located about a half a mile deep, the longest and deepest lava tube in the world. This is about 500 years old. It's from an older eruption of Kilauea, and all the lava is gone now, and now there's just this 41-mile long, empty tube. It's almost like a subway tube, and you can just walk for miles in it.

The lava flows here primarily in two forms, either as a very sort of ropy texture that we call pahoehoe or a very blocky form called aa. You've probably seen pictures of these. The two are very similar. The difference is largely just a change in the composition of the gasses in it. In fact, you can change one to the other sometimes simply by having it change the slope in which it's flowing down. The lava can sometimes fill up a crater to make a lava lake. We've seen these previously like Halemaumau and Pu'u O'o. We saw that at the end of the lecture on Erta Ale. And just the experience of driving around the volcanoes and all the different features that are there is really remarkable. One of the best drives in the world is Crater Rim Drive around Kilauea, and it's just incredible, the sites that you'll see.

One place there that left a very strong impression on me was a crater called Kilauea Iki. This is a former lava lake, with very steep walls, and steam smoking out in places, the strong sulfur smell, almost nothing growing in or around it. It looks very much like the land of Mordor from the *Lord of the Rings*, at least how I would've envisioned it. It very well could have been used for the movie version of the *Lord of the Rings*. Anything living in this area is just having a really rough time of it.

One thing that's interesting, Hawaii can get a lot of earthquakes because as the magma cracks its way up to the surface, it actually breaks open the rock. So the earthquake activity is highly monitored there as an indication of when a volcano might erupt. Most of these earthquakes are very, very small. They can be a little bit larger, because as the island grows outward you can end up with large pieces of the edges of the island sort of breaking and sliding downward. And on rare occasions, you can actually get giant earthquakes, but for a very unusual reason.

It turns out the Hawaiian Islands are decoupled from the crust below because they sit on a layer of sediments. Think about this. The Pacific Ocean seafloor was there covered with old ocean sediments long before there were islands here. And as that lava came out it spread out across this layer of sediment, which is a weaker rock and decouples it from the whole rest of the island, and sometimes the whole island can suddenly slide down a little bit across the seafloor. This has happened in 1868, 1951, and 1975, known as the Kalapana earthquake. And these have been very destructive.

One thing also that's a real hazard for Hawaii is tsunamis. Hawaii is located much within the ring of fire of all these volcanoes and earthquakes that happen around the edge of the Pacific, and when the tsunamis travel across the Pacific, which they can do at great distances, as I talked about in the lecture on Mount Fuji, when they hit shallow regions, they tend to get focused. So as they reach the broad, underwater islands of Hawaii, these tsunamis can get focused, and the Big Island has been severely hit many times within the past century by these tsunamis.

The Big Island is also large enough, and the prevailing winds blow fairly constantly enough from the northeast—these are the trade winds. But the Big Island has an incredible diversity of microclimates, making the surface geology very fascinating. The temperature here is always very moderate. It's buffered by the giant ocean, so on any given day, going back in time, the temperature only ranges by about 10 degrees. But because of the way the island is structured you can get a large variety of climates. The north side, near Hilo, has some beautiful lush areas. If you drive around the corner at one place, it's raining. You walk through a tropical jungle and see the beautiful Akaka falls. Drive around the next promontory of land, the rain stops, and you're in dry plains. Drive farther to the south, and now you're in the Ka'ū Desert. It's so dry that NASA Astronauts actually trained there for going to the moon. Drive to the top of Mauna Kea, it's so high up that there's often snow, and it's so clear that it's a great place for telescopes. There's long been an astronomical observatory there.

So, if you visit Hawaii, sure, visit the beaches on the other islands, but then take a plane over to the Big Island and experience the Earth's largest volcano and the huge variety of fascinating geologic features that are there.

Alright it's time for my top five. And what I want to do is quickly point out five other ocean hotspot chains. First, there's another chain in the Pacific Ocean that's very large. It's called the Louisville hotspot chain down in the Southern Pacific Ocean. This is a track of about 70 underwater seamounts that stretches over 4,000 kilometers from the mid-ocean ridge right into the Tonga-Kermadec Trench there, where the Pacific Plate is subducting beneath the Australian plate, which we saw in the lecture on the Fiordland National Park. This is formed by a hotspot called the Louisville hotspot, adding a chain of volcanoes onto the Pacific Plate.

Next, let's go to the Great Meteor Hotspot Track in the North Atlantic. Magma has been rising to the surface from this hotspot for more than 200-million years. This makes it the longest, continuous hotspot on Earth, both in time and distance. In fact, the length of the hotspot chain is almost 6,000 kilometers, from Northern Canada, where it first came out, to the African plate on the other side of the mid-Atlantic ridge, where the hotspot is now. The earliest record of activity up by the Hudson Bay goes back 215-million years. And as you go eastward, the volcanic activity occurred more and more recently. By 125-million years ago, it was intruding volcanic rocks up into the already-existing White Mountains of New Hampshire. Between 100- and 80-million years ago, it had formed a linear track of seamounts off the coast of Massachusetts, the New England Seamounts.

Next, I want to go to the Ninety East Ridge, which is a line of underwater seamounts that extends about 5,000 kilometers across the Indian Ocean in a north-south line at the longitude of 90 degrees, that's where it gets its name. It's this feature right here. It's this line of hotspot islands. It stretches from the coast of Sumatra, not far from where that massive magnitude nine earthquake occurred in 2004, southward all the way down into the Antarctic plates. Here it actually jumps across the ridge to Kerguelen Island, which is not far off the coast of Antarctica. This hotspot began, in fact, when the Kerguelen Island and this region of India were adjacent to each other, and it may actually be the case that this hotspot helped India breakaway from Antarctica back 120-million years ago.

Last, I want to point out another ridge that's exactly parallel to that. And that's this ridge of underwater seamounts that's parallel to the Ninety East Ridge. This is known as the Chagos-Laccadive Ridge. And this began 65-million years ago as the large outflow of lava known as the Deccan Traps in India. And as India has moved away, it left a mark of islands on the seafloor. Eventually it jumped across the mid-ocean ridge, and is now located beneath the island of Réunion just off the coast of Madagascar.

In the next lecture, I'm going look at another example of hotspot volcanism, but this time at what happens when a hotspot is underneath a continent, and I'm going to go to Western Wyoming to visit Yellowstone National Park.

Yellowstone—Geysers and Hot Springs
Lecture 25

In the last lecture, we talked about Hawaii, the last in a chain of islands and underwater seamounts that's the result of the Pacific Plate moving over a mantle hotspot. In this lecture, we'll look at what happens when a hotspots lies underneath a continent, the situation we find in Yellowstone National Park in Wyoming. As we'll see, volcanic activity occurs at Yellowstone, but it takes a different form than that in Hawaii. Before the mid-19th century, trappers reported seeing boiling mud, steaming rivers, and petrified trees in the region of Yellowstone, but organized explorations of the area didn't begin until 1869. In 1872, Yellowstone was designated as the first national park.

Visiting Yellowstone
- Yellowstone National Park has tall mountains, spectacular waterfalls, gorgeous valleys, and even a Grand Canyon of the Yellowstone, where the Yellowstone River cuts down a steep valley. It has the largest population of large mammals anywhere in North America, including a herd of bison, as well as elk, grizzly bears, wolves, lynx, black bears, moose, bighorn sheep, mountain goats, and mountain lions.

- One of the most well known places to visit in Yellowstone is Artist Point, which offers great views of the Yellowstone Grand Canyon and waterfalls. This spot is also where the artist Thomas Moran painted some of his famous images in 1871, which helped to convince Congress to make Yellowstone a national park.

- The Grand Canyon of Yellowstone formed in a similar process to the Grand Canyon in Arizona. In this case, the Yellowstone hotspot has lifted up the whole region, and the Yellowstone River has maintained its course; as the land has been lifted, the river has cut down, carving a deep canyon.

- Yellowstone is located right along the Continental Divide. This means that the two major rivers there, the Yellowstone River and the Snake River, begin close to each other but then head in different directions. The Snake River flows west into the Columbia River and, eventually, the Pacific Ocean, and the Yellowstone River flows into the Mississippi River and then into the Atlantic. These rivers make spectacular canyons as they flow through layers of soft volcanic ash that wears away sharply and dramatically.

- Of course, one major reason to visit Yellowstone is the geysers. The park has 300 geysers and a total of at least 10,000 geothermal features. Half of the world's geothermal features and two-thirds of the world's geysers are concentrated in Yellowstone National Park.

Geysers

- Geysers begin with a source of heat; in Yellowstone, this source is the magma close to the surface. Also needed are underground rocks that allow large amounts of water to percolate through them. Rainwater percolates down, sometimes as far as 2 or 3 kilometers, where it comes in contact with rock heated by the magma below. This water becomes superheated and rises up to the surface.

- Why are geysers intermittent? As it's heated, the water underneath the surface builds up pressure, but it's still water—not steam— because of the weight of all the water on top of it. Once it begins to erupt, however, the hot water turns to steam and blows out the top of the geyser. This is similar to the way a pressure cooker works. Once the water erupts, the chambers underground are emptied, and the cycle won't repeat until they are refilled.

- The most famous geyser, of course, is Old Faithful, which can spout more than 8000 gallons as high as 185 feet into the air. The popularity of Old Faithful is the result of its regularity, but Steamboat Geyser, which can spew water 300 feet in the air, is larger.
  - The eruptions at Old Faithful occur fairly regularly, though the interval changes over time, ranging from 45 minutes to 125 minutes over the last century.

- One reason the interval changes is that the water underground can cool and precipitate out minerals that begin to choke off some of the chambers, changing the interior plumbing of the geyser over time.

- Other well-known geysers include Beehive Geyser and Castle Geyser. At Beehive Geyser, the water erupts out of a small cone, only about 4 feet high, but it can reach as high as 200 feet.

- Some large geysers have an "indicator"—another, usually smaller geyser that's a precursor to the main geyser. The indicator for Beehive Geyser is a small cone 10 feet away that erupts 15 to 25 feet high. It begins its eruption between a few seconds and 30 minutes before Beehive Geyser erupts.

Other Geothermal Features

- Other geothermal features at Yellowstone fall into three general categories: (1) fumaroles, places where steam erupts without water; (2) hot springs, where water bubbles up without steam; and (3) mud pots, where hot water comes up through an area with a good deal of sediment, then boils and churns at the surface, like a giant pot of thick soup.

- The most colorful of the hot springs at Yellowstone is the Grand Prismatic Spring. The colors here are not the result of any geologic process. They are entirely due to living single-celled organisms, a particular kind of extremophile called a thermophile. These organisms thrive in areas that would cook almost anything else. They are examples of a primitive life form called archaea.
  - Each hot spring has a slightly different combination of minerals in the water and a slightly different temperature. Each color band in a spring represents a separate zone that's preferred by a particular species of archaea. The archaea themselves are different colors, resulting in the prismatic effect in the pools.

  - A research program is underway to learn about the strange life forms that exist deep inside thermal hot springs. Just as at the

The travertine terraces at Mammoth Hot Springs are formed from calcium carbonate brought up to the surface by water traveling along an underground fault.

mid-ocean ridges, all the elements are present in hot springs for the development of life: a source of heat, a source of food, and protection from the surface.

- One of the most stunning geologic features at Yellowstone is Mammoth Hot Springs. The hot water coming out at Mammoth contains large amounts of calcium carbonate that precipitates as it cools. About 2 tons of dissolved calcium carbonate—the same material that makes the shells of marine creatures and forms limestone—flows out into Mammoth every day.

  o The presence of magma underground heats water that rises up through limestone, bringing the calcium carbonate with it.

  o When the water reaches the surface and cools, minerals precipitate out, resulting in the rock called travertine.

o   Wherever the water sits in a pool, it begins to build a wall of travertine. Over time, these walls can grow very tall, creating deep pools. Water seeps out in different locations and builds a complex stairway of cascading pools.

A Giant Volcano

- The underlying cause of all this hydrothermal activity in Yellowstone is the fact that the park itself is a huge caldera, sitting on top of a volcano that could become active at any time. In fact, at 50 miles across, Yellowstone is one of the largest calderas in the world.

- A caldera forms as part of the cycle of a volcano. After an eruption from a large magma chamber, the loss of the volume of magma causes the top of the chamber to collapse. At some later point, when the magma activity is entirely done, what's left is a large depression. The caldera may still be slightly active, as evidenced by steam and geysers similar to those seen at Yellowstone.

- Yellowstone is, in fact, a supervolcano. It has had some of the largest eruptions in the world. Three large ones occurred in the past 2 million years. Volcanic activity shifted to the current Yellowstone Plateau and peaked 640,000 years ago, forming the current caldera.
  o   Since that time, a little bit of doming has occurred in the northeast and southwest sides of the caldera—magma pushing up from below. Between 150,000 and 70,000 years ago, about 1000 cubic kilometers of lava erupted within the caldera itself. No lava has erupted in the past 10,000 years or so. Are we overdue for an eruption?

  o   In 2005, GPS instruments in Yellowstone recorded that the area was lifting up at the rate of about 7 centimeters a year as magma flowed underneath. But since that time, the area has started to settle back down.

- In the past, eruptions from Yellowstone have covered much of the continent with thousands of cubic kilometers of ash. Some of the effects of an eruption are visible in the park, such as petrified trees that were essentially cooked and turned to stone when they were buried by ash.

- As mentioned earlier, Yellowstone is over a continental hotspot. The hot rock from the hotspot rises up underneath, but it doesn't come all the way to the surface. It stops underneath the crust and spreads out somewhat. It causes some melting of the granite-type composition there. That granite composition rises up to the surface and erupts, resulting in the formation of rhyolite as it flows outward.

- The path of the volcanoes at Yellowstone is heading to the southwest—the same direction in which North America is moving. It's likely that Yellowstone will last for a long time because it has an active plume underneath. It could potentially continue to poke up volcanoes all the way across North America.

Top Geothermal Features
- Geysir in Iceland is the origin of the word "geyser." This geyser can eject steam more than 200 feet high, but it is dormant for long periods of time. Geysir has a nearby partner called Strokkur that reaches only 15 to 20 meters high but erupts every 4 to 8 minutes.

- The Valley of Geysers is in a remote part of Siberia, the Kamchatka Peninsula; it has the second largest concentration of geysers in the world—about 90. The whole valley seems to be smoking and steaming, but much of it was covered in a massive mudflow in 2007. The geysers will probably return here, but they haven't done so yet.

- The Dallol Hot Springs in Ethiopia are the most spectacular colored hot springs in the world. The greens, yellows, oranges, and reds seen here are caused by various compositions of salts, iron oxides, and sulfur.

- The Pamukkale travertine terraces in Turkey are similar to the beautiful travertine terraces of Mammoth Springs in Yellowstone but on a much larger scale. The terraces may be 1.5 miles long and 2000 feet wide. Almost 2500 years ago, a Greco-Roman city, Hieropolis, was built on top of these travertine terraces.

Suggested Reading

Chapple, *Yellowstone Treasures*.

Smith and Siegel, *Windows into the Earth*.

Questions to Consider

1. Why do some geysers, such as Old Faithful, erupt regularly and some do not?

2. How could the United States prepare for a future eruption of Yellowstone? Should we do so?

Yellowstone—Geysers and Hot Springs
Lecture 25—Transcript

Hello. My name is Michael Wysession, and welcome to Lecture 25 of our course on the Geologic Wonders of the World. In the last lecture, I talked about Hawaii, the last in a chain of islands and underwater seamounts that's the result of the Pacific plate moving over a mantle hotspot. In this lecture, I will look at what happens when one of these hotspots lies underneath a continent, and I will visit Yellowstone National Park, in Wyoming.

With Hawaii, we ended up with a long chain of volcanoes stretching across the Pacific Ocean, all the way to Kamchatka, in Siberia. With Yellowstone, we still have volcanic activity, but it takes a very different form. I've tried to resist stacking my list of Geologic Wonders with U.S. National Parks. There are just so many spectacular ones. Though fortunately, with my top-five lists I've managed to slip in a few more.

It would be inconceivable for me not to include Yellowstone in that list; it's just such a remarkable place. If you've been to Yellowstone, the first thing that might come to mind is lots of people, long lines, and traffic jams. It's a difficult conundrum. Places that are geologically spectacular attract a lot of people, and that can make the place seem less spectacular. Sometimes, in the case of caves and other delicate environments, it can even damage or destroy the wonder itself, but Yellowstone is worth the crowds.

Yellowstone was the first National Park anywhere, in any country. This was passed by Congress and signed into law by President Ulysses S. Grant, back in 1872. The name Yellowstone came from the Yellowstone River, which flows through the park, which was originally called Mi tsi a-da-zi, a Native Minnetaree name that translates as Yellow Rock River. It's not certain, but it's thought that this was likely based on the color of the sandstone bluffs that are along the river as it flows through the park, though, other tribes called it different names. The Crow tribes called it E-chee-dick-karsh-ah-shay, which means Elk River.

Yellowstone actually took a while to be discovered. It was visited early on, in 1807 and 1808 by the explorer John Colter, who had been a member of the original Lewis and Clark Expedition in the years before. Colter saw at least one geothermal area in the northeastern section of the park and gave a description of a place of fire and brimstone. But he had been recovering from wounds from battles with natives at the time, and most people just dismissed his claims as delirium. They called this supposedly imaginary place Colter's Hell. And over the next forty years, there were several reports from explorers and trappers who told of boiling mud, steaming rivers, and petrified trees, but these, too, were mostly dismissed as myth. It wasn't until 1856 that an explorer named Jim Bridger reported observing boiling springs, spouting water, and what he described as a mountain of glass and yellow rock. The Civil War put an end to any exploration, but in 1869 and 1870 there were some organized explorations of the area, and they were sufficiently impressed so that two years later, in 1872, it was signed into law as the first National Park.

There are a lot of reasons to visit Yellowstone. It's a beautiful place. There are tall mountains there, gorgeous valleys, there's even a Grand Canyon of Yellowstone where the Yellowstone River cuts down a steep valley. There are spectacular waterfalls. It has the largest population of large mammals anywhere in North America. There is the largest herd of Bison, 3,000. You have about 30,000 elk, grizzly bears, wolves, lynx, black bears, moose, bighorn sheep, mountain goats, mountain lions, and so on.

One of the best-known places to visit, in terms of the scenery, is a place called Artist Point, and this gives you great views of the Yellowstone Grand Canyon and a spectacular view of waterfalls there. But this is also the place where the artist Thomas Moran painted some of his famous images, back in 1871. And this was very important because it was these paintings that helped inspire the country and actually helped convinced Congress to make this into a national park.

Incidentally, the Grand Canyon of Yellowstone there formed in a process that we've already seen in this course, very similarly to the way the Grand Canyon in Arizona formed. In this case, the Yellowstone hotspot has lifted up the whole region, and the Yellowstone River has maintained its course, and as the land has gone up, the river has cut down carving a deep canyon as the land has risen.

Yellowstone, as I said, sits high up in the mountains, and it's actually located right along the Continental Divide. What this means is that the beginnings of the two major rivers there, the Yellowstone River and the Snake River, are actually very close to each other where they begin, but the water in the Snake River flows west and into the Columbia River and eventually ends up in the Pacific Ocean, and the water in the Yellowstone River ends up in the Mississippi River and then out into the Atlantic. And because of the historical volcanic activity in the area, these rivers make spectacular canyons because they flow occasionally through layers of very soft volcanic ash that wears away sharply and dramatically.

But the reason to visit Yellowstone isn't necessarily the valleys. It's the geysers, lots of them. In fact, there are 300 different geysers in Yellowstone and a total of at least 10,000 geothermal features. In fact, half of the world's geothermal features and two-thirds of all the world's geysers are concentrated right here in Yellowstone National Park. But why does this happen? There are a couple of factors that have to come into play and happen in just the right way to get so many geysers. First of all, you need a source of heat, and you've got it. There's magma right close to the surface. You also need to have the right kind of rocks underground that will let large amounts of water percolate through them, and you have to have that water heated to just the right temperature. In fact, in places it's more than 400-degrees Celsius.

So what happens is the rainwater percolates down, sometimes two or three kilometers down, and here it comes in contact with very hot rock, heated by the magma that's sitting below, and this water becomes super heated and rises up to the surface. But, this doesn't really answer why the geyser occurs. In particular, why is it intermittent? Why isn't there constantly hot water bubbling up? I can show you this with an animation. If you have water percolating down, it comes all the way down into the ground, you have heat that heats up that water, turns it into hot water and steam. A tremendous amount of pressure builds up and, it eventually bursts out the surface. There are a couple of factors here. First of all, the water is more than the boiling temperature at the surface, but it's not turning into steam way down deep; it's still water. Why is this happening?

You may have seen this in your own kitchen if you've ever used a pressure cooker. If you take water and you don't give it room to expand into water vapor. You can superheat it higher than its boiling point at the surface of the Earth. One thing you don't want to do is take the lid off a pressure cooker because that water is going to flash into steam and can be very dangerous. That's essentially what happens here. This hot water builds up a lot of pressure, but it's still water because of the weight of all the water on top of it. Once the water begins to erupt, however, all this hot water begins to turn to steam, and it's a runaway effect, and the steam and hot water blow out the top of the geyser. Then you have empty chambers, which have to fill up with water again, and once the fill up, the cycle can then repeat. There are other places around the Earth where water can be seen bursting out of the ground, most notably around coastal regions. These are features that we call coastal blowholes where waves will hit a shoreline rock that has holes in it and will blow water off the surface. It's a totally different process, even though it actually may look similar.

The most famous geyser, of course, is Old Faithful. Old Faithful can spout over 8,000 gallons up into the air in a few minutes, as high as 185 feet. It's actually not the biggest geyser in Yellowstone. That's Steamboat Geyser, but its popularity is due to its regularity. I've been there and waited with my camera, and it's just tremendously rewarding to wait, and you have a sense from the guide as to when it's going to come, and there it is. It erupts and you get your pictures. It's just fantastic.

The eruptions occur fairly regularly, though the interval actually changes over time. Over the last century this has ranged from between 45 minutes and 125 minutes. It's currently about 90 minutes between eruptions, and that's just the right amount of time to build up suspense. If it erupted every few minutes you'd get there, you'd see it erupt, you've seen it, and you move on. Here, people stand around and they talk and they wait. It's sort of like waiting for the climax at the end of a movie, and then it erupts, and then you can go on and see something else in the park.

I mentioned that it changes its interval over time. Why would it change over time? There are a couple of reasons here. One important one is water supply. If you're there during a dry period when there's not a lot of rain, it just takes longer for that groundwater to refill the chambers of that geyser. Another thing that can happen is as the hot water sits in there and cools it can actually precipitate out minerals that can begin to choke off some of the chambers. This material is called sinter. So the interior plumbing of the geyser itself can actually change over time.

Steamboat Geyser, as I mentioned, is the largest geyser in Yellowstone. And it can spew water more than 300 feet in the air, and this can go on for 40 minutes at a time. However, Steamboat is much less predictable. It can take a few days between eruptions. It can actually take 50 years between eruptions. It didn't erupt at all between 1911 and 1961. Other well-known geysers include Beehive Geyser and Castle Geyser. Beehive geyser is understandably named because of the way it looks. The water erupts out of a small cone, only about four-feet high, but its sort of shaped like a beehive. Eruptions there go up as high as 200 feet, actually higher than Old Faithful and can last about 5 minutes. But the interval is long; it can be eight, or even 20 hours, before it happens again.

Interestingly there are some large geysers that have an indicator, another, usually smaller, geyser that's a precursor to the main geyser and lets you know when the large one is going to occur. In the case of the Beehive Geyser, its indicator is a small cone located just 10-feet away, and it will erupt only 15 to 25 feet high, but it begins anywhere between a few seconds to 30 minutes before, so it gives you warning that the large eruption is going to occur. I have to stress, geyser activity, if you go and visit, is usually very variable, and that's what makes Old Faithful such a wonderful site to visit because it's so unusual in its regular intervals. During the 1990s, Beehive Geyser was actually totally dormant. And during this time it was Beehive's indicator that erupted, and it could sometimes erupt for as much as an hour at a time. Castle Geyser is another popular geyser. It gets its name because deposits have built up around the vent that give, very much, the appearance of a castle with turrets. And when Castle Geyser erupts, these eruptions are often 10 to 12 hours apart, it can erupt water for 20 minutes, going almost 100 feet high, and then it erupts steam for the next 30 or 40 minutes.

At Yellowstone, as I mentioned, you don't just have geysers, you have many different forms of what we call geothermal features, over 10,000 of them.

And these occur in sort of three general categories. You have what are known as fumaroles, which are steam without water, you have hot springs, which are water without steam, and mud pots. The way these work for fumaroles is you are venting gasses, mostly water vapor, that come out. There's not much to see, but it often makes a strong sound as this jet of hot gas is ejected out.

The hot springs involve water sort of bubbling out regularly, and I'll show you these in a moment. And the mud pots are just fascinating, because if the hot water comes up through an area with a lot of sediment, these mud pots can just sit there and boil and churn and bubble away like a giant pot of some very thick soup or something.

There are actually several different regions throuhout Yellowstone Park that contain huge numbers of these geothermal features. The most colorful of these are the hot springs, like the Grand Prismatic Spring, and these are truly incredible. The colors are amazing. This isn't dye put in here. This is what it actually looks like. Can you imagine stumbling across this in the 1800s? What's even more fascinating is the colors are not due to any geologic process. They are entirely due to living, single-celled organisms called extremophiles, in fact, a particular kind of them called thermophiles. These are single-celled organisms that like heat. They thrive in areas that would otherwise cook most anything else. These are examples of the very primitive life form called archaea.

You may remember back in the lecture on the Burgess Shale, I talked about archaea being one of the three branches of life, very primitive, single-celled organisms, and some of the first archaea were discovered here in the Yellowstone hot springs. Each spring has a slightly different combination of minerals in the water, and also slightly different temperatures, and in fact, even in the same pool you'll have a range of temperature from the middle towards the edge. Each color band represents a separate zone that's preferred by a particular species of archaea. And the archaea themselves are different colors, so the result is this prismatic effect where the color changes according to the types of archaea that are present there in the pool. It's really incredible.

Remember when I talked about all the strange life forms that are at mid-ocean ridges and the possibility that life on Earth actually started at a mid-ocean ridge? This is another possibility, deep inside a thermal hot spring. I mean, you have everything you need. You have a source of heat; you have a source of food, all the rich minerals that are there; and you're protected from the surface. Because remember, early on in Earth's history there wasn't any oxygen in the atmosphere, and so there wasn't any ozone, and so ultraviolet radiation just bombarded the surface and would've been deadly to anything living there. There are actually large research program underway to learn about these strange life forms that exist in this hot water that is just incredibly hot and that most organisms cannot survive. There are scientists that go and sample a pool in many different locations, pulling out and identifying the different single-celled organisms that live there.

One of the most stunning geologic features at Yellowstone, and personally, my favorite, is Mammoth Hot Springs. The hot water coming out at Mammoth contains large amounts of calcium carbonate that precipitates as it cools, the same material that makes the shells of marine creatures. About two tons of dissolved calcium carbonate flows out into Mammoth every day. Where does this calcium carbonate come from? This is the same stuff that limestone is made of. And just like Mammoth Caves in Kentucky, same name, Mammoth, no connection, and many other places we have seen already in this course, it comes from a deep layer of limestone. However, here, the presence of magma underground heats water that rises up to the surface coming through the limestone, bringing the calcium carbonate with it. This is just the opposite of caves where rainwater percolates down through a layer of limestone, making spectacular formations underground. Water from the Norris Geyser Basin nearby travels along a fault underground; the fault is from an old earthquake that happened long ago, and this water travels through the rock, dissolves away the limestone, and the water is hot, it's 170°F, but when it comes up to the surface and cools, those minerals precipitate out. That happens more so as the water evaporates and it causes the spectacular rock called travertine. This isn't snow or ice here; this is solid rock, travertine, and as the water comes down and evaporates on this, it causes these shields and walls to continue to grow these spectacular, beautiful colors.

Wherever the water sits in a pool, it begins to build a wall. And over time, these walls can grow very high, creating very deep pools. Water will seep out in a variety of different locations, and over time builds up a complex stairway of these cascading pools. I mean, it's really remarkable.

So, what's the underlying cause of all this hydrothermal activity that's spread out all over the park in so many stunning ways? Well, it's because nearly the whole park itself is a giant volcano. It's a huge caldera that sits on top of an active, not at the moment, but could be any time, an active volcano. In fact, Yellowstone is one of the largest calderas in the world. It's actually 50-miles across, about 85 kilometers. How does a caldera form? A caldera forms as part of the cycle of a volcano. So you may have a large eruption with a magma chamber underneath, and after that eruption occurs, the magma drains back down underneath, and the top part actually collapses because of the loss of the volume of magma underneath. At some later point, when the magma activity is entirely done, at a later stage, what you're left with is a large depression here. This is the caldera, and it may still be slightly active in terms of steam and geysers, and that's what we have in Yellowstone, but the magma is still there.

It's part of this cycle and we don't fully understand how this happens, but it seems as if large volcanoes like Yellowstone—they're certainly not living, but they breathe in a sense—where the magma comes up towards the surface, the whole region lifts up. You may have eruptions, and the magma then drains back down again, and it goes through this cycle. Many of you may have seen shows about Yellowstone or read about it as a supervolcano. And Yellowstone is, indeed, a supervolcano. It's had some of the largest eruptions in the world that we know of. It has many past eruptions, both big and small. But there were three big ones in past two-million years that have really captured people's attention; 2.1 million years ago there was an eruption of ash that created what's called the Huckleberry Ridge Tuff, T-U-F-F. We've seen this earlier in the course. This is when hot ash falls down and compacts into a hard rock. This is 2.5-thousand cubic kilometers of ash. And when that volcanic eruption ended the surface collapsed down to make the island park caldera; it's farther to the west from the current volcanic activity, but it was also huge, about 75 kilometers long. This was the last part of a volcanic cycle that concluded with the next large eruption. This was about 1.3-million years ago, and this created the Mesa Falls Tuff, and it formed a 16-kilometers-wide caldera called Henrys Fork, and that's also at the west end of the first caldera. Volcanic activity then shifted to the present Yellowstone Plateau and peaked 640,000 years ago with the eruption of more than 1,000 cubic kilometers of the Lava Creek Tuff and the formation of the current present caldera.

Since then, there's a little bit of doming occurring in the northeast and southwest sides of the caldera, magma pushing up from below, and there's been about 1,000 cubic kilometers of lava that have erupted within the caldera itself that happened a long time ago, about 150,000 to 70,000 years ago. No lava, however, has erupted in the past couple 10,000s of years, and the question remains, are we gearing up for the next one?

If you had asked me this question back in 2005, I would've said very possibly, because at that point we had a network of GPS instruments in the area; all of Yellowstone was actually lifting up at the rate of about seven centimeters a year as magma was flowing up underneath. The temperatures were getting hotter, and then it started to go down. So this is this breathing process I was talking about, so it's really hard to tell. But these eruptions are enormous. They cover the continent, or much of it, with ash, thousands of cubic kilometers.

If you want to see some of the effects you can actually see this in Yellowstone. There are places where there are petrified trees where the ash fell down, buried, and essentially cooked these trees turning them into stone. Water continues to flow through the ground and heat up, but the ground doesn't cool off, and where does this continuous supply of heat come from? Of course this is because Yellowstone is a hotspot, like Hawaii. But it's under a continent, as I mentioned at the start of the lecture.

So if it's a hotspot, we should see a track, and indeed we do. What happens is the hot rock for the hotspot comes up underneath, but it doesn't come all the way to the surface. It actually stops underneath the crust and spreads out somewhat. And it causes some melting of the granite-type composition here. This rises up to the surface where it erupts sometimes with the same composition as granite, but it forms a rock that we call rhyolite as it flows out of the surface.

You can look at the history of volcanism in Yellowstone and see this progression of volcanism. The current volcanoes are located over here, but if you look back in the past two-million years, six-million years, 14-million years, you can see this path heading to the southwest. Why in this direction? Because that's the direction that North America is moving. And the hotspot began down here about 17 million years ago. In fact, some of that magma actually rose up underneath the Columbia River basalt area in Washington and Oregon and caused an enormous outpouring of lava at that time, 17-million years ago. One thing that you also see that's very puzzling, or was puzzling, and now we understand, is a ring of earthquakes that make a funny parabolic shape. What's happening here is as the hotspot, which is stationary, moves, apparently across North America, that's moving to the southwest, it creates a thermal front that spreads out, causes the rock to expand and crack as earthquakes. So you get the earthquakes occurring in this parabolic shape, pointing directly towards the current hotspot. By the way, these orange lines here represent the historic past calderas of Yellowstone going back into the past.

One other question obviously is going to be, how long will Yellowstone last? Well, probably for a while because we have an active plume coming up from underneath. We can get a sense of this by looking at the seismic tomography here. And this is really remarkable. The picture on the right here is a model that was made a long time back on a computer of what you would expect to see for the Yellowstone hotspot coming up to the surface and then begin dragged off to the west by the motion of the North American plate. What you see on the left here is an actual picture made from seismic imaging, and it's not exactly the same, you wouldn't expect it to be, but what you very clearly see is the plume rising up and then being dragged off to the west. How long will this continue? We don't know. We've seen places like Hawaii where you've had eruptions go on for tens of millions of years. Will it be under Minnesota one day? Quite possibly! It could potentially continue to poke volcanoes underneath North America all the way across.

It's time for my top-five list. And let me start at the place where the word geyser came from. And this is in Iceland. There is indeed a geyser there, it's pronounced Gay'-sr, but that's where we get the name geyser from, which, in Icelandic, means to gush, not surprisingly. Geysir can eject steam up to 70-meters high, more than 200 feet, but can also be dormant for long periods of time. Fortunately, if you ever go to Iceland as a tourist, it also has a partner called Strokker, which is just 50 meters away, and it's a smaller geyser; It only erupts 15 to 20 meters, but it's remarkably frequent and regular. It erupts every four to eight minutes or so. I'm going to talk more about Iceland a little bit later in Lecture 27.

Next, let me go to one of the most difficult places you can get to in this course to see one of these geologic wonders, and that's the Valley of Geysers in a remote part of Siberia, in the Kamchatka Peninsula. This has the second largest concentration of geysers anywhere in the world, about 90 geysers. The whole valley is a volcanic region; it seems to be smoking and steaming. Unfortunately, a massive mudflow covered over two-thirds of the valley in 2007, which is important in a way because it shows not all of these geologic wonders are going to stick around forever. Probably, in this case, the geysers will likely return, eventually breaking their way up through the mud, but it hasn't happened yet.

Next, we'll go to Ethiopia for the Dallol Hot Springs. I already talked about these in the lecture on Erta Ale, but I just can't leave it off the list here. The region contains the most spectacular colored hot springs in the world with colors of greens, yellows, oranges, and reds. Hot springs are found in many parts of the world, even in Arkansas, far from any volcanoes. But these extreme colors, here in Ethiopia, caused by various compositions of salts, iron oxides, and sulfur, are extremely rare.

And last, let me go to Turkey for the Pamukkale travertine terraces. Imagine the beautiful travertine terraces of Mammoth Springs in Yellowstone, but on a much larger scale. These things are a mile-and-a-half long, 2,000 feet wide. *Pamukkale* in Turkish means "Cotton Castle," and it certainly looks that way. Two-and-a-half-thousand years ago, there was a Greco-Roman city, Hieropolis, that was built right on top of the travertine terraces because of the hot springs. And in fact, people have been bathing here for thousands of years, which has actually considerably damaged the pools. This got a lot worse in the mid-20th century. However, since it was declared a World Heritage Site by UNESCO, as are most of the geologic wonders I've talked about here, a lot more care has been taken to keep the tourism from destroying the delicate travertine terraces.

I haven't mentioned this up until now, but there has been a fantastic effort undertaken by UNESCO to identify those parts of the world that are especially important for either natural or cultural reasons. In many cases, simply having the distinction of being a world heritage site has actually provided the justification for protecting and preserving a natural wonder in the face of so many forces that would otherwise cause its degradation, and sometimes even destruction. So, I take my hat off to UNESCO for carrying out this important work, since 1972.

In the next lecture, we're going to travel to Indonesia to visit a very strange feature, the world's most acid lake, Kawah Ijen.

Kawah Ijen—World's Most Acid Lake
Lecture 26

In the last lecture, we looked at the features that result when magma and water are mixed underground: the beautiful geysers and hot springs of Yellowstone National Park. In this lecture, we'll look at a different result of mixing water with volcanoes; for this, we'll visit the acid lake at Kawah Ijen on the island of Java. Ijen is the name given both to a group of stratovolcanoes and the 20-kilometer-wide caldera in which they sit. It's also the name given to a small acid lake that sits in the midst of this caldera. Unlike some of the heavenly beautiful beaches and waterfalls we've visited so far in this course, Kawah Ijen is a vision of hell.

The Island of Java

- The area of Indonesia in which Kawah Ijen is located consists of a large number of islands. Ijen happens to be on the far eastern end of Java, across from the island of Bali, but Sumatra, Java, Bali, and numerous other islands form the longest continuous island-arc volcanic chain in the world. The chain is almost entirely made of volcanoes and is a direct result of the subduction of the Australian Plate underneath Southeast Asia.

- On the island of Java, the volcanoes are spread out about 80 kilometers from each other. They are each about 3 kilometers high and run right down the spine of the island. Though some of Java's 38 major volcanoes are currently dormant, any or all of them could erupt in the future. The most active volcano here is Mount Merapi in central Java. Smoke comes out of its summit about 300 days a year, and it has erupted regularly since it became known in 1548.

- Java and the surrounding islands have been populated for a long time. Fossils from an early human found here, *Homo erectus*, known as "Java man," date back 1.7 million years. Evidence of *Homo sapiens* has also been found, dating back more than 130,000 years. Most of the modern humans in Java are related to a second wave of modern humans that settled in the islands about 40,000 years ago.

- o In 2003, a dwarf species of human was discovered, *Homo floresiensis*, only about 1 meter tall. This species lived just 18,000 years ago on the island of Flores, east of Java.

- o The remains of dwarf elephants have also been found in the area, in the same deposits as the humans.

Chemistry of Kawah Ijen

- The volcano Kawah Ijen has a deep crater at the top that's filled with water; gases bubble up out of the crater into the water, forming a lake of boiling acid that is one of the most inhospitable places on Earth. Kawah Ijen is a little less than 3 kilometers in elevation, and the lake is 200 meters down from the crater rim.

- The lake on Kawah Ijen is only about 360 meters across and about 200 meters deep. Fumaroles—gas vents—bubble up into the water

Local people harvest about 4 tons of nearly pure sulfur every day directly out of the fumaroles at Kawah Ijen.

at the bottom; the water temperature is between 93° and 100°F. The fumaroles contain water vapor, carbon dioxide, nitrous oxides, and sulfur dioxide.

o Oxygen is a hyperreactive material. It often forms a negative ion that bonds with anything nearby. In fact, almost all rocks are mostly made of oxygen. The crust of the Earth is 93 percent oxygen by volume. Many gases also contain large amounts of oxygen.

o A common gas that comes out of volcanoes is sulfur dioxide. In the atmosphere, sulfur dioxide mixes with water vapor and forms sulfuric acid. Particles of sulfuric acid make a common aerosol in the atmosphere.

o As the gas bubbles its way up through the water, it forms both sulfuric and hydrochloric acid. The acid is in such high concentrations that the lake water has a pH of 0.5—about the same pH level as the sulfuric acid in batteries.

o Note that pH is a measure of the activity of hydrogen atoms, which are also highly reactive. Neutral water has a pH of 7; anything with a pH of less than 7 is an acid, and anything with a pH of greater than 7 is a base. A pH of 0.5 is so acidic that it will burn away skin.

o The small lake on Kawah Ijen is estimated to have dissolved more than 0.5 million tons of hydrochloric acid and 0.5 million tons of sulfuric acid.

• The liquid sulfur emitted at Kawah Ijen is so hot that it actually burns, but it's about 99 percent pure. It hardens as it cools and is collected by local workers to be used in various industrial processes, such as refining sugar and vulcanizing rubber.

Effects of Volcanoes on Climate
• The sulfur released into the air from Indonesian volcanoes has had a profound influence on life, including our own.

- The sulfur reacts with oxygen to form gaseous sulfur dioxide, which then combines with water vapor in the atmosphere to make an aqueous sulfuric acid. These droplets are aerosols; they're particles that are so tiny they can stay suspended in the air.

- The acidic liquid begins as a vapor but needs something to condense onto to form the small liquid particles, such as ice crystals within clouds, dust carried up from the surface, or ash emitted from volcanoes. These liquid particles eventually grow in size; in the atmosphere, the sulfuric acid droplets are about 0.1 to 1.0 micrometers in diameter. These sulfuric acid aerosols can powerfully block out sunlight and cool the surface of the Earth.

- Only stratovolcanoes produce atmospheric aerosols, but when one of these erupts, the effect is like a giant umbrella, essentially blocking out sunlight.

- In recent history, eruptions from even small volcanoes, such as Pinatubo and El Chichón, produced enough aerosols to drop the amount of solar radiation reaching the surface by tens of percents. Pinatubo dropped global temperatures by a degree for about a year.

- When global climates are cold, more dust tends to be in the atmosphere. More dust in the atmosphere means that there are more particles for the sulfuric acid vapor to condense on to make aerosols and block sunlight. A feedback mechanism develops: more dust, more aerosols, less sunlight, and so on. Thus, a volcano that erupts when it's already cold will have a greater impact on climate, making it even colder.

- A good example of the climate effects of an Indonesian volcano is the eruption of Tambora in 1815. This volcano ejected about 100 to 160 cubic kilometers of material into the atmosphere; it was 100 times larger than the eruption of Mount Saint Helens in 1980. Almost 100,000 people were directly killed, but more significantly, the volcano created the worst famines of the 19th century in 1816, known as the year without a summer.

- The effects of Tambora pale in comparison to the eruption of another Indonesian volcano not far from Kawah Ijen, Toba, about 73,000 years ago. This is the largest known volcanic eruption, even larger than the Yellowstone eruptions. When Toba erupted, it released about 2800 cubic kilometers of ash into the atmosphere. This eruption occurred during a period of glaciation and probably triggered an extension of that period. Genetic research suggests that most of the world's humans did not survive this long period of extreme cold following the massive eruption.

- At some point, it may be possible for humans to control the temperature of the planet by deliberately introducing sulfuric acid aerosols into the atmosphere to counter the effects of the release of greenhouse gases. This approach might be the cheapest way to prevent global warming, perhaps 100 times cheaper than producing the same amount of global temperature change by reducing carbon dioxide emissions.

Top Extreme Lakes
- The Poás Volcano in the Central Valley region of Costa Rica is the site of another extremely acidic lake. The volcano has two separate crater lakes; the northern one, Laguna Caliente ("Hot Lake"), has pH levels of less than 1. This lake is larger than Kawah Ijen—about 1 mile wide and 1000 feet deep.
  - At the Poás Volcano, acid fogs sometimes develop above the lake, drift away, and precipitate out as acid rain; thus, the whole surrounding area has been burned.

  - Poás has erupted about 40 times in the last 200 years, most recently in 2009. Sometimes it emits hot eruptions of gas, called phreatic eruptions, that eject the acid lake water high into the air as acid geysers.

- About 20 kilometers off the coast of the north island of New Zealand is White Island, a small, circular volcano that also has an acid lake in the crater. The temperature of this lake is about 50°C, and the lake has a pH of about 1. As a result of its chemical composition and, remarkably, the presence of single-celled organisms, the lake has an unusual bright green color.

- Lake Natron in Tanzania is the world's most alkaline lake. It has a pH of about 10.5, similar to ammonia. The temperature of this lake is about 50°C, and it's also fed by hot springs that are triggered by volcanic activity in the African Rift Valley. But instead of bringing such minerals as sulfur into the water, these hot springs bring salts, such as sodium carbonate, or soda ash. Types of cyanobacteria and blue-green algae, such as spirulina, give the lake a red color and support large populations of fish and birds, including flamingos.

- The most acidic water found anywhere on Earth is at Iron Mountain in California, which is actually an abandoned mine, not a natural cave. The rock here naturally contains high concentrations of metals—iron, silver, gold, copper, zinc, and others—and as water seeps into and out of the cave, it reaches a pH level of –3.5. This is the equivalent of half-strength pure sulfuric acid.
  - o This area is considered one of the most toxic waste sites in America, but geologically, it's fascinating because new types of minerals are forming here that don't exist anywhere else in the world.

  - o Almost all life has been eliminated from the streams that are downstream of the mine, with the exception of a few new kinds of extremophile bacteria and archaea. Remarkably, even this extreme environment created on our planet has resulted in the evolution of new life.

Suggested Reading

Lockwood and Hazlett, *Volcanoes*.

Oppenheimer, *Eruptions That Shook the World*.

1. Historically, why has there been a demand for sulfur?

2. Why do you think there aren't more acid lakes in the calderas of volcanoes around the world?

Kawah Ijen—World's Most Acid Lake
Lecture 26—Transcript

Hello. My name is Michael Wysession, and welcome to Lecture 26 of our course on the Geologic Wonders of the World. In the last lecture, we looked at what happens when you mix magma and water underground, the beautiful geysers and hot springs of Yellowstone National Park, in Wyoming. In this lecture, we will look at a very different result of mixing water with volcanoes, and we're going to visit the acid lake at Kawah Ijen, on the island of Java.

Ijen is the name given both to a group of stratovolcanoes and the 20-kilometer-wide caldera that they sit in. And it's also the name given to a small acid lake that sits here in the midst of this caldera. We've seen some places in this course with beautiful beaches or waterfalls that look like heaven. In this lecture, we're going to visit a location that's more like that other place. It's about as hellish a place as you could visit. Imagine a place where hot steam has so much sulfuric acid in it that it would burn away your lungs if you breathed it in directly. Imagine hot, flaming, liquid sulfur condensing from this steam. Imagine a lake filled with the equivalent of battery acid that would dissolve you away if you fell in it. Such a place exists here on Earth. It's the crater lake of Kawah Ijen on the island of Java in Indonesia.

We've already seen stratovolcanoes like Mount Fuji a couple of times in this course, and we've also seen a couple of large calderas, like Santorini, and Yellowstone. These places are beautiful tourist-friendly attractions. The same is not true for Kawah Ijen. Let me put Kawah Ijen in its setting. This whole area of Indonesia consists of a large number of islands. Ijen happens to be on the far eastern end of Java, right across from the island of Bali. But Sumatra, Java, Bali, and the other islands of Sumbawa, Sumba, Flores, and Timor, and others form the longest, continuous island-arc volcanic chain in the entire world. This whole chain is almost entirely made of volcanoes, and is a direct result of the plate tectonic process of the Australian plate moving northward and subducting down underneath Southeast Asia.

On the island of Java, the volcanoes are spread out about 80 kilometers from each other. They're tall; they're each about three-kilometers high, and they run right down the spine of the island. I say almost entirely made of volcanoes because at a subduction zone you also have the rock of an accretionary wedge; there are other geologic processes going on. For instance, here you have the Australian plate sinking beneath the islands here, and the sediment gets scraped off to form new land that gets added on to the Indonesian islands. You can also flood the island during globally warm periods and deposit sediments on top of the land that will form platform sedimentary rocks.

But the islands are there because of the volcanism, and they're, essentially, a chain of interconnected volcanoes. Though some of Java's 38 major volcanoes are currently dormant, and haven't erupted for a while, any or all of them could still erupt in the future, and geologically speaking, they're still active. Some of them are incredibly dangerous. The most active of these is Mount Merapi, in central Java. There's smoke coming out of its summit probably 300 days a year, and it's erupted regularly since it was known, in 1548.

This island is incredibly dangerous, and it can kill in many different ways. In fact, there was an explosion in 1994 that killed 27 people, just from the compositions of the gases that were released. Java and the surrounding islands have had a people for a long time and actually have a very varied interesting human history. There are fossils from what's known as Java Man that go back almost two-million years, 1.7-million years. This was an early human, a homo erectus. There's evidence of Homo sapiens, our species, going back more than 130,000-years ago here. Although, interestingly, most of the modern humans there are related to a second wave of modern humans that settled here in the islands about 40,000-years ago. And this is going to be very important later on in the course.

Back in 2003, an entirely new species of human was discovered, a dwarf human called now *Homo floresiensis*, and these people are colloquially referred to as hobbits because they were incredibly short, only about a meter tall. They lived recently, just 18,000-years ago, on the island of Flores, just east of Java. Not only were they hobbit-sized people there, but there were also the remains of dwarf elephants found in the area in the same deposits as the humans. And the reason for all these small sizes is still being debated.

But it's at one of the volcanoes on Java, Kawah Ijen, that we see a very interesting combination of factors. Kawah Ijen has a deep crater at the top that's filled with water; it rains a lot here, and there are gases that continue to come up out of the crater, bubbling up right up into the water. The result is a hot, boiling acid lake that's one of the most inhospitable places on Earth. Kawah Ijen is just under three kilometers in elevation, but it's just a short ways down, 200 meters from the crater rim, that you reach the lake. The lake isn't very big. It's only about 360-meters across and about 200-meters deep. But there are fumaroles that bubble right up into the water at the bottom. Remember from Lecture 25, fumaroles were gas vents; these were holes where hot gasses were ejecting out quickly from the surface. This causes the temperature of the water to rise and can be anywhere between 93°F and 100°F.

But the fumaroles contain more than just water vapor. They also contain carbon dioxide, nitrous oxides, and sulfur dioxide. A quick word about chemistry, oxygen is a very hyperreactive material. It often forms a negative ion that will bond with anything nearby. In fact, most all rocks are mostly made of oxygen. The crust of the Earth is 93 percent oxygen by volume. And many gases, as well, contain large amounts of oxygen. A very common gas that comes out of volcanoes is sulfur dioxide. It's a gas where the molecules contain one atom of sulfur and two atoms of oxygen. In the atmosphere, sulfur dioxide will mix with water vapor, and it will form sulfuric acid. Particles of sulfuric acid actually make a very common aerosol in the atmosphere, and I'll get back to this in just a moment.

As the gas bubbles its way up through the water, it forms the acid there, both sulfuric and hydrochloric acid as well. And the acid is in such high concentrations that the lake water has a pH of 0.5. This is about the same pH level as the sulfuric acid in batteries. pH is a measure of the activity of hydrogen atoms, which are also very reactive. And let me just give you a sort of brief discussion of how the pH scale works. The pH is a logarithmic scale, and it's a measure of how much free hydrogen is in a solution. So, for example, if I have hydrochloric acid at 10 percent strength, what that means is I have 90 percent water and 10 percent hydrochloric acid. if I write that 10 percent as a decimal, that's 0.1; I have one decimal place so it has a pH of one. Let's say I take one-percent-strength hydrochloric acid, 99 percent water, one percent hydrochloric acid, if I write that as a decimal, that's 0.01. I have two decimal places, so that's a pH of two; 0.1 percent hydrochloric acid would be 0.001, and so the pH for that would be three, and so on. Neutral water has pH of seven, and that means that it contains free hydrogen ions at the very low fraction of only 0.0000001—seven decimal places. Anything with a pH less than seven, we call that an acid. Anything with a pH of greater than seven we call that a base. And in order to get pHs over seven, you actually have to dissolve some other material, we call that base, in the water, which will remove the remaining hydrogen ions. You can look at a picture of this scale to get a sense of different materials that you might come across and what their pHs are. So pure distilled water has a pH of seven, sea water is eight, baking soda is nine, Milk of Magnesia is 10, ammonia is 11, very soapy water is 12, and 13 would be bleach. You can see as you go higher up, the material becomes increasingly reactive. If you go down the pH scale, you get to things that are more, increasingly acidic, urine, coffee, tomato juice, orange juice, lemon juice, gastric acids, and down at zero would be battery acid. A pH of 0.5 is so acidic that it will burn away your skin. There are scientists who go out onto the lake at Kawah Ijen, out in rubber boats, and they measure the temperature and the acidity, the pH, of the water there. It's kind of like tightrope walking over the Niagara Falls. If they tip over, they're done for.

The lake is estimated to have dissolved within it over half a million tons of hydrochloric acid and over half a million tons of sulfuric acid, in this one, small lake. You would think that the local people would stay away from this a place like this. It's not so. Remember I talked earlier about how volcanic processes can concentrate the minerals that we need as resources. In other words, rather than having to dig up large amounts of rock in order to get sulfur, we can go to a volcanic area, and through natural volcanic processes the sulfur can reach high concentrations that allow us to feasibly, economically retrieve the material. This is particularly true at subduction zones. And people here at Kawah Ijen harvest the sulfur directly out of these fumaroles. Local people work at the mountain day and night, and they harvest about four tons of pure sulfur every day, carrying it up and out of the crater. There are probably at least 30,000 tons of sulfur available in the crater at any given time. An individual worker can carry up and out of the crater probably about 750 pounds of sulfur during a single shift. It's very interesting, they actually put pipes directly over the tops of these gas-emitting fumaroles. The sulfur-rich gasses come out, and they condense into liquid sulfur from the sides of the pipes. The sulfur is so hot when it comes out, though, that it actually burns. It makes a blue flame, and it flows down as this blood-red liquid. The liquid sulfur is about 99 percent pure, however. It runs down, cools, hardens, and they collect it. They use the sulfur nearby for a variety of processes like refining sugar and vulcanizing rubber for tires.

Not surprisingly, it's incredibly hazardous, and the workers here suffer from severe lung damage. But here's the really significant thing; It is this same sulfur in Kawah Ijen and other volcanoes like it that when these volcanoes erupt becomes deadly, not just at a local scale, but on a global scale. The sulfur gets released into the air from Indonesian volcanoes, and this has had a profound influence on life, including our own. The sulfur reacts with oxygen to form gaseous sulfur dioxide, which then combines with water vapor in the atmosphere to make aqueous sulfuric acid. These droplets, as I mentioned, are aerosols; they're small, little particles that are so tiny they can stay suspended in the air.

The acidic liquid begins as a vapor but needs something to condense onto to form the small, little liquid particles. Ice crystals within clouds are good, dust carried up from the surface works, or the ash emitted from volcanoes. These little liquid particles bump into each other, eventually grow in size, and in the atmosphere, the sulfuric acid droplets are about 0.1 to 1.0 micrometers in diameter. This is really tiny; a micrometer is one millionth of a meter. Here's the thing. These sulfuric acid aerosols can powerfully block out sunlight and cool the surface of the Earth. It turns out the maximum scattering of sunlight occurs for particles with a diameter of about 0.3 micrometers. That's right in the range of these sulfuric-acid aerosols. Not all volcanoes make atmospheric aerosols. It turns out only stratovolcanoes do. The basaltic eruptions at shield volcanoes like Hawaii, they don't create those massive plumes of ash and dust that reach high up into the stratosphere. You have to get this stuff up into the stratosphere, but when it happens from these stratovolcanoes, the effect is like a giant umbrella, essentially blocking out sunlight.

We can go back and look at some of the recent volcanic eruptions. Now, fortunately, for us, we have not had a large volcano erupt, at least on geologic scale, for quite some time. But look at a couple of the eruptions that happened in the 20th century here, Pinatubo in 1991, El Chichón, these were not big volcanoes, but nonetheless, the amount of aerosols they produced managed to drop the solar radiation reaching the surface by tens of percents. Over a short period, as I had mentioned previously when Pinatubo had erupted, it dropped global temperatures by a whole degree for about a year, but again, these are small volcanoes as far as volcanoes go. An interesting point here is there's also a feedback mechanism that can happen. When global climates are already cold, they tend to have more dust in the atmosphere. This is one thing that we've learned from examining the Antarctic ice cores. If you have more dust in the atmosphere, you have more particles for the sulfuric acid vapor to condense on to make aerosols. More aerosols, less sunlight, it's colder, more dust, more aerosols, less sunlight, and so forth. So a volcano that erupts when it's already cold will have a greater impact on making it even colder.

A good example of the climate effects of an Indonesian volcano is in 1815 with the eruption of Tambora. This was the biggest volcano to erupt in the past 200 years. I mentioned Tambora very briefly at the end of the first lecture. It ejected about 100 to 160 cubic kilometers of material into the atmosphere, so 100 times bigger than the eruption of Mount Saint Helen's in 1980. Almost 100,000 people were directly killed, but more significantly, it created the worst famines of the 19th century, in the year 1816. This was the year known as the year without a summer. It snowed in New England during the summer. There was extensive crop and livestock loss. In fact, this was a large motivation for Americans to settle the West. They were starving in the East, so why not look for greener pastures elsewhere.

The 1810s were the coldest decade on recent record, and disease often accompanies famine; there's a disruption in practices, sanitary practices, etc. In the 1810s, there were typhoid outbreaks in Europe and the Mediterranean; cholera outbreaks in Bengal etc. This actually pales in comparison to the eruption of another Indonesian volcano not from Kawah Ijen, Toba volcano; 73,000-years ago, the largest-known volcanic eruption occurred, bigger even than the Yellowstone eruptions. When Toba erupted, it released about 2,800 cubic kilometers of ash up into the atmosphere that settled out as ash all throughout that part of the world. The remaining caldera there is 100-kilometers long. Ice records show that this happened at a very cold time and that the following 1,000 or so years were even a colder, extreme, extended period of glaciation role. There is some debate in the climate community as to the exact role that this volcano played, but very clearly it happened at a time of glaciation and probably triggered an even extensive period of glaciation.

Here's the thing, remember how I said that the generation of aerosols is increased during a dustier time, such as during peak Ice Ages? Well, this was already a very cold period, so the production of aerosols would have been amplified, making it colder.

Here's the third coincident thing, we have a volcanic eruption, we have an extreme Ice Age. Research led by Stanley Ambrose at the University of Illinois has looked at genetic records of a large number of people. And if I take everyone in a class, and I look at their genetic records, in particular, I look at the DNA of the mitochondria of their cells, it turns out that most of us would share common ancestors going back sometime not too long before about 50,000 years. Homo sapiens lived long before then; the earliest fossils of Homo sapiens back in Ethiopia go back almost 200,000 years, but we likely didn't descend from most of them. This Toba Catastrophe hypothesis, as it's known, suggests that there was a population bottleneck somewhere about this time. The exact time is not yet identified. The idea is that most of the world's humans would have died off. They couldn't have survived through this long period of extreme cold following the massive eruption. In other words, the sunlight would have been blocked for decades, or maybe centuries, by all of these aerosols up in the atmosphere. And a small number of people, maybe just thousands of individuals, would've survived through this time.

There was added support for this theory that's come from looking at other mammals. It turns out there are similar population bottlenecks observed for chimpanzees in East Africa, or orangutans in Borneo, or macaques in Central India, cheetahs, tigers, gorillas, et cetera. It's hard to determine the exact causation for things that happened so long ago, especially something that happened 70,000 years ago, and it's important to remember that correlation doesn't always imply causation. But nonetheless, when you have these three things happening at the same time, it's a signal that they might be related.

And I have to say, the Toba Catastrophe hypothesis has its opponents. But nonetheless, it's very possible that this Toba eruption caused a massive volcanic winter that killed off a significant portion of the megafauna, including humans. The sobering thought is, these volcanoes, including Toba are all still active. And if this has happened in the past, it certainly can happen again in the future.

Another interesting point here, on this topic of sulfur-dioxide aerosols, and that is the subject of geoengineering. I often point out how humans are now powerful enough as a species that we move rock around the planet up to 10 times more than any other natural process. For instance, how we dig up in America as much rock to make our roads, and buildings, and cities; it's 10 times more than all the rock carried by the Mississippi River each year. It may be, at some point, possible for us, as a species, to actually control the temperature of the planet, to be able to adjust that thermostat wherever we want it to go. There is discussion of the process of deliberately putting sulfuric acid aerosols up into the stratosphere to counter the effects of the release of greenhouse gases, like methane and carbon dioxide, in order to stabilize global temperatures.

The idea is to use airplanes or high-altitude balloons to release these aerosols. You wouldn't want to release them down low in the troposphere because then you get acid rain, and actually, we've been remarkably successful with clean air regulation in preventing the acid rain that had been such a problem in the 1940s, and '50s, and '60s. You also have to be careful because we don't know what the effect on the stratosphere ozone layer would be from putting the sulfuric acid up there, but nonetheless it is possible that this could be the cheapest way to prevent global warming, perhaps 100-times cheaper than producing the same amount of global temperature change by reducing carbon dioxide emissions. There are some estimates, for instance, by the Council on Foreign Relations, that one kilogram of very-well placed sulfur in the stratosphere could theoretically offset the warming effects of hundreds of thousands of kilograms of carbon dioxide. Again, though, this is still a ways off. But it's remarkable to me that we have now reached the power as a geologic agent that we're even talking about the possibility of undertaking something like changing the global climate at will.

It's time for my top five. And first, let me take you to Poás Volcano in the Central Valley region of Costa Rica. This is another, extremely acidic lake. The volcano has two separate crater lakes, and it's the northern one that's called Laguna Caliente, literally, Hot Lake, and it's the one that has pH levels of less than one, actually, it's had a pH as low as zero. It depends on the amount of rainfall at that time of year. The lake is larger than Kawah Ijen; it's about a mile wide and 1,000 feet deep. There're a couple of strange things that happen here at the Poás Volcano. There sometimes are acid fogs that will develop above the lake and will drift off the lake and then precipitate out as acid rain, so the whole surrounding area has been burned bare. There's another very strange phenomenon, Poás is very volcanically active. It's erupted about 40 times in the last 200 years; the last was just in 2009. You can get hot eruptions of gas, we call these Phreatic eruptions, that will eject the acid lake water high up into the air as acid geysers.

Next, let's go to New Zealand, the north island of New Zealand, and we're going to go off the coast to about 20 kilometers to get to a region called White Island. White Island is a small, circular volcano; it's about two kilometers in diameter, and it also has an acid lake in the crater. It's also very hot, about 50°C, and it's also extremely acidic. It has a pH of about one. This lake is unusual, it has a very bright green color to it, and there are two factors to this. One is the chemical composition of materials like sulfur that are in there, and the other, remarkably, is the presence of single-celled organisms. Yes, there are creatures that will live in this acid material. It's a type of archaea that we've discussed before, simple, single-celled organisms. These are extremophiles called thermo-acidophiles; in other words, they like both high temperature and high acidity. They actually eat the sulfur. Like Kawah Ijen, White Island had been used for mining sulfur. It actually started back in the 1800s, but the process stopped when part of the crater rim collapsed at one point, allowing part of the lake to drain out with a massive acid mudflow that ended up killing all the miners. The mining equipment is still there. You can go see it, but it's been corroded almost beyond recognition by the sulfuric acid fumes.

And next, let me go to Lake Natron, in Tanzania. This is going to be for a contrast to what we've just seen. Kawah Ijen, Poás Volcano, and White Island in New Zealand, are the world's most acidic lakes. Lake Natron, in the African rift valley, is just the opposite. It's the world's most alkaline lake. It has a pH of about 10.5, this is similar to ammonia. The temperature of the lake is also hot, like the others, about 50°C, and it's also fed by hot springs that are triggered by the volcanic activity there in the African Rift Valley. But instead of bringing minerals like sulfur into the water, these hot springs bring salts like sodium carbonate, which we call washing soda, or soda ash. However, just like the acid lakes, there are also extremophiles that like these conditions and live here. Types of cyanobacteria and blue-green algae like spirulina; they give the lake a red color. These strange salt-loving organisms end up supporting large populations of birds and fish that also manage to survive in this ultra-caustic, ammonia-like water.

The most remarkable site at Lake Natron, however, happens during the breeding season for birds. You have an ocean of flamingos. Over a million flamingos come here to mate every year, 75 percent of the world's population of one species of flamingo, called lesser flamingos. Even stranger, it turns out that flamingos are not pink. These birds are naturally white, but they live off of the pink spirulina algae that thrives in this ultra-basic water, and it turns their feathers pink.

Last, I want to go to the place on the Earth with the most acidic water found anywhere in the world, and this is Iron Mountain, in California. I'm cheating a little bit with this one, because this is actually an abandoned mine, and not a natural cave. But the mine has been empty and abandoned since 1963. The rock here naturally contains very high concentrations of metals, iron, silver, gold, copper, zinc, and others, and as water seeps into and out of the cave, it becomes acidic to the level of a pH of −3.5. I didn't even know that pHs could go that low. This is the highest acidity ever measured in the field anywhere. It's equivalent to half-strength, pure sulfuric acid. This area is considered, obviously, one of the most toxic waste sites in America, but geologically, it's fascinating, because whole new types of minerals are forming here that don't exist anywhere else in the world. They've never been seen before because there has never been a climate as acidic as this one. Almost all life has been eliminated from the streams that are downstream of the mine, with the exception of a few new kinds of extremophile bacteria and archaea that are living there and aren't found anywhere else in the world. It's really a remarkable thing about our planet. If you create a new environment on this planet somewhere, something is going to evolve to enjoy it.

In next lecture, I will visit a place that is a paradise for geologists, a place where volcanoes and glaciers go hand in hand—literally—fire and ice. We're going to visit Iceland.

Iceland—Where Fire Meets Ice
Lecture 27

Iceland is a geologist's paradise, offering mountains, canyons, waterfalls, geysers, and most important, volcanoes and ice. It even has volcanoes under the ice of glaciers. Iceland is a hotspot, sitting right on top of the Mid-Atlantic Ridge. In fact, it's one of the few places on Earth where you can walk along the mid-ocean rift above land. Eruptions can take place on any one of many segments of the rift here. Eruptions are infrequent, but when they occur, they result in bizarre features, such as entire curtains of lava that rise up along the rift segments. In this lecture, we'll explore some of these features to see what happens when lava and ice are combined.

Volcanism in Iceland

- Iceland has more than 30 separate active volcanic systems. In March of 2010, the Iceland volcano Eyjafjallajökull erupted and shut down airplane flights in parts of Europe for weeks. The volcano Hekla in Iceland has had large eruptions at least 20 times over the last 1000 years. The layers of ash from these eruptions are found across many parts of Europe and serve as good archaeological time markers.

- Recent research has shown that over the past 1000 years, multiple significant ashfalls have blanketed many parts of Europe, disrupting agriculture and civilization. The average interval for these ashfalls is about 56 years, and the majority of them have come from Iceland.

- On a rare occasion, at least from a human perspective, we get to see the process by which a new volcano is born; this happened famously with the emergence of Surtsey in 1963 off the southern coast of Iceland. Surtsey is kept off limits to people in order to allow researchers to learn how an island becomes biologically populated once it emerges.

o   Life can arrive on a new island in several ways. It may float in on logs or seaweed; seeds may be dropped by migrating birds; or birds or insects may be blown in by a storm. Surtsey gives us an opportunity to follow this process.

o   The island emerged in 1963, and by 1965, the first plants and fungi were already present. Two years later, there were mosses, and by 1970, there were lichens. By 2008, 30 plant species had become established. The island also has birds and hundreds of species of insects. Earthworms and slugs help to break down the rock and make soil, which will allow for much more plant life in the future.

Geothermal Power

- The heat from the volcanoes in Iceland provides a source of energy for most of the island. In fact, most homes are heated directly by the magma underneath the island. Electricity produced at geothermal power plants supplies about 20 percent of the island's electrical needs.

- Geothermal power plants work by pumping water down into the rock, which is heated by magma. The water is heated above its surface boiling temperature. When the superheated water then returns to the surface, the pressure is released, and the water expands into steam and runs a turbine to generate electricity. Essentially, this process is the equivalent of creating a geyser.

- The volcanic regions of Iceland produce steam at very high temperatures, about 1100°C. This temperature is three times more than is minimally needed for a geothermal power station, resulting in incredibly efficient energy.

- Magma that is not far under the ground in Iceland also heats the groundwater and causes a wide variety of geothermal features, including hot springs, geothermal baths, and geysers. One of the most visited attractions of Iceland is the Blue Lagoon geothermal spa, not too far from the capital of Reykjavik. The lagoon there is not a natural feature but is filled with water from a nearby geothermal power plant.

A Harsh Region

- Iceland is generally a difficult place to live; not only does the island have volcanoes, but it also has cold climates and, as a result, poor soil.
  - The people who live in Iceland now are descendants of the Vikings, who settled the island in the late 1800s, just as the rest of the world was entering the medieval warm period. During this period, the Sun gave off slightly more energy.

  - Before this time, the sea around Iceland had been impassable—frozen for much of the year. But during the medieval warm period, people were able to sail back and forth from Scandinavia with no difficulty.

- Most of the ice in Iceland is located in one large glacier called Vatnajökull, which is one of Europe's largest glaciers. It has more than 3000 cubic kilometers of ice within it. During the summer, the melting ice creates spectacular waterfalls.

- Because Iceland has both volcanoes and glaciers, a volcano sometimes erupts beneath a glacier, causing an enormous outrushing of water. This phenomenon is called a *jökulhlaup*. In 2011, a large glacier called Grímsvötn erupted, pouring water into the ocean. Grímsvötn also erupted in 1783, as did the nearby Laki volcano.
  - At that time, these volcanoes poured out about 14 cubic kilometers of basaltic lava and released large clouds of poisonous hydrofluoric acid, as well as sulfur dioxide compounds. The eruption killed more than half of Iceland's livestock, and the famines that followed killed about one-quarter of the population.

  - The drop in global temperatures following these eruptions caused crop failures in Europe, droughts in India, and famine

The multi-stepped Gullfoss ("Golden Falls") is among the stunning waterfalls created by glacial melting during the summer in Iceland.

in Japan. The crop failures likely galvanized political unrest in France and contributed to the outbreak of the French Revolution.

Causes of the Iceland Hotspot

- No geologist doubts that Iceland is a hotspot, with an enormous outpouring of lava at this one location, but there is significant debate about what is causing this hotspot.

- Seismic tomographic images show a region of warm rock that extends from the surface deep down into the mantle, but it's not clear how far down it goes. It may not extend all the way into the lower mantle. Geologists are not sure if this is the same kind of hotspot that comes out at Hawaii. The rock coming out of Iceland also doesn't seem to be as hot as the rock at Hawaii.

- A large gravity anomaly is present under this region, which means that the whole tectonic plate structure here seems to be lifted up from below. This would support the idea of a rising mantle plume underneath. We saw this with the Afar hotspot rising up underneath the north end of the African Rift Valley.

- Another hypothesis is that this isn't a hotspot as much as a wet spot, a region of slightly higher water content in the mantle. As mentioned in an earlier lecture, water allows rock to melt (and become lava) at a lower temperature.

- What's coming up at Iceland could also be ancient ocean crust that was subducted down into the mantle during some other time of plate collisions and has been floating there. Now that the plates are opening and this ancient ocean crust is brought toward the surface, it simply melts more voluminously.

- One thing about the Icelandic hotspot is certain: When it first appeared on the surface, it had an effect much greater than changing European climates or shutting down airports—it actually ripped off a whole piece of Europe.
    o When Pangaea was starting to break up, Greenland was part of Europe, directly adjacent to Scandinavia. The Mid-Atlantic Ridge, at that point, ran up between Canada and Greenland through what is now the Labrador Sea.

    o The first outpourings of lava in this region occurred about 70 million years ago. Some geoscientists think that the plume that is now underneath Iceland was, at that point, under Greenland or even on the west side of Greenland and that lava came out in several locations on the border between Greenland and Canada.

    o About 35 million years ago, however, the bulk of the Iceland hotspot lava began to come out between what is now the border of Greenland and Scandinavia. In fact, volcanic rocks from that time can be seen on both sides of the Atlantic, and the Mid-Atlantic Ridge suddenly jumped to a new location.

o   The splitting away of Greenland from the rest of Europe was probably due to the Iceland hotspot in much the same way that the Tristan hotspot helped to split Africa and South America.

o   It may be the case that when a supercontinent breaks up, mantle plumes are responsible for determining exactly where the plates break. In the case of Iceland, the hotspot is strong enough that it has captured the location of the Mid-Atlantic Ridge. For smaller mantle plumes, the ridge eventually drifts away from the hotspot.

Top Mid-Ocean Ridge Islands

- Jan Mayen Island in Norway is a small volcanic island, about 50 kilometers long, covered partly by glaciers. It also sits along the Mid-Atlantic Ridge, a little bit northward from Iceland. This island grew a few additional square kilometers during a volcanic eruption in 1970.

- Bouvet Island is also part of Norway, but it's located at the southern end of the Atlantic Ocean, near Antarctica. This island is along the spreading ridge between the African and Antarctic plates. It's a small, glacier-covered, dormant volcano that is inhabited only by lichens, mosses, and a few seals, seabirds, and penguins. It has the distinction of being the single most remote land on Earth. Bouvet is 1600 kilometers away from any other bit of continent or other island.

- The Saint Peter and Saint Paul Rocks, under the sovereignty of Brazil, are a small group of islets and rocks at the equator along the Atlantic Ocean. These islets have the unusual distinction of being the only place in the world where rock from the mantle can be seen directly. Faulting that occurs at the mid-ocean ridge there has pulled the crust off the mantle, exposing the rock peridotite, which is found elsewhere in the world directly beneath the crust.

- The Azores, which are part of Portugal, are a cluster of nine volcanic islands and some islets that sit at the junction of the North American, Eurasian, and African plates. There are only a few places in the world where three plates meet at a single point, and it's often the case that they move away from each other, which happens here. Not surprisingly, this area is volcanically and seismically active.

Suggested Reading

Krakauer and Roberts, *Iceland*.

Thordarson and Hoskuldsson, *Iceland (Classic Geology in Europe)*.

Questions to Consider

1. Why do Iceland's volcanic eruptions affect Europe more than North America?

2. Iceland gets much of its electricity from geothermal and hydroelectric resources. Why doesn't it have any resources of coal or oil?

Iceland—Where Fire Meets Ice
Lecture 27—Transcript

Hello. My name is Michael Wysession, and welcome to Lecture 27 of our course on the Geologic Wonders of the World. In the last lecture I focused on volcanoes in Indonesia, places like the acid lake at Kawah Ijen, places that are incredibly inhospitable. In this lecture, I'm going to look at what happens when you combine lava and ice, and I'm going to look at the volcanoes and glaciers of Iceland.

Iceland is a geologist's paradise, though it also has some hellish aspects to it that I'll get to. There are giant geologic features, mountains, canyons, waterfalls, geysers, and most importantly, volcanoes and a lot of ice. It even has volcanoes that are under the ice of glaciers. Iceland is a hotspot, and it sits right on top of the Mid-Atlantic ridge. So if you look at a map of the globe, the Mid-Atlantic ridge is the line that divides North and South America from Europe and Africa, and Iceland actually sits right along it. It's one of the very few places on Earth where you can walk right down along a mid-ocean rift above land.

There are many other hotspots at ridges, you may remember I talked about this in Lecture 11, on the Iguazu Falls, when I talked about how the Tristan hotspot, which is located near the Mid-Atlantic ridge, had helped create the lava that the waterfalls were actually flowing over. This is the only place in the world, however, where you can walk down that rift itself. Imagine if you took the Galapagos Rift we saw in Lecture 3, and brought it up above the surface. That's what you see here in Iceland.

Eruptions occur on any one of many segments of the rift here. They're infrequent, but when they do erupt, you can get bizarre features like entire curtains of lava that rise up along these rift segments. Iceland is obviously very volcanically active. It fact, it has more than 30 separate active volcanic systems. In March of 2010, the Iceland volcano, Eyjafjallajökull started erupting. It shut down airplane flights in parts of Europe for weeks. It was actually a fairly small and insignificant eruption, at least as far as Iceland eruptions go. But it still cost Europe billions of dollars because of the shutdown in air traffic.

One of the most active volcanoes in Iceland, Europe too, for that matter, is the volcano Hekla. Hekla has had large eruptions at least 20 times over the last 1,000 years. It's also had enormous eruptions going back before that, around 3,000, 4,000, 6,000, and 7,000 years ago. The layers of ash from these eruptions from Hekla are found across many parts of Europe, and they're actually very good archaeological time markers. I mean, if you find this layer of ash in the geologic record somewhere, you can use that to date the ages of the civilization that lived there.

Following a particular big eruption of Hekla during the Middle Ages, in the year 1104, and actually, for many hundreds of years after, Hekla was considered by many to be the gateway to hell. In fact, it shows up this way in a very famous 1585 map made by the famous Flemish mapmaker Abraham Ortelius. In fact, recent research of the geologic record in many places around Europe has shown that over the past 1,000 years, multiple significant ashfalls have blanketed Europe, and therefore, extremely disrupted the life, agriculture, and civilization in parts of Europe.

The average interval for these ashfalls is about 56 years, sometimes as short as six years before eruptions, the longest was 115 years. The majority of these have come from Iceland. And there's another way that Iceland was considered to be the gateway to hell, or at least to the Earth's interior. If you ever read Jules Verne's *Journey to the Center of the Earth*, you may remember that in this 1864 science-fiction story, the German professor, Otto Lidenbrock, and the rest of his team actually descend into the Earth through a volcano in Iceland. There were actually some scientists, at the time, who proposed that Earth's interior might indeed be hollow and that there was a hole down into it that was located somewhere near the North Pole.

On a rare occasion, at least from a human perspective, we also get to the see the process where a new volcano is born, and this happened famously with the emergence of Surtsey, in 1963, off the southern coast of Iceland. This map shows some of the various volcanic zones that are found around the island, and Surtsey is located right down off the southern coast. What we got to see here was the birth of a new island coming above the waves. The island, unfortunately, of Surtsey, is still off limits to people; you can't visit there, and that's in order to see how an island actually becomes biologically populated once it emerges. It's a very interesting thought. I mean, think of islands like Tahiti, in French Polynesia, thousands of kilometers away from the nearest continent. They also started, like Surtsey, as volcanoes rising from the sea. And yet, when the Polynesians landed there, there were all kinds of plants and animals already there. How did they get there? How does life get to a new island?

It actually gets there in several ways. Life sometimes floats on rafts of logs or seaweed that may float for months, or even years, out at sea. You have seeds that can be dropped by migrating birds or perhaps birds blown off course by a storm, and you can also get insects that are blown there by the wind. Surtsey gives us a chance to see how this process happens. The island came out in 1963, and by two years later, in 1965, there were already the first plants and fungi there. Two years later, there were mosses, and by 1970 you had lichens. In fact, mosses and lichens now cover most of the island. The first bush, a willow actually, didn't get there until 1998. By 2008, you had 30 plant species that had become established. Lots of birds visit the islands, of course, and they have helped bring a variety of other plants and insects with them. There're now hundreds of species of insects that have either washed or blown there, or come attached to birds. There are even earthworms and slugs there now helping to break down the rock and make soil, which will allow for much more plant life in the future.

For the people of Iceland, the volcanoes pose both a blessing and a curse. The heat from the volcanoes provides an incredible source of heat and energy for most of the island. In fact, most homes are heated directly by the heat from the magma underneath. You can also create electricity using geothermal power plants, and that supplies about 20 percent of the island's electrical needs. Essentially you take water and pump it down into the rock; it comes in contact with hot rock heated by the magma, which heats the water up above its boiling temperature at the surface; as that superheated water comes up to the surface; the pressure is released and it expands into steam; and it runs your turbine to generate electricity. Essentially, you are making your own geyser. Remember in the lecture on Yellowstone I talked about this very same process led to geysers. You had hot water there that only turned to steam once the pressure left and it could expand outward, only with a geothermal power plant you're capturing that steam, letting it condense back into water, pumping it back into the ground to create a cycle. The volcanic regions here produce steam at very high temperatures, about 1,100 degrees Celsius, about the temperature that the magma sits at. And this is three times more than is minimally needed for a geothermal power station, so it's incredibly efficient energy. Magma that's not far under the ground also heats the groundwater and causes a wide variety of the geothermal features that we saw previously in Yellowstone. There are many hot springs, there are geothermal baths, there are lots of geysers. Remember I said in the lecture on Yellowstone that the original word geyser came from Iceland. It's actually pronounced "Gay'sr."

One of the most visited attractions of Iceland is the Blue Lagoon geothermal spa, which is not too far from the capital of Reykjavik. The Lagoon is filled with water from a nearby geothermal power plant. It's actually not a natural feature. What they do is they use magma-heated water to run the geothermal plant; the water left over is then used to provide heat for the region's hot water heating system, and the water that's left over after that is put into the Lagoon. But at this point, the water is about 98°F or 100°F. It's just perfect for a hot bath in a cold region. So, if you ever look at tourist literature from Iceland, it almost always shows people bathing in the Blue Lagoon geothermal spa. There can sometimes be hazards from the geothermal energy. Recently, a group of researchers were trying to find a new site for geothermal energy and they were drilling down. They were planning to go to a depth of over four kilometers, but just below two kilometers they hit magma, which started rushing up their well. The good news is that well is now providing enough dry steam that's providing energy to power over 30,000 homes.

But the volcanoes can also be destructive as well. In 1973, a very famous eruption occurred; a volcano appeared right behind the town of Vestmannaeyjar on the island of Heimaey, just off the coast of the main island, not far from the island of Surtsey, in fact. The volcano's ash and lava crushed most of the village, but the people battled it and managed to cool if off. They drove up on the front with tractors with hoses, and they sprayed it down. They stopped the flow, and the lava ended up extending out into the harbor to actually improve the harbor.

Iceland is generally a pretty rough place though. You not only have the volcanoes, but you have very cold climates, and as a result you have very poor soil. It takes a pretty hearty people to survive there. And in fact, the people who live there now are descendents of the Vikings, and they really were pretty tough people. The Vikings began to settle Iceland in the late 800s, just as the rest of the world was entering a period called the Medieval Warm Period. This is a period when the sun was giving off a little bit more energy. The sea around Iceland had been impassable. It had previously been frozen for much of the year and actually would be again during the Little Ice Age that followed later on. But during this time—the Medieval Warm Period—the people were able to sail from Scandinavia back and forth with no trouble. The modern people of Iceland still carry some of those Old Norse traditions that used to hold throughout all of Scandinavia. For instance, people in Iceland still take the name of their father as their last name, so the name Magnusson, for example, means "Son of Magnus," or Ragnarsdottir, "daughter of Ragnar." The unfortunate thing is there're actually very few different names in the Iceland phone book.

Iceland, I said, has a lot of ice, and these are the locations of the major glaciers in Iceland, and they are in a few different regions, but most of the ice is located in one very large glacier called Vatnajökull, which is actually one of Europe's largest glaciers. It has over 3,000 cubic kilometers of ice within it. The melting of the ice that occurs during the summers off of these glaciers creates some of the world's most spectacular waterfalls. Two very famous ones are the multi-stepped Gullfoss, which means Golden Falls, and Dettifoss, which is actually the most powerful river in Europe. It carries water that melts off of north side of the, Vatnajökull glacier.

Because Iceland has both volcanoes and glaciers, you sometimes get a volcano erupting beneath a glacier. And when this happens, an enormous outrushing of water can occur. This is a phenomenon called a *jökulhlaup*, and you can see here beneath the large glacier here, Grímsvötn, a volcano, is located. This happened in the year 2011. Grímsvötn erupted, and an enormous outflow of water happened rushing to the ocean. Grímsvötn also erupted back in 1783, as did nearby Laki volcano. And I mentioned these briefly at the end of the first lecture, on Santorini.

At that time, these volcanoes poured out about 14 cubic kilometers. For scale, that's about 3.5 cubic miles of basaltic lava releasing large clouds of poisonous hydrofluoric acid, as well as sulfur dioxide compounds. The eruption was devastating for Iceland. It killed over half of Iceland's livestock. The famines that followed killed about a quarter of the population. But the effects extended far beyond the borders of Iceland. This Laki-Grímsvötn eruption killed over six-million people globally, due to the change in climate, making it the deadliest volcanic eruption in historic times. The drop in temperatures caused crop failures in Europe, droughts in India, Japan's worst famine of the time, and you could document this. In fact, Ben Franklin, who was living in Paris at the time, actually recorded how much weaker the sun was shining through the haze from all the aerosols released by this volcano. As I have mentioned previously, this likely galvanized the political unrest in France and directly caused the French Revolution.

No geologist doubts that Iceland is a hotspot, with an enormous outpouring of lava at this one location. But there actually is a significant debate as to what is directly causing it. Seismic tomographic images, these are three-dimensional pictures made using the seismic waves from earthquakes. They do indeed show a region of warm rock that extends from the surface deep down into the mantle, but it's not clear how far down it goes. It might not go all the way down into the lower the mantle like it does with Hawaii. So we're not sure if this is the same kind of hotspot that comes out at Hawaii. The rock coming out of Iceland also doesn't seem to be as hot as the rock at Hawaii. There just seems to be a whole lot it, a whole lot of lava flowing out.

There is a very large gravity anomaly under this whole region, and what this means is the whole tectonic plate structure in that area seems to be lifted up from below, which supports the idea of a rising mantle plume underneath. We saw this with the Afar hotspot rising up underneath the north end of the African Rift Valley. Another hypothesis, though, is that this isn't a hotspot as much as a wet spot, a region of slightly higher water content in the mantle. Water, as I discussed before, lets rock melt more easily, at a lower temperature. You add just a little bit more water into the rock, and it's just going to erupt, it's going to turn to lava much more easily.

Or, what's coming up at Iceland could also be ancient ocean crust that got subducted down into the mantle during some other time of plate collisions and maybe has been floating around in the mantle there, and now that the plates are opening and rock is being pulled to the surface, as this ancient ocean crust gets brought towards the surface, it simply melts more voluminously. One thing is for certain, however, and that is when the Iceland hotspot first appeared on the surface, it had an effect much greater than changing European climates or shutting down airports. It actually ripped off a whole piece of Europe.

When Pangaea was starting to break up, Greenland was actually on the other side; it was actually part of Europe, directly adjacent to Scandinavia. The Mid-Atlantic ridge, at that point, ran up between Canada and Greenland through what is now the Labrador Sea. The first outpourings of lava in this region happened about 70-million years ago. Some geoscientists think that the plume that's now underneath Iceland at that point was under Greenland, or maybe even on the west side of Greenland, and that lava came out in several locations in the border between Greenland and Canada.

About 35-million years ago, however, the bulk of the Iceland hotspot lava began to come out between what is now the border of Greenland and Scandinavia. In fact, volcanic rocks from that time can be seen on both sides of the Atlantic there, and the Mid-Atlantic ridge suddenly jumped to a new location. Remember in the lecture on the Iguazu Falls, how the Tristan hotspot started to erupt when Africa and South America were connected? The process here for the splitting of Greenland away from the rest of Europe is probably due to the Iceland hotspot in the very same manner.

The Labrador Sea, a spreading center between Greenland and Canada, is now an extinct, inactive, mid-ocean ridge, though the rift is still there under the rock, and it still gets a few large earthquakes now and then. It's this process I've talked about before, like perforating a piece of paper; you make this weakness in the crust, and later on, even maybe millions of years later, you're still likely to get earthquakes there because the faults remain there.

It may be the case that when a supercontinent like Pangaea breaks up, mantle plumes like Iceland are what are responsible for determining exactly where the plates break up. In the case of Iceland, we see that the hotspot is strong enough that it has actually captured the location of the Mid-Atlantic ridge. Recent research has found that over the past 15-million years, the Mid-Atlantic ridge has repeatedly tried to wander away from the Iceland hotspot and then jumped back on to it again.

For other, smaller mantle plumes, the ridge eventually drifts away from the hotspot. Remember in the lecture on Hawaii, we saw how some other hotspots, like the Kerguelen and Reunion hotspots down in the Indian Ocean, we saw in that case where a mid-ocean ridge could drift right over and then past a hotspot, essentially ignoring it. Not here in Iceland. Iceland controls the location of where the Atlantic Ocean was forming. The Iceland hotspot is big enough, and the speed of the moving ridge is slow enough that Iceland seems to have permanently captured the ridge. And that's why you have such a large island sitting right on top of a plate boundary, and the island is still growing.

It's time for my top five. Let's go to other islands that also sit along, if not exactly on top of, Mid-Ocean ridges. There are two places that would have been at the top of my list, but I've already discussed them and talked quite a bit about them in this course, so I won't take any more time with them; they are the Galapagos Islands, which sit along the ocean-spreading ridge between two plates in the Pacific Ocean—the Nazca and Cocos Plates. And as I just mentioned, Tristan de Cunha, the hotspot along the southern of the Mid-Atlantic Ridge, halfway between Africa and South America, so four more interesting islands along the mid-ocean ridges.

First, let me go to Jan Mayen Island, in Norway, which is north of Iceland. It's along the Mid-Atlantic Ridge, a little bit northward. It's a small volcanic island, about 50-kilometers long, covered, as is Iceland, partly by glaciers. The area of the island is quite small, but because it's very volcanic it's actually growing. It grew a few additional square kilometers, in fact, during a volcanic eruption from the center of the island, back in 1970.

Next, I'm going to go to another island that's also part of Norway, but it's located at the southern end of the Atlantic Ocean down near Antarctica. This is Bouvet Island. It's actually along the spreading ridge between the

African and Antarctic Plates. It's a small, glacier-covered, dormant volcano that contains only lichens, mosses, and a few seals, seabirds, and penguins. It has the distinction of being the single, most-remote land on Earth. In other words, it is 1,600 kilometers away from any other bit of continent or other island. The closest point, actually, is the coast of Antarctica.

Next, I'll go the Saint Peter and Saint Paul rocks, which are owned by Brazil. This is a small group of islets and rocks that are at the equator along the Atlantic Ocean. The Saint Peter and Saint Paul rocks have the unusual distinction of being the only place in the world where you can actually see, directly the rock from the mantle. Faulting that occurs at the mid-ocean ridge there has pulled the crust off the mantle, exposing the rock peridotite—that is the rock that you would find anywhere else in the world directly beneath the crust. It's the only place on the Earth where the crust is missing and you can peer right down to what that rock of our mantle looks like.

I talked previously about Charles Darwin and his discoveries on the Galapagos Islands. These small rocky outcrops of the Saint Peter and Saint Paul rocks were actually the first stop of Charles Darwin and the HMS Beagle, back in 1832. At that time, Darwin found two birds, a crab, a fly, a moth, a beetle, and a bunch of spiders. And he viewed this as the first step in life settling on a new island, just like the way we saw life has begun to settle on the Icelandic Island of Surtsey. Incidentally, Darwin also noticed that these islands, strangely, were not volcanoes; he was very perceptive, like most other ocean islands that you find in the ocean, which are volcanoes. But he had no way of knowing, at the time that what he was actually looking at was rock from Earth's mantle pushed up to the surface by faulting.

And last, I want to go to the Azores, which are part of Portugal. And this is a cluster of nine volcanic islands and some islets that sit at the junction of three plates, the North American Plate, the Eurasian Plate, and the African Plate. There are a few places in the world where you will have three plates all meeting at a single point, and it's often the case that they move away from each other, which happens here. So this is a very volcanically active area, and also, it has lots of earthquakes as well.

Unlike the other islands I've been talking about, the islands of the Azores are in a region with very good climates, and it actually supports a very large population. You have about a quarter of a million of Portuguese who live across this set of nine islands. Since the late 1600s, large numbers of people have moved to the United States from the Azores, particularly into the east coast, places like Rhode Island and Massachusetts. And incidentally, there are some Portuguese bakeries in the northeast, places like Rhode Island, that make, in my opinion, the best-tasting bread in the world. It's called Portuguese sweet bread, but you won't find this bread anywhere in Portugal. It comes from the remote Mid-Atlantic islands of the Azores.

In the next lecture, we're going to look at what happens to ocean islands when they get very old and become coral atolls, and we're going to visit the Maldives in the Indian Ocean. We're going to see, essentially, the conclusion to this process that I've talked about of hotspots erupting up out of the surface of the Earth as massive islands, places like Hawaii or places like Iceland where we can build enormous islands, but of course, the work of erosion over time will tear these away. And what we will see is what is left over after tens of millions of years of these exposed at the surface. And incidentally, in the process, we're also going to get to visit some of the world's most beautiful beaches.

The Maldives—Geologic Paradox
Lecture 28

In this course, we've seen some spectacularly tall mountains—countries at the roof of the world—but the entire nation of the Republic of the Maldives has an average elevation of just 5 feet above sea level. In fact, the highest point anywhere on any of the islands is 7.5 feet. The Maldives consists of 1192 separate islands in the Indian Ocean. They are distributed among a north-south double-chain of 26 ringlike coral atolls over an area of 90,000 square kilometers. These islands make for an unusual-looking country and allow us to see what happens when old ocean volcanoes die.

A Tropical Paradise

- The Maldives is a tropical paradise, where the temperature remains between 75° and 90°F. Currently, tourism is the chief industry, and the islands have a large number of beautiful resorts. In the past, the major industry here was the collection of cowry shells, which were used as a form of money.

- Only about 400,000 people live in the Maldives today, primarily on about 300 of the islands. The country is strictly Islamic, and most of the local people do not mingle with tourists.

- The Maldives was the first country to hold a government cabinet meeting underwater. The purpose of the meeting was to make a statement about the importance of controlling greenhouse gas emissions to combat global warming. Obviously, a rising sea level would not be a good thing for a country where more than 80 percent of the land is less than 1 meter above sea level.

A Country at Sea Level?

- As we've noted in several lectures, the sea level rose 400 feet at the end of the last ice age. Were all of these islands sitting at 400 feet above sea level 20,000 years ago so that the sea level came right up

The capital of the Maldives is Male, a busy, bustling city in the middle of the ocean.

to their level? The answer is no; the islands at that time were still right at sea level, but they were 400 feet lower.

- It may be hard to imagine, but all of the islands of this nation are ancient volcanoes. Of course, they didn't look the way they do now when they formed. Initially, they looked like any other volcano ocean island—tall, with steep cliffs. But then, they followed a certain progression in changing from a volcano to a coral atoll.

- Over time, when the volcanism that formed an island stops, the island begins to sink down. Its barrier reef of coral, however, stays at sea level, even when the original volcano has been torn away and sunk under the waves. Three factors are involved in this process: erosion of the island, a sea level rise, and the sinking of the ocean plate.
  - As we've seen, any land that is left alone for long enough, with no features being added to it, will eventually wear down by erosion. We've also seen that the sea level rises and floods island volcanoes. A third reason that ancient volcanoes become

sea mountains, with their tops far below the surface of the water, has to do with the sinking of the ocean plate.

o   When the ocean floor forms at a mid-ocean ridge, the rock is hot and rises high off the surrounding seafloor. As the plate moves away from the ridge, it gets colder, becomes heavier, and sinks. Anything on top of it, such as an island, will sink, too. In other words, over time, the top of a volcano can end up a long way below the sea surface.

o   But if the relative rise of sea level and the erosion are slow enough, the coral reef can keep pace; it can keep growing upward and stay right at the sea level surface.

o   If the sea level rise occurs too quickly or some environmental factor kills off the corals, the atoll will sink for good; the result is a flattop underwater sea mountain.

o   During the recent rise of the sea level, the tops of the Maldives were a few meters under water. But as the sea level rose, the coral reefs kept growing, as well. In fact, the Maldives has grown in height from the seafloor about 400 feet in the past 20,000 years.

Formation of Atolls

•   If the atoll grows from the growth of coral and coral live under the water, then why are parts of the atolls above sea level? The answer to that question can be found in ocean waves. The waves grind up the coral of the reef into a calcium carbonate sand. Further, certain fish, such as the parrot fish in the Caribbean, eat coral and excrete a carbonate sand.

•   As we've seen, water can hold sediment when it's moving quickly. It drops sediment when it slows down; that's why a delta forms in front of a river. A similar thing happens here. The waves slow down as they reach and then cross over the atolls.

- Waves tend to have very long wavelengths out in the ocean, but that wavelength is a function of the depth of the water. As a wave approaches land, its wavelength shortens. Because energy must be conserved, if the wavelength is shortened, the wave must become taller. That's why waves get high as they approach a beach.

- The waves carry ground-up sand and deposit it up on top of the atoll; thus, the atolls are layers of ground-up coral sand deposited over time by wave action.

Volcanoes in the Ocean

- Why are volcanoes present in the first place in the middle of the ocean? And why are they aligned in a north-south direction?

- Beginning 65 million years ago, India had just recently broken away from Antarctica and was starting to move north, crossing the Tethys Sea. At around the same time, there was a tremendous outpouring of lava from the Deccan Traps in India. This outpouring occurred over a broad region from about 60 to 68 million years ago; it was probably on the order of about 0.5 million cubic kilometers of lava.
  o It's likely that the lava from the Deccan Traps contributed to the extinction of the dinosaurs; this outpouring occurred at the same time as the Chicxulub meteor impact in the Yucatan Peninsula.

  o Interestingly, an impact on one side of the planet can cause seismic waves that are focused on the other side. This phenomenon has been seen on Mercury. At the time of the meteor impact, India was on the exact opposite side of the planet from Mexico.

  o Some scientists have proposed that the impact of the Chicxulub meteor created waves that hit India and caused the melting of the Deccan Traps. However, it seems likely that the energy from those seismic waves would have been many orders of magnitude too small to cause the volcanism in India. The two events may be just an interesting coincidence.

- After the initial outpouring of lava of the Deccan Traps, even more lava came out. Because India was moving north, it ended up making a chain of islands across the Indian Ocean, similar to what we saw in Hawaii.

- At some point, the ridge between the Indian Plate and the African Plate crossed over the hotspot; thus, the islands that had been forming on the Indian Plate began to occur on the African Plate. The hotspot is now located under Réunion Island, just east of Madagascar.

- The Deccan Traps in India, the Maldives, and Réunion Island are all related; they are all the result of the same hotspot. But there is something puzzling about the ages of the islands.
  - If the hotspot is on the African Plate, we would expect that as the plate moved away, it would carry old islands far from the ridge. In other words, the islands should go from younger to older as we move away from the ridge. But we see just the opposite.

  - Both the African and the Indian plates are moving northward. For this reason, the hotspots are essentially anchored in the underlying mantle. In this case, both Africa and India are moving across the hotspot. The ridge is moving northward, as well; thus, we can see that the plates sometimes move significantly relative to the deep underlying mantle.

The Future of the Maldives

- Over the next century, the sea level is projected to rise 1 to 2 meters. Even though the atolls will continue to grow slowly, recent research has shown that this growth is unlikely to keep pace with the rising sea level, and most of the islands will eventually be underwater.

- For this reason, the country is one of the most outspoken against the burning of fossil fuels, which contributes to global warming. As we know, variations in the Sun's output also play a major role in shaping global climates.

- The government of the Maldives plans to create a fund from tourism to buy land in India, Sri Lanka, or Australia and move the country at some point in the future.

Top Transition Sites from Volcanic Island to Coral Atoll

- The Society Islands in French Polynesia include Bora-Bora, Tahaa, Raiatea, Huahine, and Maupiti. They occur in a cluster and represent the first step in the transition from a volcanic island to an atoll. These islands have volcanic summits covered with jungles, steep valleys, and waterfalls, but they're also surrounded by a beautiful lagoon and a ring of coral because they've already begun to sink. The coral ring shows the previous coastline of the islands.

- Aitutaki is in the Cook Islands, north of Rarotonga, about halfway between French Polynesia and Tonga. Aitutaki is what we might call an "almost atoll." The maximum height here is about 123 meters, about 400 feet above sea level. The lagoon, however, is about four times larger than the island; the island already makes up a smaller part of the total area. Over time, the mountains in the middle of the island will wear down entirely to form a raised atoll.

- The Aldabra Atoll is one of the outer islands of the Seychelles, north of Madagascar in the Indian Ocean. It is the tallest raised atoll, about 8 meters above sea level. This island is practically untouched by humans, but it has the world's largest population of giant tortoises. Again, over time, the amount of land here will decrease, resulting in a formation similar to the Maldives.

- Bikini Atoll is in the Marshall Islands of the northwestern Pacific. The atoll here is the set of about 23 islands that are part of a long coral reef surrounding a much deeper, broader lagoon of about 100 square kilometers. Bikini Atoll is in a remote part of the northwest Pacific called Micronesia and was, of course, the site of nuclear bomb testing by the United States from 1946 to 1958.

Suggested Reading

Davidson, *The Enchanted Braid*.

Pilkey and Young, *The Rising Sea*.

Questions to Consider

1. Why doesn't coral grow well more than a few tens of meters below the surface?

2. Changes in ocean chemistry have caused corals in many parts of the world to die off. What are the implications of this for the appearance of oceans a million years in the future?

The Maldives—Geologic Paradox
Lecture 28—Transcript

Hello. My name is Michael Wysession, and welcome to Lecture 28 of our course on the Geologic Wonders of the World. In the last lecture, I talked about Iceland, a hotspot volcano along the mid-ocean ridge. In this lecture, I'm going to take us way over into the Indian Ocean to look at what happens to old ocean volcanoes when they go off to die. To do this, I'm going to take us to the islands of the Maldives. We've seen some pretty spectacularly tall mountains, countries at the roof of the world. Here's something even stranger, the entire nation of the Republic of the Maldives, often just called the Maldives, is so flat that its average elevation above sea level is 1.5 meters; that's five feet. In fact, its highest point anywhere on any of the islands is 2.3 meters, that's 7.5 feet, and it's in the midst of the Indian Ocean, south of India.

The Maldives consist of 1,192 separate islands, and they're distributed among a north/south double chain of 26 separate ring-like coral atolls. They're distributed over a total area of 90,000 square kilometers. So you can see, it's a very unusual looking country. Each one of these small rings is a separate coral atoll. And what's more, if you zoom in on any one of these, you can see how remarkably flat this is; more than 80 percent of the land here is less than a meter above sea level.

This area is a tropical paradise. I mean, the climate never varies outside of about 75°F to 90°F. In fact, the southern part of the islands is actually right at the equator. Currently tourism is its number one industry, and there's a large number of beautiful resorts. But interestingly, it actually used to have a very different industry. It used to make money, not so much make it as harvest it. In fact, people would come here from all over the world, India, Africa, China to get money. I happen to have some loose change here in my pocket. It's not coins; it's shells.

The major industry here was the collection of cowry shells, which were used as a form of money, not just any cowry shells, but a particular species called monetaria moneta. It's found throughout the Indian Ocean and also parts of the Pacific, but it was especially abundant here in the Maldives. So much so, in fact, that from the second century onward many parts of the Arabic world knew of the Maldives as the money islands. The Chinese started using cowry shells as currency back as far as 3,000-years ago. And there are parts of Africa that continued using them through the late 1800s.

The Maldives today, currently have a fairly small population. There're only about 400,000 people who live there. That's about the size of Tulsa, Oklahoma. And the local people there primarily live on about 300 of the over 1,000 islands. But they don't mingle with tourists who go to other islands for vacation. It's actually a very strict Islamic country, one of the few that does not practice religious tolerance.

If you look at some of the islands here, they're spectacular. You can go here on vacation. There're a lot of tours that will take you to some spectacular beach resorts. In fact, you can sometimes have your own island, but don't expect to see any of the local people here, because they don't go to the islands that you will go to. The government is actually very modern in some ways. In fact, it's the first government to open up a virtual embassy within Second Life; it's an online, virtual world where you can go and hear lectures, or go to conferences, or even have classes.

The capital Male is actually a very cosmopolitan place. You can see there's not a lot of room for horizontal expansion, so they build up here, and it is quite a remarkable thing to come across this busy, bustling metropolis with absolutely nothing else around it. It was the first country to hold a government cabinet meeting underwater. This actually wasn't a tourist gimmick. The government was making a statement about the importance of controlling greenhouse gas emissions in order to combat global warming. Obviously, if sea levels continue to rise, this would not be a good thing for a country where more than 80 percent of the land is less than a meter above sea level. As it is, being at such a low elevation in the middle of the ocean creates some significant hazards. During some of the large Indian typhoons, cities like Male undergo significant flooding and severe damage.

How can it be that nearly the entire country is right at sea level? If you look, it's just remarkably flat for a huge expanse. It can't possibly be a coincidence, after all, because the sea level just rose 400 feet at the end of the last Ice Age.

We've seen this in several of the previous lectures. So how does this work? I mean, had all of these islands been sitting at 400 feet above sea level just 20,000-years ago so that the sea level came right up to their level? No, of course not. The islands back then were still right at sea level, only they were 400-feet lower. So how does this happen? You would never imagine it, but all of the islands of this nation are volcanoes, just very ancient volcanoes. These volcanoes didn't look the way they do now when they formed. When they formed they looked like any other volcanic ocean island, like Hawaii, you know, tall, and lava initially, and then steep cliffs. But there's a progression that happens as you go from a volcano like Hawaii to a coral atoll like the Maldives. They are part of a single progression.

Initially, you have a volcano, and we've seen the eruptions that happen. And over time, though, when the volcanism stops, these islands will begin to sink down. The barrier reef of coral, however, will stay at sea level while the volcanoes have long since been torn away and actually sunk under the surface of the waves.

There're a couple of things that are involved here, there are three factors. First of all, there's the erosion of the islands that happened, and then there's a sea level rise that's climate related, and then there's a process that involves, actually, the sinking of the ocean plate. If you leave any land alone long enough and you don't add anything to it, no more volcanoes, no more mountains being pushed up by plate tectonics, they will eventually wear down by erosion. The processes we've seen of rain, and ice and, wind will just tear them away. It doesn't take long, maybe millions of years, or maybe even hundreds of thousands—a really short time geologically. And we've also seen, of course, that the sea level is rising, and that also wants to flood these volcanoes.

But there's a third reason, and it's actually why very old volcanoes become sea mounds with their tops far below the surface of the water. When the ocean floor forms at a mid-ocean ridge, the rock is really hot, it's warm, and it rises up high off the seaflood. We've seen pictures of the Mid-Atlantic ridge or the East Pacific Rise, or in this case, the Indian Ridge, places where new crust is being formed. And if you look at the elevation you see it's risen quite a bit higher off the surrounding seafloor. As that plate moves away from the ridge, it gets older, it cools, it gets colder, and in the process it becomes heavier and it sinks. And anything on it, like an island, will sink too. So in other words, over time, the tops of the volcanoes can end up a long ways below the sea surface.

Another very important part of this is the ocean plate itself actually grows in thickness as it moves away from the ridge. There's really not a lot of difference between the rock of the asthenosphere and the rock of the lithosphere. It's just a matter of temperature, so as both of these move away from the mid-ocean ridge, some of the asthenosphere slowly turns into lithosphere. And interestingly, both the depth of the ocean seafloor and the thickness of that plate follow a very simple curve; they're parabolas. This is because the temperature of the tectonic plate is directly proportional to the square root of the age of the plate. And you may remember from algebra, if you make a graph of an equation, like $y = x^2$, the shape of the curve you get is a parabola. It is remarkable that such a complex process as seafloor tectonics follows a simple shape with such a simple mathematical curve. But here's the interesting part here. If the relative rise of sea level and the erosion are slow enough, the coral reef can actually keep pace, it can keep growing upward and stay right at the sea level surface.

You may remember back in the third lecture on the Galapagos Ridge I mentioned that Charles Darwin made some really important geologic discoveries during his voyage on the HMS Beagle. He made many wonderful biological discoveries, but one of the geological discoveries he made was he was the first to document how ocean islands actually sink in the ocean over time. He had no idea why. He couldn't; plate tectonics was discovered for another 135 years. But if the sea level rise occurs too quickly or some environmental factor kills off the corals, the atoll will sink for good, and you'll end up with one of these flat-top, underwater seamounts. This actually was a huge puzzle to geologists when the ocean seafloor was first being mapped in great detail in the 1940s and 1950s, the discoveries that led to the discovery of plate tectonics. This puzzle was a huge mystery, how you could possibly get a flat-top seamount.

During the recent rise of the sea level, 400 feet, the tops of the Maldives were a few meters under water. As sea level rose, the coral reefs kept growing as well. So in fact, the Maldives have actually grown in height from the seafloor about 400 feet in the past 20,000 years. And here's another question, if you think about it, if the atoll grows from the growth of coral and coral live under the water, then why are there parts of the atolls above sea level? The answer to that is waves, ocean waves. The waves grind up the coral of the reef, pulverize it, grind it into a calcium-carbonate sand. Actually, there's also a biological component to it as well. There are certain fish, like the parrot fish in the Caribbean, that actually eat the coral and excrete a carbonate sand. So in fact, when you walk on some of those beautiful beaches in tropical areas, you're actually walking on fish excrement.

Water can hold sediment when it's moving fast. We've seen that previously. And it drops its sediment when it slows down; that's why you get a delta in front of the river. A similar thing happens here. The waves slow down as they reach and then cross over the atolls. What happens here, a wave is just propagating energy, and there is a law, the conservation of energy, that has to be satisfied here. The waves tend to have very long wavelengths out of the ocean, but that wavelength is a function of how deep the water is. And as the wave approaches land, that wavelength shortens. But to conserve energy, if you shorten the wavelength, you have to make the wave taller. That's why waves get high as they approach a beach. So the waves carry that ground-up sand and dump it up on top of the atoll, so essentially, what you have is these atolls are layers of ground-up coral sand deposited over time by wave action. This sand can accumulate with a circular lagoon that ends up being surrounded by the atoll. Inside the water flows very slowly, and that sand gets deposited.

But here's another question. Why are the volcanoes even there in the first place in the middle of the ocean? And why are they aligned in a north/south direction? I've already briefly mentioned this region with my lecture on Hawaii. It was one of my top five hotspot island tracks, the Chagos-Laccadive hotspot chain of islands and seamounts. That was this chain here that I showed previously. It's a very interesting story here. It actually has many different parts. Beginning a long time ago, 65-million years ago, India was still down in the southern hemisphere. In fact, it had just recently broken away from Antarctica and was starting to move north crossing what we call the Tethys Sea. You may remember I talked about this in the lecture on the Tibetan Plateau. Well, 65-million years ago, there was a tremendous outpouring of lava that we call the Deccan Traps. It actually occurred over a broad range of time for about 60- to 68-million years ago, and it was an incredible outpouring of lava, probably on the order of about half a million cubic kilometers. At least, that's what we see now today, and it's quite possible with erosion that the original mound of lava was at least three times that, covered half of India.

By the way, the name the Deccan Traps comes from a Swedish word for stairs. If you go to India and you look at this, the layers of basalt, the multiple layers, have this stair-like appearance to them. It has a very interesting point. Sixty-five-million years ago is also the time that the dinosaurs went extinct, and it's quite likely that the Deccan Traps contributed to the extinction of the dinosaurs. After all, most of the lava came out in a fairly brief period, maybe 30,000 years long, right about 65-million years ago. And this would've had an enormous impact on climate. We've already seen the effect that volcanoes can have on a changing climate. This is exactly the same time as the Chicxulub impact of a meteor in what's now the Yucatan Peninsula. So you have two totally different things happening at the same time. Sometimes coincidences do happen in history, and it's possible that sometimes there is more than one cause for something. Here's another interesting point, though, 65 million years ago, India was not in its current location. It was still in the southern hemisphere moving northward, as I just mentioned. And in fact, it was 180 degrees, at the exact opposite side of the planet as the Chicxulub impact, in Mexico.

There's an interesting phenomenon that has been observed on moons and small planets where an impact on one side of the planet can cause waves that are focused from the other side and can blow the back side of the planet off to some degree. We see that on Mercury. There's an enormous 1,600 kilometer basin, the Caloris Basin, an impact basin from probably four-billion years ago and exactly 180 degrees away. On the other side of the planet there was this fractured and rifted terrain that is thought to be due to the focusing of the seismic waves at the back end. People have proposed the same thing here, that the impact with the Chicxulub crater created these waves that focused and hit India and caused the melting there of the Deccan Traps. However, a lot of people have looked at this, scientists have calculated the energy involved, and it seems like the energy from those seismic waves would've been many orders of magnitude too small to cause the volcanism. So maybe it really is just an interesting coincidence.

Anyway, this is all a hotspot. So after the initially outpouring of lava of the Deccan Traps, more lava kept coming out. But India was moving north, so it ended up making a chain of islands across the Indian Ocean, much like we saw with Hawaii. And, 55-million years ago it was making the volcanic islands that would become the Maldives today. At some point, even the ridge between the Indian Plate and the African Plate crossed over the hotspot, so the islands that had been forming on the Indian Plate now find themselves emerging on the African Plate on the other side. The hotspot, in fact, is now located under Réunion Island here just east of Madagascar. And so the Deccan Traps in India, the Maldives, and Reunion Island are all related. They're all the result of the same hotspot. But there's also something a little puzzling here about the ages of the islands. You can go underwater and dredge up rock and determine its ages. And what we see is this progression I mentioned, 65-million years ago lava in India 55-million years ago lava coming out in the Maldives. Today we see it in Reunion Island, but the ages of the islands on the African Plate seem to go the wrong direction. On the African Plate you would expect if the hotspot was there that as the plate moved away it would carry old islands far from the ridge. You should go from younger to older as you move away from the ridge. In fact, we see just the opposite. Why could this occur? Actually, we've already seen the answer to this.

We know that the African Plate, as well as the Indian Plate, are both moving northward. Remember, we saw that the African Plate was rotating up into Europe. That was what caused the volcanoes like Santorini. And of course, we know India is moving northward. So it turns out that the hotspots are essentially anchored in the underlying mantle. And in this case, both Africa and India are moving across the hotspot. The ridge is moving northward as well, and so we can see sometimes the plates can move significantly relative to the deep, underlying mantle. Reunion Island, as I said, is now the southernmost of the islands, and by the way, it is a beautiful place. It's part of France. It is a spectacular island, a resort with much tourism, very much like the Hawaiian Islands.

What will happen to the Maldives in the future? Well, sea level is projected to rise one to two meters over the next century. Even though the atolls will continue to grow slowly, recent research has shown that this is likely not going to be able to keep pace with the rising sea level, and that most of the islands there will eventually be under water. Because of this, the country is one of the most outspoken against the burning of fossil fuels, which is contributing to global warming. Burning fossil fuels is not the only cause of the rising global temperatures, of course. And remember? I talked about things having more than one cause. It turns out that variations in the sun's output plays a very major role in shaping global climates, as we've already seen with the Medieval warm period and the Little Ice Age, both of which were driven largely by changes in solar output. It turns out an increase in the sun's output has contributed to the warming over the past century, but the human production of carbon dioxide doesn't help. After all, everything is all interconnected. The government of Maldives has a plan therefore. It's going to create a fund from tourism to buy land in India, or Sri Lanka, or Australia, and they will move at some point. They know at some point in the future they will have to move their whole population because their country will be under water.

It's time for my top-five list. And for this I thought I would show islands in various stages of going from a volcanic island to a coral atoll. In the process, I also get to show some really beautiful places. First of all, let me start with the Society Islands in French Polynesia. The islands here include Bora-Bora, Tahaa, Raiatea, Huahine, and Maupiti. They occur in a cluster, and they represent the first step going from a volcanic island to an atoll. They are also, in my opinion, the perfect islands. They still have wild, jagged-edge, volcanic summits covered with juggles, steep valleys, and waterfalls, but they're also surrounded by a beautiful lagoon and a ring of coral because they've already begun to sink. And the coral ring shows the previous coastline of the islands.

Bora-Bora is about 10-kilometers long, about four-kilometers wide, and it rises almost a half a mile in the middle. And it has many square miles of shallow, turquoise water over stunning coral reefs that are just perfect for scuba diving and snorkeling. The islands of Tahaa and Raiatea are close enough that the coral atoll contains them both. Each one is actually a separate former volcano, however. Over time, these islands will all wear down so that the land of the lagoon inside is just a small part of the inside lagoon. And when this happens, the island will look something like the next example.

Aitutaki in the Cook Islands, north of Rarotonga, about halfway between French Polynesia and Tonga. Aitutaki is what we call an almost atoll. The maximum height here is about 123 meters, so we're looking at on the order of about 400 feet above sea level. The lagoon, however, is about four times larger than the island. So we already see the island making up a smaller part of the total area. The island here was first settled by Polynesians more than a thousand years ago, though the first westerners to discover it were Captain Bligh and the crew of the HMS Bounty, back in 1789, back before the famous Mutiny on the Bounty.

Over time, these mountains in the middle of the island will wear down entirely until you get something called a raised atoll, and that's what we see in the next example, the Aldabra Atoll. This island is one of the outer islands of the Seychelles, another beautiful place, north of Madagascar in the Indian Ocean. It's the tallest raised atoll, up to about eight meters above sea level. It's actually the second largest atoll of any kind by area. It covers about 155 square kilometers. And this particular island is practically untouched by humans. Incidentally, it also has the world's largest population of giant tortoises. There are more than 100,000 of the giant Aldebaran tortoise on this island. But again, over time, the large amount of land here will decrease as well, and when this happens you'll have something like the Maldives.

For the last example I want to show one more classic example of an atoll. And I want to take you to Bikini Atoll in the Marshall Islands in the Northwestern Pacific. The atoll here is the set of about 23 islands that are part of a long coral reef that surrounds a much deeper, broader lagoon of about hundred square kilometers. It's in a very remote part of the Northwest Pacific, called Micronesia. It's actually part of the greatly dispersed Republic of the Marshall Islands. Micronesian people have lived here on Bikini for over 3,000 years. Bikini, by the way, means coconut surface. However, the atoll will forever be connected with two non-geologic things.

This was one of the first nuclear test-bomb site grounds for the United States. There were 20 nuclear bombs tested here between 1946 and 1958. Some of the images of giant battleships dwarfed by massive nuclear explosions that sink some of them. These are some of the most iconic images of the entire nuclear test program. The largest nuclear bomb ever detonated by the United States was here, in fact. It was 1954; it was a 16 megaton Castle Bravo test. It made a fireball seven-kilometers in diameter and blew out a two-kilometer chunk of the coral of the Bikini Atoll. Unfortunately, it was this test also that created the deadly nuclear fallout that fell across other atolls to the east, Rongelap and Rongerik Atolls.

However, most people know the word bikini in relation to the bathing suit, but I'm sorry to tell you that the bikini bathing suit has absolutely nothing to do with the actual islands or the people who live there. The Micronesians on Bikini never wore bikini bathing suits. It was actually all part of a marketing ploy. Another bathing suit, a one-piece suit, had just come out at the time and it was called Atom, and it was advertised as being the world's smallest bathing suit. So just days after the first nuclear test on Bikini Island in 1946, another bathing suit company came out with a two-piece bathing suit, and they called it the bikini. Their ad was that they had split the atom.

In the next lecture I'm going to switch directions somewhat. We've now seen a lot of volcanoes and islands. Starting in the next lecture, and for several after that, I will look at the strange geologic features that you find in desert regions, and I'm going to start with the Dead Sea along the border of Israel and Jordan.

The Dead Sea—Sinking and Salinity
Lecture 29

In the last lecture, we talked about the country with the lowest average elevation in the world, the Maldives, a chain of coral atolls in the Indian Ocean. In this lecture, we'll get even lower, with the body of water that has the lowest elevation anywhere on Earth: the Dead Sea, along the border of Israel and Jordan. The surface and shores of the Dead Sea are 1388 feet below sea level, but it's also dropping at the rate of about 1 meter per year. If you look at the shorelines and surrounding hills, you can see multiple rings of these past shorelines.

Description of the Dead Sea

- The Dead Sea is only about 67 kilometers long and about 18 kilometers across at its widest point. It sits in a long, narrow valley that stretches from the Red Sea north to Syria, and it separates Israel and Jordan.

- Most lakes eventually drain to the ocean, but that obviously can't happen with the Dead Sea because it's below sea level and most rivers can't flow uphill. What happens to the water here?
  - The Jordan River runs down from the north, first draining into and out of the Sea of Galilee and then flowing down the narrow valley into the Dead Sea.

  - The Dead Sea is a closed basin; the water evaporates as fast as it enters. In fact, it is now evaporating faster than it's being filled because the water from the Jordan River is being drawn off for a variety of purposes by Israel and Jordan.

  - Once the water evaporates, it leaves behind salts. The Dead Sea is one of the saltiest lakes on Earth. It's 33.7 percent salt, which is 8.6 times saltier than the ocean.

- We can see evidence of the salinity of the water here in the unusual salt features that have precipitated along the shore. Some of the formations look like small castles sticking up out of the water.

- The composition of the salts in the Dead Sea is a function of the geology of the surrounding rocks. About 30 percent of the salts are sodium chloride, and 50 percent are magnesium chloride. The remainder includes calcium chloride, potassium chloride, and others. The exact salts vary by season, depth in the water, and temperature.

- The amount of salt makes the water extremely dense. If you go swimming in the Dead Sea, you'll be surprised by how easily you float.

History of the Dead Sea
- The entire region of the Dead Sea has an enormous amount of salt because the valley was flooded by the Mediterranean Sea multiple times.

Salt crystals form on anything in the water of the Dead Sea, such as rocks or sticks.

- About 3 million years ago, the climates were much warmer, and there was much less ice in Antarctica and Greenland; sea levels in general were higher. The Mediterranean flooded in through the Jezreel Valley, which cuts to the Mediterranean just to the southwest of the Sea of Galilee. Each time the Mediterranean receded, the long lake would slowly dry out, depositing another layer of salt. The ancient ancestor of the Dead Sea, the prehistoric Lake Sodom, had an accumulation of salt 3 kilometers thick.

- About 2 million years ago, the land between the Jordan Valley and the Mediterranean was uplifted by tectonic forces. When this happened, the Dead Sea was cut off, and it became a long lake, known as Lake Gomorrah, and no longer flooded.

- The region's climate was wetter at the time, and Lake Gomorrah was a freshwater lake with significant sediments deposited in the lake bottom. These rocky sediments weighted down the layer of salt underneath and pushed the salt up and around the edges of the lake, forming ridges and hills made entirely of salt. For instance, the Lisan Peninsula to the south and Mount Sodom to the west are both made of salt.

- Going back tens of thousands of year, the lake was generally much higher than it is now, but the level has fluctuated greatly. The drop in water level has caused the salinity to increase to the wildly high levels seen now.

- The salinity of the Dead Sea is so high that the bottom part of the lake water is at its saturation point. That means that salt is currently precipitating out of the water, making a new layer of salt on the bottom.

- The shallow levels of the Dead Sea are having some unfortunate geologic consequences around the area. As the sea shrinks, underground layers of salt have dissolved away, leading to the sudden formation of large numbers of small sinkholes that are causing roads and bridges to collapse. More than 2500 sinkholes now line the shores of the Dead Sea, most of which have appeared just since 2000.

Location of the Dead Sea

- The fact that the Dead Sea is so far below sea level can be traced to the breakup of Africa that began 30 million years ago. As we discussed earlier, the Arabian Peninsula had been part of Africa for a long time. Then, it started to break away to the northwest. First, the area experienced volcanism; then, the crust was stretched, thinned, and rifted.

- Starting about 12 million years ago, the Red Sea began as a real ocean. It started as a continental rift, just like the African Rift Valley, but it kept opening up. The strange shape of the Red Sea, the Gulf of Suez, and the Gulf of Aqaba stems from the Dead Sea transform fault, a fault that is allowing the Arabian Peninsula to slide past the Sinai Peninsula.

- The Dead Sea transform fault is not straight; it makes a bend. As the two plates slide past each other, a hole develops at the bend, and that is the Dead Sea. The seafloor of the lake is dropping continuously and could do so for some time because the plate boundaries show no sign of stopping their movement.

Human Occupation

- Civilization in the West began in the Dead Sea region. Jericho, just to the north, is one of the world's oldest cities, dating back before 10,000 years ago. The early cities of Sodom and Gomorrah, mentioned in the Hebrew Bible, the New Testament, and the Koran, were somewhere along the southeastern shore of the Dead Sea. One important implication of the Dead Sea's location along a major plate boundary is that it can have large earthquakes. Some have proposed that an earthquake caused the famous destruction of Sodom and Gomorrah.

- The Dead Sea region is also one of the few places in the world where asphalt seeps directly to the surface, similar to the La Brea

Tar Pits in Los Angeles. This asphalt was prized by the early Egyptians; in fact, many Egyptian mummies were embalmed with Dead Sea asphalt.

- One of the most famous archaeological discoveries in the region is the caves of Qumran, where the 2000-year-old Dead Sea Scrolls were found. These scrolls contain alternate versions of many parts of the Hebrew Bible, as well as many stories that didn't make it into the canonized Bible. The scrolls were from Jewish tribes who lived in the area from about 150 B.C.E. to 70 C.E.

- The unique geologic conditions of the Dead Sea make it a popular tourist destination. More than 1 million people visit each year, largely for the spas that exist along the coast. The high mineral content of the water, the fact that there's low pollen in the area, and the low ultraviolet radiation from the thicker air contribute to the popularity of the site.

Extremophiles in the Dead Sea

- As we have seen in other environments, single-celled extremophiles live in the ultra-saline waters of the Dead Sea. Scientists are interested in these strange organisms because they might be models for the kinds of life that could possibly survive on another planet. One day, we might even discover similar organisms on solar system bodies, such as Mars.

- In times of flood, the salt content of the Dead Sea can drop from its usual 33 percent to about 30 percent or lower. In the wake of this influx of fresh water, the Dead Sea temporarily comes to life. In 1980, after one rainy winter, the normally dark blue Dead Sea turned red. It was teeming with a type of algae called *Dunaliella* that nourished red-pigmented halobacteria, causing the color change.

- Since 1980, the Dead Sea basin has been extremely dry, and the algae and the bacteria have not returned in measurable numbers.

Top Saltwater Lakes

- Tiny Don Juan Pond is in the Dry Valleys of the Transantarctic Mountains, not far from McMurdo Base in Antarctica. The amount of water here is almost insignificant. The pond is currently on average about 4 inches deep, but this depth varies over its extent, which is about 300 meters by 100 meters. The pond seems to be fed from underground water and has the saltiest water found anywhere in nature. When it was first found, its salinity was 40 percent at a temperature of $-30°C$.

- Lake Assal in the small coastal African country of Djibouti is the saltiest real lake in the world. Its salinity at the surface is 34.8 percent, just edging out the Dead Sea, at 33.7. Like the Dead Sea, Lake Assal is below sea level, about 155 meters, making it the lowest point anywhere after the Dead Sea and the Sea of Galilee. The composition of Lake Assal is primarily sodium chloride, similar to seawater. The small lake is continuously fed by water flowing underground from the Indian Ocean.

- The Salton Sea in southern California, along the San Andreas Fault, formed through the same mechanism of shearing along a bend in a transform fault as the Dead Sea. The Salton Sea is an extension of the Gulf of California, forming as the arm of Baja, California is tearing away from Mexico. The Salton Sea sits about 69 meters below sea level.

- The Turpan Depression in the Xinjiang region of western China also formed from a sheared, pull-apart basin, about 250 million years ago. The Xinjiang region is the hottest and driest part of China and has the lowest elevation of anywhere in Asia, at 154.5 meters below sea level.

- The Caspian Sea is the largest salt lake and the largest lake of any kind in the world, but it has only about one-third the salinity of the ocean. The Caspian Sea has more than 130 rivers draining into it, but it has no outlet; its water never reaches the ocean. Like the Black Sea, the Caspian Sea used to be part of the ancient Tethys

Sea. When Africa, Arabia, and India all crashed into Eurasia and the Tethys Sea closed up, the Caspian Sea became landlocked, forever to be an interior sea.

Suggested Reading

Haviv, *Trekking and Canyoning in the Jordanian Dead Sea Rift*.

Neev and Emery, *The Destruction of Sodom, Gomorrah, and Jericho*.

Questions to Consider

1. The Sea of Galilee sits in the Jordan Valley, just like the Dead Sea, and it drains to the Dead Sea. Do you think it is fresh water or salt water?

2. If Arabia keeps moving northward into Eurasia, what will eventually happen to the Dead Sea?

The Dead Sea—Sinking and Salinity
Lecture 29—Transcript

Hello. My name is Michael Wysession, and welcome to Lecture 29 of our course on the Geologic Wonders of the World. In the last lecture I talked about the country with the lowest average elevation in the world, the Maldives, a chain of coral atolls in the Indian Ocean. In this lecture, I get lower than low, and I'm going to take us to the body of water with the lowest elevation anywhere on Earth, the Dead Sea along the border of Israel and Jordan.

The Dead Sea is also one of the very saltiest places on Earth; about a third of the water is dissolved mineral salts. I have visited some very high places so far in this course, and the big problem if you actually go visit these, is the air gets very thin. It's hard to breathe. I mean, the slopes of Everest are scattered with empty oxygen canisters and bodies too. This is actually a very predictable phenomenon. You can easily find charts that show you what the air pressure will be as you go up above sea level. These charts all start at sea level, and that makes sense, right, because you can't go below sea level right? Wrong.

First of all, we've already talked about places far below the surface of the Earth, down in caves. But there are also places you can go to on land where the surface itself is far below sea level. I briefly talked about one of these places in the lectures on the African Rift Valley and Erta Ale, the lava lake, when I talked about the Danakil Depression in Ethiopia being about 100 meters below sea level. It turns out there are several places around the planet where the surfaces of the continents actually sit some distance below sea level. The deepest of all of these is the Dead Sea.

The surface and shores of the Dead Sea are 423 meters, 1,388 feet below sea level. And if you visit here, you will be able to breathe more easily than anywhere else, because the air pressure is actually five percent more than at sea level. You breathe in more air. I talked a little bit about this phenomenon, how it works, in the lecture on Gibraltar, when I described what it would have been like at the bottom of the Mediterranean Sea when all the water evaporated and it dried up. However, I have to add that the exact elevation of the Dead Sea below sea level is not constant. If you go there, you will see signs all over the place that will list the elevation below sea level of the shores of the Dead Sea. The funny thing is if you look at different signs in different areas, they all give you different numbers for the elevation. It's not the case that they've all made mistakes, it's because they were put up at different times. It turns out that the level of the Dead Sea is rapidly dropping, about a meter per year. You can see it clearly if you look at the shorelines and the surrounding hills; you can see multiple rings of these past shorelines. And it can still drop a long way. The Dead Sea is still 375-meters deep, so the record books may have to keep being changed for awhile.

The Dead Sea is not terribly big; it's about 67-kilometers long, and it's about 18-kilometers across at its widest point. And it sits in a long, narrow valley that stretches all the way from the Red Sea, way up north to Syria, and it separates Israel and Jordan. The border, in fact, runs straight down through the middle of the Dead Sea. Most lakes eventually drain to the ocean; that's how it works. This obviously can't happen here with the Dead Sea because it's below sea level, and rivers can't flow uphill. Well, okay, they do sometimes if they are tidal bores, like I talked about with the lecture on the Bay of Fundy. I have to be a little bit careful with what I say here when it comes to geology, because there're often exceptions to the rule.

But it's clear that the water here is not flowing to the ocean. So what happens to the water? There is a main river, the Jordan River that runs down from the north. It first drains into and out of the Sea of Galilee and then flows down the narrow valley into the Dead Sea. But the Dead Sea is a closed basin; the water evaporates as fast as it enters. In fact, now it's actually evaporating faster than it's being filled because the water from the Jordan River is being largely drawn off for a variety of purposes by Israel and Jordan. There's a very dry climate here. It only rains about 10 centimeters per year. I mean, this is a desert. So rivers flow into the Dead Sea, the water evaporates, and that leaves behind salt. Well, salts really because it turns out there are many different kinds of salts. The Dead Sea is one of the saltiest lakes on Earth. It's 33.7 percent salt; that's actually 8.6 times saltier than the ocean. In fact, there are only a handful of places that are saltier. Lake Assal, in Djibouti, and one very shallow, less-than-a-foot-deep pond in Antarctica, and I'll talk about these two places at the end of the lecture.

You can see evidence of how salty the water is by the unusual salt features that have precipitated all along the shore. It creates some really bizarre-looking rock formations. Some of them look like small, little castles sticking up out of the water. And the salt crystals form on anything there, rocks, sticks, anything that's in the water. But as I mentioned, the salt here is not the same as ocean salt, which is mostly sodium chloride. It actually has a very different taste than ocean salt. You can go to some specialty gourmet shops and buy different salts from around the world; they have slightly different tastes depending on the exact chemical composition. You may have noticed already that ocean sea salt, if you cook with it, tastes slightly different than table salt, which is just sodium chloride.

Here the salts form by being dissolved out of the surrounding hills by rainwater and then carried into the lake, so the composition of the salts in the Dead Sea is a function of the geology of the surrounding rocks within the lands nearby. They're almost all chlorides. You don't get the sulfates, like gypsum, that you see in other parts of the world and that we've seen in previous lectures. It's just not only sodium chloride, or halite, or table salt. In fact, only about 30 percent of the salts here are sodium chloride. Half of the salts are magnesium chloride. You also have calcium chloride, potassium chloride, and a variety of others. In fact, the exact salts vary by season, depth in the water, and temperature, and time of year.

There is so much salt in the water that it makes the water extremely heavy, very dense. And if you go swimming in the Dead Sea you'll be surprised at how easily you will float because the water is just so much denser, but make sure you don't have any cuts or scrapes. The extreme saltiness will be very painful if you do. In fact, there's an enormous amount of salt in the entire region here. The reason for this is that the whole valley in here used to be flooded by the Mediterranean Sea. In fact, it happened multiple times.

About three-million years ago, there were much warmer climates here—in fact, all over the world. There was much less ice in Antarctica and Greenland, so sea levels were generally higher. And the Mediterranean actually flooded in through the Jezreel Valley; it's a valley that cuts to the Mediterranean just to the southwest of the Sea of Galilee. Here's the Sea of Galilee, and here's the Jezreel Valley. The Mediterranean flowed in and flooded this whole valley multiple times. Each time it left, the long lake would slowly dry out, depositing another layer of salt, so much so that the broad region of the Dead Sea, referred to for that time as prehistoric Lake Sodom, accumulated three-kilometers thick of salt. About two-million years ago, the land between the Jordan Valley and the Mediterranean was uplifted by tectonic forces; you can see the high elevation for the hills here. And when this happened, this cut off the Dead Sea and it became a long lake in here, know as Lake Gomorrah, and it no longer flooded.

The region's climate was wetter back then, and it was actually a fresh water lake that deposited significant sediments in the lake bottom. More typical sediments that we've seen like silts and muds that become rocks like shale. The weight of these rocky sediments, heavier than the salt, pushed down on the layer of salt underneath and actually pushed the salt up and around the edges of the lake. And this formed ridges and hills made entirely of salt. For instance, the Lisan Peninsula to the south and Mount Sodom to the west, are both made of salt.

Salt is a solid, it's a solid material, but it actually flows much more easily than other rocks. In fact, if you go in the Gulf of Mexico region in the United States, the surface of the rock there in the states in places like Texas and Louisiana is underlain by large numbers of salt domes that are being squeezed and rising up through the overlying sediments, squeezed up by the heavier sediments pushing down, exactly like what's happened here.

Mount Sodom is five miles long, three miles wide, and it sits over 740 feet above lake level, and it's all salt. In fact, there's a very famous feature here, a popular feature, a column made of salt that's referred to as Lot's wife after the story in the Hebrew Bible. Going back tens of thousands of year, the lake was generally much higher than it is now, but the level has fluctuated greatly, and the drop in water level now has actually caused the salinity, the salt level, to increase to the wildly high levels that we see there now. In fact, the salinity is so high the bottom part of the lake water is actually at its saturation point. And that means salt is currently precipitating right out of the water making a new layer of salt on the bottom. The southern region of the Dead Sea is much shallower than the rest; that's this region down here, and that's actually been segregated into a separate set of salt ponds that you can see in this satellite image here, and that's being used to harvest the salt for human use.

The shallow levels of the Dead Sea are having some unfortunate geologic consequences around the area. As the sea shrinks in size, underground layers of salt have actually dissolved away. And that has led to a strange phenomenon, the sudden formation of large numbers of small sinkholes that are causing roads and bridges to collapse. We've seen sinkholes before in limestone, but this is a very different phenomenon. And there are over 2,500 sinkholes that now line the shores of the Dead Sea, and most of them have appeared just since 2,000. In order to deal with this issue and others related to the rapidly dropping water levels, there's actually serious talk about bringing a pipeline up from the Red Sea, from the Gulf of Elat, or the Gulf of Aqaba, to fill the Dead Sea from ocean water.

There is a bigger question here. Why is the Dead Sea even here? I mean, how do you get a region to drop so far below sea level? The answer involves forces operating over a much greater area. This is all related to the breakup of Africa that began about 30-million years ago. I talked about this process a little bit in the lecture on the African Rift Valley. Though there I focused more on the rifting that was going on within the African mainland itself. But the rifting of Africa actually started up here first. The Arabian Peninsula had been part of Africa for a very long time, and then it started to break away to the northwest. First there was volcanism in the area, then the crust got stretched and thinned and rifted, and starting about 12-million years ago, the Red Sea began as a real ocean. It started as a continental rift, just like the African Rift Valleys, but it kept going, and now you have the Red Sea opening up, the Gulf of Aden opening up towards the Indian Ocean, and then you have the African Rift Valley heading on towards the south.

A very interesting phenomenon here, there's a strange appearance to the shape of the Red Sea, the Gulf of Suez, and the Gulf of Aqaba, in here, that stretches right up through the Dead Sea, the Sea of Galilee, and north. How do you end up with something like this? The key was the Sinai Peninsula, here, used to be part of Arabia but got separated from Arabia, and is now actually part of Africa. The reason is, it's a lot easier to slide rocks past each other than it is to break them apart. Take two bricks, you can slide them easily past each other, but it's hard to break it apart. So plate boundaries will often arrange themselves to be transform faults for as much of the length as possible rather than rifts. I make it sound like it's a premeditated thing on the part of the Earth. What's actually happening, of course, is that things in nature tend to occur in the easiest way possible. Remember when we looked at the hexagonal fracturing in the lecture on the Devils Tower, things happen in their lowest energy state and it's the same thing here.

What we have here is what's called the Dead Sea Transform and it is a fault that is allowing the Arabian Peninsula to slide past the Sinai Peninsula, but it's not perfectly straight. It takes a couple of bends in here, and that's what's going to actually cause the Dead Sea. I can do a demonstration of this using clay. Let me take this very simple set of pieces of clay, and you see, I've taken this block of clay, and I have simply made two cuts in it. This is going to demonstrate Africa, the Sinai Peninsula, and Arabia. Initially we had the situation where the Sinai Peninsula was part of Arabia, and it began to rift away from Africa, and so this is the Red Sea here. The Gulf of Aqaba was part of that. However, at some point the Arabian Peninsula stopped breaking away from Africa, and the Sinai Peninsula stayed connected to Africa, and the Arabian Peninsula began to slide past the Sinai Peninsula. And this funny shape here of the Suez Gulf, the Red Sea, and then the Gulf of Aqaba, and the Dead Sea Transform is what we have happening in a tectonic level. So we have Arabia crashing up into Eurasia, pushing Turkey out of the way to the west, which then collides with the African Plate, and that causes the volcanoes in Greece and Italy. So everything is all connected here. This is part of the whole story that we saw in the very first lecture on Santorini.

We have another process going here because we haven't explained why the Dead Sea is dropping. And to do this, I need to look at another demonstration. Let me take another piece of clay now. And you see I've covered this piece of clay with a layer of peanut butter, and I did that because it's a nice, thick, viscous material. And if I take a stick and I carve a set of lines here, and you'll see in a moment why I'm going to do this. I'm making these straight across. What I want to demonstrate the process by which the Dead Sea will open up along the Dead Sea Transform. What I'm going to do is take these two pieces and begin to slide them past each other. There's a plate boundary underneath that you can't always tell by looking at the rocks at the surface, so as I continue to push this, you get a sense now by where the lines are bending where that plate boundary is. It's here, and it's here. You notice I didn't score the middle, but something very strange is happening to the peanut butter in the middle. It is beginning to drop down in elevation. It is sinking down. The whole surface there is actually dropping below the surface that it started. Why did this happen?

Let me show you what the plate boundary actually looked like here. You can see that the transform fault is not straight. It makes a bend, and so as the two sides slide past each other, a hole develops, and it is that hole that is the Dead Sea. And the seafloor of the lake is dropping continuously, and really, we have no idea how long that's going to go, because the plate boundaries show no sign of stopping soon.

There is a long history of human occupation here around the Dead Sea. Civilization in the West began in this part of the world. The city of Jericho is just to the north, and it is one of the world's oldest cities. It dates back before 10,000 years ago. The early cities of Sodom and Gomorrah, mentioned in the Hebrew Bible, the New Testament, and the Koran, were somewhere here along the southeastern shore of the Dead Sea. One very important implication of the Dead Sea sitting along a major plate boundary is that it can have large earthquakes. And it has been proposed that it was an earthquake that caused the famous destruction of these cities, Sodom and Gomorrah.

This is also one of the few places in the world where you have asphalt seeping directly to the surface, kind of like the La Brea Tar Pits in Los Angeles. You have nodules of hard asphalt that naturally rise up. And this material was prized by the early Egyptians who came over and mined it. In fact, many of the Egyptian mummies were embalmed with Dead Sea asphalt. But one of the most famous archaeological discoveries in the Caves of Qumran, along the northwest shore of the Dead Sea, what's now the West Bank, is a large number of intact papyrus scrolls from around 2,000 years ago. These are known as the Dead Sea Scrolls. And these scrolls contain alternate versions of many parts of the Hebrew Bible, as well as many storied that didn't make it into the canonized Bible. And these were from Jewish tribes who lived in the area from about 150 before the Common Era to about the year 70.

Currently, the unique geologic conditions of the Dead Sea make it a popular tourist destination. There are over a million people who visit each year, largely for the spas that exist along the coast. The water is considered to have great rejuvenating properties. It has more bromine than any other body of water on Earth. The high mineral content of the water, the fact that there's very low pollen in the area, and the low ultraviolet radiation from the thicker air make it a popular site. It's hard to imagine, but even though it's so hot and dry here, the thicker air means it's harder to get sunburned.

The giant lake here is called the Dead Sea, but amazingly, it's not dead. There is life that can survive there. We've previously seen places like Lake Natron, in Tanzania, that can support large populations of these single-celled extremophiles that will thrive in the ultra-basic water there that turn the waters and the feathers of flamingoes a red color. Something very analogous happens here in the Dead Sea. Here there are similar types of extremophiles that survive in these ultra-saline waters. Scientists are very interested in these strange organisms, because they might be models for the kinds of life that could possibly survive on another planet, and we could one day discover on some body like Mars.

In times of flood, the salt content of the Dead Sea can actually drop from its usual 33 percent salinity to about 30 percent or lower. And when this happens, the Dead Sea, temporarily, comes to life in the wake of this influx of freshwater. In 1980, after one such very rainy winter, the normally dark blue Dead Sea turned red. The Dead Sea was teeming with a type of algae called *Dunaliella*. The *Dunaliella*, in turn, nourished red-pigmented halobacteria, causing the color change. Since 1980, the Dead Sea basin has been extremely dry and the algae and the bacteria have not returned in measurable numbers.

It's sometimes difficult to categorize the biggest or the most of something when it comes to the Earth. I've said the Dead Sea is the lowest land surface on Earth. But would you call it the deepest? I mean, we've seen natural caves that extend much deeper. And the deepest lake is Lake Baikal, it's at an elevation of 450 meters or so, but it reaches a depth of 1.6 kilometers, so it extends more than a kilometer below sea level. And there's a place in Antarctica, the Bentley Subglacial Trench, that's 2.5 kilometers below sea level, but it's currently covered with ice. But if the ice melted, then it would now be below sea level, and it would also be flooded by the ocean. And as far as sea trenches go, the deepest part of the seafloor anywhere is the Mariana Trench, and that's almost 11 kilometers below sea level. So, the Dead Sea is a low point, but it's not all that low.

It's time for my top five. And first I want to go to Antarctica, for the tiny Don Juan Pond. This exists in the Dry Valleys of the Transantarctic Mountains, not far from McMurdo Base, which we saw in the lecture on Antarctica. The amount of water here is almost insignificant. The pond is currently, on average, about four-inches deep, but varies over its extent, which is about 300 meters by 100 meters. We're talking about the area of about three soccer fields. However, it has the saltiest water found anywhere in nature. It seems to be fed from underground by water. And when it was first found, its salinity was 40 percent, at a temperature of –30 degrees Celsius. It's so salty that it doesn't freeze, even in the Antarctic winters, but there's really so little water here.

Next, I want to go to Lake Assal in the small coastal African country of Djibouti. And this is the most salty real lake in the world. It's salinity at the surface is 34.8 percent salt, which just barely edges out the Dead Sea, which is at 33.7. Like the Dead Sea, Lake Assal is below sea level, about 150 meters, actually 155 meters below sea level, and that makes it the lowest point in Africa, and the lowest anywhere after the Dead Sea and the Sea of Galilee. The composition of Lake Assal is different from the Dead Sea, however. It's primarily normal halite, sodium chloride. In fact, its composition is very similar to that of sea water. This is not an accident. Lake Assal, which is about 10-kilometers across or so, is not far from the coast of the Indian Ocean, actually, it's about 10 kilometers from the ocean. And though the region is incredibly hot and dry—it's routinely over 120 degrees Fahrenheit during summer—and the evaporation rates are extremely high, the small lake doesn't dry up because it's continuously fed underground by water flowing through the ground from the ocean. Remember, the lake is down below sea level, so water flows from the ocean downhill underground from the ocean into the lake. Lake Assal has played a very important role in the ancient economics of North Africa. In fact, many of the Sahara camel caravans involve trade routes that had the sale of this region's salt as their economic foundation.

Next, I want to go to the Salton Sea in Southern California, along the San Andreas Fault. This sea here, this inland lake, has formed through the same mechanism of shearing along the bend in a transform fault as the Dead Sea. It's what we call a pull-apart basin. In fact, the Salton Sea is actually an extension of the Gulf of California, which we saw previously as forming as the whole arm of Baja California is tearing away from Mexico. In fact, the Salton Sea also sits below sea level, like the Dead Sea by about 69 meters. The whole area would actually be underwater, including many towns there like Coachella and Indio, which is just south of Palm Springs, except for one thing. The Colorado River delta has actually blocked it off and separated it from the ocean. All that sand carried down from the west side of the Rockies has been dumped here and has cut off the Salton Sea from the rest of the ocean. At the time of the huge runoff of melted ice water at the end of the last Ice Age, the Salton Sea was actually huge, but it has since dried up. However, there are, periodically, lakes that form within the broad depression, known as the Salton trough.

The current Salton Sea, however, is there for entirely accidental human reasons. There was a flood along the Colorado River, in 1905, and the flooding topped the Alamo Canal head gates, which are right near Yuma, Arizona. It, for awhile, brought the entire volume of the Colorado River through that canal and into the Salton Sea, which had been dry and began to fill up. The Southern Pacific Railroad finally stopped the flooding, but not before the new flooding had cut a channel so deep it made a waterfall 80 feet high in what used to be the Alamo Canal. Water from the Colorado River continued to flow into the Salton Sea during flood times for the next 30 years, and this was only finally stopped with the completion of the Hoover Dam, in 1935.

Next, we go to the Turpan Depression in the Xinjiang Region, of China. This is a large depression in Western China that also formed from a sheared pull-apart basin, but it happened a really long time ago, 250-million years ago. This is the hottest and driest part of China and has the lowest elevation of anywhere within Asia. It's 154.5 meters below sea level, just half a meter less than Lake Assal in Djibouti, so that makes it the third lowest region on land.

And last, I want to go to the Caspian Sea, the largest salt lake in the world. The largest lake of any kind, by area. In fact, it's 50 percent larger than all of the Great Lakes combined, or of the size of Texas. But it isn't all that salty, at least compared to lakes like the Dead Sea. It's only about a third of the salinity of the ocean. The Caspian Sea borders many countries, Russia, Iran, Turkmenistan, Azerbaijan, Kazakhstan, and has over 130 rivers draining into it, including some larger ones—the Volga and Ural rivers. But it has no outlet. Water never reaches the ocean. And it's so large that many people in history likely thought that it was a sea, part of the ocean, and thus its name. And actually, geologically, it used to be. Like the Black Sea, the Caspian Sea used to be part of the ancient Tethys Sea, the sea that closed up when Africa, and Arabia, and India all crashed into Eurasia. And at that time, the Caspian Sea got landlocked by the closing up of the continents, forever to be an interior sea.

In the next lecture, I will look at what happens to a salt lake like the Dead Sea when you have all the water evaporate and all you have left is the salt. And I will take you to the flattest place on Earth, the Salar de Uyuni or, the Uyuni salt flats in Bolivia.

Salar de Uyuni—Flattest Place on Earth
Lecture 30

In the last lecture, we discussed some of the saltiest lakes in the world, starting with the Dead Sea, along the border of Israel and Jordan. In this lecture, we'll again go a step farther and look at what happens when the salty water disappears and all that's left is salt. For this discussion, we'll visit the world's largest salt flat: the Salar de Uyuni in Bolivia. This area is about 4000 square miles—almost the size of Connecticut and about 25 times larger than the Bonneville Salt Flats in Utah. The Salar de Uyuni has about 10 billion tons of salt.

The Saltiest, Flattest Place on Earth

- The Salar de Uyuni is located high in the Altiplano of Bolivia, the High Plateau of the Andes Mountains. It is exactly 11,995 feet in elevation over almost its whole extent of 4000 square miles. The process for such a large region to become so perfectly flat requires the constant wetting and recrystallizing of the layers of salt.

- Some of the salt may be slightly rough in some places, but then it rains, the salt dissolves and levels out a bit, the water dries off, and the salt may buckle and crack. The rain comes again, dissolves the salt, and fills in all the cracks. Over time, the region becomes perfectly flat for hundreds of miles in any direction.

- Features in the Salar de Uyuni generally measure less than 1 meter. The flat has a slight general trend to increase its elevation slightly—by centimeters—from the south to the north. In addition, there are ridges and mountains on the surface, but these are only centimeters high.

- The flatness of the Salar de Uyuni is analogous to the change in sea level over ocean ridges and trenches.
  - Averaging out the waves, you might think that the ocean surface would be flat, but that isn't the case. Because the composition of the Earth varies in different regions underground, it exerts a

varying gravitational force in different parts of the world that causes the sea surface to rise and fall.

o   In a place where cold ocean seafloor is subducting, mass is added, and thus, gravity increases. A rising, hot mantle plume would be more buoyant and have less mass; thus, it would pull with decreased gravity. The effect is to make the whole Earth somewhat lumpy so that even the shape of the ocean surface varies from an ellipsoid.

o   In some places, such as around Iceland, the sea surface is significantly elevated, probably because of the rising mantle plume that causes the Iceland hotspot. Just south of India, the sea surface is depressed, a condition that is probably related to the motion of India northward.

o   The varying sea surface is called the geoid. The Salar de Uyuni is the only place on Earth where the ground is so flat that we can actually see and measure the centimeter-high variations in the Earth geoid, the true shape of the Earth.

•   When the Salar de Uyuni gets a thin layer of water on top, it becomes the world's largest mirror. It is used by some satellites to calibrate their elevation above the surface of the Earth.

•   Salt polygons on the Salar de Uyuni represent an expansion of the salt that is analogous to the columnar basalts we saw at the Devils Tower. There, cracks formed from the contraction of cooling basalt. Here, the salt expands slightly when it crystallizes, pushing up tiny ridges, primarily in the shape of hexagons and pentagons.

Effects of Salt in Water
•   Salt significantly changes the properties of water in which it's dissolved. An experiment with a hard-boiled egg shows that the density of salt water is greater than fresh water. This higher density explains why you float when you go swimming in a salt lake. Because the salt water is significantly denser than normal, you float higher.

- If you put a beaker of fresh water and one of salt water in the freezer overnight, the fresh water will be frozen in the morning, but the salt water will still be liquid. The presence of the salt decreases the melting point of ice. We see this effect at Don Juan Pond in Antarctica, the 4-inch-deep pond that doesn't freeze during Antarctic winters.

  o At the Salar de Uyuni, the elevation is so high that the temperature at night is often below freezing—for fresh water at least—but the salty water doesn't freeze. Daytime temperatures are fairly stable, about 55° to 70°F, which means that even normal ice would be melted.

  o In an indoor skating rink, salty water at temperatures much lower than 0°C is run through a network of pipes to chill a slab of concrete to below the freezing temperature for pure water. When fresh water is poured on top of the chilled slab, it freezes.

Sources of Salt

- As we saw with the Dead Sea, the whole region of the Salar de Uyuni is a closed basin; water flows into it but not out. The water evaporates and leaves the salts behind. The Altiplano has an extremely low rainfall, but it experiences enough rain to eventually dissolve the salts out of rocks in the surrounding mountains and deposit them in the basin. Water also flows in from streams around the perimeter, such as the Rio Grande river along the southern border.

- Most of the water for the salt flat here comes from the north. During the rainy season, Lake Titicaca overflows its banks, and the rainwater flows down into two small lakes, Uru Uru and Poopó. These lakes, in turn, overflow their banks, and the water flows to two salt flats, the Salar de Coipasa, the smaller one to the northwest, and the Salar de Uyuni. The water eventually evaporates away, leaving behind another layer of salt.

- Most of the salt here dates back to 46,000 to 36,000 years ago, when Uyuni was a large lake, now called Lake Minchin. About 26,000 to 13,000 years ago, at the end of the last ice age, Lake Minchin transformed into another paleolake, Lake Tauca, with a depth of about 140 meters. About 13,000 to 11,500 years ago, the smaller Lake Coipasa formed, and when it dried, it left behind the lakes Uru Uru and Poopó and the two salt deserts.

Structure and Composition of the Salt Flats

- The structure of the salt flats is strange. A thin crust of salt on the surface—perhaps tens of centimeters to a few meters thick—rests on top of a thicker layer of slushy liquid brine—perhaps 2 to 10 meters thick.

  o This brine contains salt crystals that gradually dominate deeper into the layer; eventually, the layer reaches a region where there are no pore spaces between the salt. There is no water here—just solid salt.

  o Because the evaporation rates are so high at the surface, a crust forms over the top of the brine, but right underneath that crust, the salt is porous and there's a good deal of liquid brine. When flooding occurs, the layers alternate between solid and liquid.

- The salt here also has an interesting composition. It's primarily halite, or sodium chloride, but it's highly enriched in other salts, such as magnesium chloride, potassium chloride, and lithium chloride. These other salts are largely concentrated at the top of the briny layer.

Tourist Highlights

- Though the salt stretches out flat for hundreds of miles, some small islands poke up through it in places. Some of these islands are the tops of ancient volcanoes, and some have salt hotels, with walls made of blocks of salt.

- During the rainy season, when a thin layer of water sits on the surface, all you can see is the reflected image of the sky in the water, and it looks as if you are driving across the sky. Because all you see is sky in all directions, it's almost impossible to keep your bearings.

- One highlight for tourists in this area is the train cemetery. In the 1800s, the British built a railway system here to serve the mining industry in the area. When that industry collapsed in the 1940s, the trains were no longer used and were left in one long line.

© iStockphoto/Thinkstock.

The reflection from the thin layer of water that sits on top of the Salar de Uyuni during the rainy season gives drivers the impression of traveling across the sky.

- Very little life is found in the Salar de Uyuni. The salt itself is entirely devoid of life. During the rainy season, a bloom of pink cyanobacteria takes place in the saltwater layer, and the area becomes a nesting ground for flamingos and other birds. The islands host small microenvironments with cacti, rabbits, foxes, and other animals.

- Because the Salar de Uyuni contains more than 40 percent of the world's known lithium, used in batteries, the area is harvested extensively, but removing all the lithium would destroy the appearance of the salt flat.

Top Salt Flats
- The Salar de Atacama in Chile is a salt flat similar to the Salar de Uyuni. It's about one-third the size of the Salar de Uyuni and not nearly as smooth because in many places it no longer floods and is permanently dry. This area contains 27 percent of the world's known lithium but provides about one-third of the world's annual supply.

- The Bonneville Salt Flats in Utah is the largest of many salt flats that are west of the Great Salt Lake. Both Salt Lake and the Bonneville

Flats are the remnants of the once huge Lake Bonneville, which at its peak, 20,000 to 30,000 years ago, was about the size of Lake Michigan but much deeper. Some of the ancient shorelines of the former Lake Bonneville can still be seen high up on the sides of the mountains in Utah. This lake seems to have been a recurrent feature of the cycles of ice ages. It has filled up and dried away at least 25 times over the past 3 million years.

- Lake Eyre is both the lowest point in Australia, about 15 meters below sea level, and the largest lake there—but only when it rains. Lake Eyre is largely a salt pan with some small salty lakes, but occasionally over the course of a century, heavy winter rains fill in the lake. The last time this occurred was in 1976.

- The Makgadikgadi Salt Pan sits in the middle of the dry savanna of northeastern Botswana. It is all that remains of the formerly enormous Lake Makgadikgadi, which once covered a vast area but dried up several thousand years ago.

Suggested Reading

Arrieta, *From the Atacama to Makalu*.

Fletcher, *Bottled Lightning*.

Questions to Consider

1. How did the structure of the salt layers at the Salar de Uyuni (with a layer of liquid brine in between two solid layers) initially form?

2. The valuable lithium is concentrated in one region in the south but still is found throughout the Salar de Uyuni. In your opinion, how much (all, some, or none) of the lithium should be removed from this salt flat?

Salar de Uyuni—Flattest Place on Earth
Lecture 30—Transcript

Hello. My name is Michael Wysession, and welcome to Lecture 30 of our course on the Geologic Wonders of the World. In the last lecture, we looked at some of the saltiest lakes in the world, starting with the Dead Sea, along the border of Israel and Jordan. In this lecture, we're going to take a step further and talk about what happens when that salty water is gone and all that's left is the salt. And to do this, we're going to visit the world's largest salt flat by far—the Salar de Uyuni, in Bolivia.

Salar de Uyuni literally means the salts of Uyuni, and this is huge. It's about 4,000 square miles. It's almost the size of Connecticut. It's about 25 times the size of the Bonneville Salt Flats in Utah. There's a lot of salt here, about 10-billion tons of salt. And it's located very high up in the Altiplano of Bolivia. This is the High Plateau of the Andes Mountains. It's about two miles high, in fact. In fact, it's 3,656 meters, or 11,995 feet, in elevation, exactly, over just about the whole 4,000 square miles. Which also makes it, by far, the flattest place in the world.

How do you possibly get such a large region to be so perfectly flat? It's actually a long process. It requires the constant wetting and recrystallizing of the layers of salt there. What happens is you may have the salt that might be slightly rough there, there's some water, it rains, the salt dissolves, levels out a little bit, and then the water dries off and the salt might buckle and crack a little bit. And then the water comes again, and it melts again. And then it dissolves and fills in all the spaces. And over time what you end up with is a perfectly flat region of salt for hundreds of miles in any direction.

There are actually features here. It's not perfectly flat, but these features are less than a meter total. First of all, there is a slight general trend to increase its elevation slightly as you go from the south to the north, by just centimeters. In addition, there are ridges, and mountains on the surface, but they're only centimeters high. And this has an analog somewhere else on the Earth. This is actually analogous to the change in sea level over ocean ridges and trenches. You would probably think that the ocean surface would be flat, and I'm not talking about waves, so average out the waves. But you would think that if you sailed around over the ocean, the sea surface should be flat. It turns out that the surface of the sea isn't level. This is a somewhat odd concept, but the Earth is not a perfect ellipsoid shape. First of all, the Earth isn't a sphere, as we know, because it rotates and it bulges out along the equator to make the shape of an oblate ellipsoid. This is sphere that's been flattened due to sort of the merry-go-round effect of the rotation. But because the composition of the Earth varies in different regions underground, it exerts a varying gravitational force in different parts of the world that actually causes the surface of the sea to go up and down. You could have a cold ocean seafloor that's subducting, sinking down into the mantle. That's adding mass there, so the gravity increases. Or you could have a rising hot mantle plume, so that would be more buoyant; that would be less mass; it would pull with less gravity. The effect is to make the whole Earth somewhat lumpy, so that even the shape of the ocean surface varies from this ellipse. It's not a lot; it's by plus or minus about 200 meters, a couple of football fields in length.

In some places, like around Iceland, the sea surface is significantly elevated. And this is probably due to a rising mantle plume that's causing the Iceland hotspot. If you go just south of India, the sea surface is depressed. And this is unusual; this is a strange phenomenon. This is the lowest location of the ocean surface in the world, and it seems to be related to the motion of India northward. The rock of the deep asthenosphere, that layer beneath the plates, actually has to flow out of the way and around the deep continental root as India moves forward. And that leaves a low pressure zone behind India in the mantle just south of India. It's sort of like if you were in a fast boat. The boat would push the water in front but leave a depression in the wake behind it. Well, the sea surface does something similar. This whole varying sea surface has a name; it's called the geoid. You're probably wondering what this has to do with the Salar de Uyuni. Salar de Uyuni is the only place on Earth where the ground is so flat that you can actually see and measure the centimeter-high variations in the Earth's geoid—the true shape of the Earth.

The Salar de Uyuni is so flat, that when it gets a very thin layer of water on top of it, it becomes the world's largest mirror. It's actually used by some satellites in order to calibrate their elevation above the surface of the Earth. Lakes are also flat. You would think that they would work, but the water of the lakes tends to absorb most incoming radiation. Here, up in the Altiplano, the air is very dry, and the surface ends up reflecting about 70 percent of ultraviolet light, so it provides a perfect condition for satellites to use this as a mirror. In fact, using Salar de Uyuni as the target, the Ice, Cloud, and Land Elevation Satellite, ICESat managed to achieve an elevation measurement accuracy of about two centimeters or less across the whole salt flat, and was then able to map out all the small variations across the surface of the salt flat.

There are other unusual features that you will find. You do find very, very small ridges. Many of them that are called salt polygons. And we can see this if you look at this photograph. Each one of these represents expansion of the salt that's very analogous to the columnar basalts we saw at Devils Tower, only with Devils Tower, there were cracks that were forming from the contraction of the cooling basalt. Here, the salt expands slightly when it crystallizes, and that pushes up these tiny ridges. But again, it's largely in the shape of these hexagons and pentagons. It's trying to maximize the expansion with the least amount of actual cracking. One very important thing about salt is that it significantly changes the properties of water when it's dissolved in it. And I can do a demonstration. Suppose I have two beakers of water. They're identical beakers. They look the same, but one has pure water, and the other has a lot of salt dissolved in it. How could I possibly tell them apart? There are a couple of things I could do. I could taste them, and actually, frankly these props have been moved around so much, I'm not sure which is which, so that would be one way to do it. I could taste them. I could do something else. I can do a demonstration with something that's very close to the density of water. Let me take hard-boiled eggs. So if I take this egg and I drop it into this beaker here and see what happens. I see that this egg sinks down to the bottom. Let me take this egg here and drop it down and see what happens. It floats. This one's the salt.

How do I know this? Well, when the salt gets added to the water, the density of the water increases. The density of the fresh water is slightly less than the hard-boiled egg, so the egg sinks to the bottom. The density of the water with the salt in it is much higher, and so the egg floats on top of it. There's another way I could've told which was which here. I can take these two beakers of water, and I can put then in the freezer, and I can leave them there overnight. And what will happen is the fresh water in the morning will be entirely frozen. The salt water will still be liquid. Why? The presence of the salt actually changes the chemical properties of the water. It makes it harder to freeze.

I wasn't entirely truthful at the start of this. It turns out you can tell by looking which is the salt water, but you have to look very closely and measure to a high degree of accuracy. You know the phenomenon that if you put a pencil or a spoon or something in water and look at it, it looks bent, and that's because the presence of the water will actually refract light that passes through it. If I were to take two laser beams and shoot them in through the side of the water here, they would get bent slightly different amounts. The salt water would actually bend the light more and you can measure that.

So what happens here? The high density explains why you float if you go into a salt lake and go swimming some place like the Dead Sea or the Great Salt Lake. The water with the salt is significantly denser than normal, so you end up floating higher. The temperature effect explains why the salt lakes don't freeze easily. Remember Don Juan Pond in Antarctica, the little four-inch deep pond that doesn't freeze during Antarctic winters? By the time you get to a salinity of just 25 percent, the melting point has dropped to more than −20 degrees Celsius. And go all the way down to the 40 percent salinity of Don Juan Pond, it's really hard to freeze this.

Here at the Salar de Uyuni, the elevation is so high that the temperature at night is often below freezing, for fresh water at least, but the water is so salty it doesn't freeze. Daytime temperatures are pretty stable controlled by sun shining through the thin atmosphere, and it tends to be about 55 to 70 degrees Fahrenheit, so normal water would be melted anyway. You also have, probably, some experience with salt lowering the freezing point of water in your own life. Have you ever gone skating in an indoor skating rink, or watched an indoor hockey game? How do they do this? They don't lower the temperature of the whole room below freezing, right? What they do is they run very salty water at temperatures much lower than zero degrees Celsius through a network of pipes, and this chills a slab of concrete to below the freezing temperature for pure water, and then when fresh water is put on top of that chilled slab, it freezes. Actually, most skating rinks use calcium chloride salt and not sodium chloride, but it's a very similar process.

Where does all this salt come from? Just like other salt lakes and salt flats, like what we saw with the Dead Sea, the whole region is a closed basin, water flows into it, but not out. The water just evaporates and leaves the salts behind. The salts don't evaporate with the water. The area here, up on the Altiplano, has an extremely low rain fall, but not zero. It can rain as much as an inch per month during the rainy season. That's not a lot of rain, I mean, this is a very dry desert, but it is enough rain to eventually dissolve the salts out of the rocks of the surrounding mountains and deposit them at the bottom.

Water flows in also from streams around the perimeter, like the Rio Grande River along the southern border. Rio Grande just means big river, and here it's a little bit of a misnomer; it's a fairly small stream. But most of the water for the salt flat here actually comes from the north during the rainy season. The water starts with Lake Titicaca up here in the north, which is a beautiful lake. I should say, in this satellite image here, these ridges off to the right here are the highest parts of the Andes Mountains. The very dry region along the coast there is the driest place on Earth, the Atacama Desert, and I will talk about that in the next lecture. All these little circular features here, these are volcanoes. After all, this is a subduction zone. The Nazca Plate of the Pacific Ocean seafloor is sinking beneath South America here, creating all of these volcanoes. You have Lake Titicaca here, which is the largest lake in all of South America, actually. It's also one of the worlds very highest, and it's a fascinating place. It has 41 distinct islands, each one ecologically different from the other. It's also interestingly the home of the Bolivian Navy. Bolivia is entirely landlocked; there is no connection to the ocean, but it still has a Navy up here on the lake.

During the rainy season Lake Titicaca overflows its banks, and the rainwater flows down across this normally dry area into two small lakes, Lake Uru Uru and Lake Poopó, which then, in turn, overflow their banks, and the water flows from here across to two salt flats, the Salar de Coipasa here, the smaller one to the northwest, and then the Salar de Uyuni here, the very large one. The water eventually evaporates away, leaving behind another layer of salt. It is during this time, with a very thin layer of water on the top of the salt, that the surface of the flats becomes that giant mirror I talked about. Most of the salt here dates back to much earlier times, times when there was a lot more water here and Uyuni was actually a large lake, a real lake; 46,000, 36,000 years ago, based on radiometric carbon-14 dates. This area was a large prehistoric lake that has the name, Lake Minchin. The climate before then had been extremely dry, and there wasn't much in the way of lakes at all. Lake Minchin, afterwards, transformed into another lake, paleolake Tauca, and that was fairly substantial. It had a depth of about 140 meters of water. That's about 460 feet, and this was the period 26,000 to 13,000 years ago. This is just the end of the last Ice Age. In fact, this lake filled in up to half of the whole basin.

Most recently it was the smaller lake, called Lake Coipasa. And this was 13,000 to 11,500 years. And when it dried, it left behind these two lakes I mentioned, Uru Uru and Poopó, and the two salt deserts here, Salar de Coipasa, and the larger, Salar de Uyuni.

The structure of the salt flats is very strange. There's a thin crust of salt at the surface, maybe tens of centimeters to a few meters thick, that actually rests on top of a thicker layer of slushy liquid brine, very ultra salty water that's maybe 2 to 10 meters or more thick, so more than 30 feet in places. That brine contains salt crystals that gradually dominate as you go down, and eventually you get to a region where there are no pore spaces between the salt, so there's no water; there's just solid salt down there. A crust forms over the top of this brine, because the evaporation rates are so high at the surface, but right underneath that crust the salt is very porous, and there's a lot of liquid brine. So it's a very unusual structure. When it floods, the water coming down from Lake Titicaca, you have this alternating layer of solid, liquid, solid, liquid.

The salt has an interesting composition. We looked at the salts of the Dead Sea and noticed how they were different than the salts of the ocean. This is a different composition again. It's primarily halite, or sodium chloride, but it's highly enriched in other salts such as magnesium chloride, potassium chloride, and in particular, lithium chloride. These other salts are very largely concentrated at the top of the briny layer. The unusual nature of the salt flat has made it a very interesting tourist destination. Despite its relative inaccessibility, there are more than a half-million people who visit each year. Because it's perfectly flat, it's a preferred driving route for traffic and many trucks routinely take a shortcut going right across it. Though the salt stretches out flat for hundreds of miles, there are some small islands that poke up through it here and there. They sometimes serve as resting places for travelers. Some of these are actually the tops of these ancient volcanoes I mentioned before. Some of the islands even have salt hotels. The walls are made of blocks of salt. I mean, you have to work with what you have available, right. During the rainy season, when there's a thin layer of water on the surface, it looks as if you are driving across the sky. All you can see is the reflected image of the sky in the water, so top or bottom, wherever you look, all you see is sky. It's one of the most bizarre sights you could ever imagine. And because all you see is sky, in all directions, it's almost impossible to get your bearings and figure out where you're going.

One highlight for tourists in this area is what's called the Train Cemetery. It turns out there was a lot of mining in this area, in the 1800s, and the British built a whole railway system here. But when the mining industry collapsed in the 1940s, the trains were no longer used, and all the trains are left here now in one long line. Another very unusual spot and frequently visited by tourists is a strangely eroded rock that kind of looks like a big umbrella, it's called the Stone Tree, that rises right up out of the salt.

There's very little life here. The salt itself is entirely devoid of life. But during the rainy season there is a bloom of these pink cyanobacteria in the saltwater layer that we've seen elsewhere in very salty lakes. And as a result, just like Lake Natron, in Africa, it becomes a nesting ground for birds. Every November, three species of flamingoes, Chilean, Andean, and James's flamingo, and about 80 other bird species descend upon Uyuni to feed on the bacteria. So it just becomes covered with birds. And again, just like with Lake Natron, it's the pink cyanobacteria that gives the flamingoes here their pink color. They would otherwise be white. The islands in the salt, however, have quite a bit of life on them. And they host small, little microenvironments. It's much like an island in the ocean. It's very similar. They're dominated by these tall cacti that can grow 40-feet high, and there are different species of rabbits, foxes that live off of them, but they're almost entirely cut off from other islands.

Like many other geologic wonders, there are human-related conflicts with respect to the use of the Salar de Uyuni. And there's a large current debate about its very future that focuses on the fact that this salt flat contains more than 40 percent of the world's known lithium, this one place. It's the largest known lithium reserve, of course, by far. Lithium is a very important material. It's used for batteries, largely. If you use a laptop computer, or a cell phone, or an electric car, you rely on lithium, and especially with a push towards electric cars that we're expecting in the future, there is going to be a booming need for lithium. But it's only abundantly found in a very few places in the world. Lithium tends to prefer to stay dissolved in the briny liquid, long after most of the other salts have crystallized out, so that's actually very convenient, because it's right here at the surface.

The largest producer of lithium, which actually provides 30 percent of the world's current supply, is another salt flat just south of Uyuni. It's called the Salar de Atacama, in Chile. It has a slightly higher density of lithium in the water. It's about 0.3 percent of the water. It's also drier there, so there are higher rates of evaporation, so it's a little bit more efficient to harvest the salts there. After all, you have to wait for the water to evaporate out of the salt ponds to leave the salt behind. For Salar de Atacama, you also have a thicker layer of the lithium salts, and they're spread out over a smaller region. For Uyuni, the lithium is spread out over a much broader region, and the layer of brine is thinner. So here, percentages of lithium are generally much lower than Atacama, except in one region in the south and that's where the Rio Grande River enters.

People have long harvested the salts here for its many uses. It's easier to harvest the liquid brine, but because the topmost layer of the crust here is so high in lithium, people still remove it by hand, even though it's painstaking work. Still, one shovelful of this salt has about $6 worth of lithium in it, and there are a lot of shovelfuls here. They tend to shovel it into cones that are then picked up by trucks. So if you actually visit here and drive across you'll see all these little cone shapes all over the surface, and they're not naturally formed, that's done by people.

As I mentioned, it's less costly to pump out the liquid brine. And this is what they do in a large, sort of factory-style process. They mix that liquid with a set of chemicals that then allows the salts to be extracted. You put the liquid in a sequence of evaporation ponds, and different salts come out with each successive pond, and then what's leftover at the end is the lithium. These lithium processing plants, as I said, are very common in the Salar de Atacama, but one has now opened in Salar de Uyuni by the mouth of the Rio Grande.

Certainly removing all the lithium here would destroy the appearance of the salt flat, which is a geologic wonder. And there are some locals who favor it. It means jobs, wealth, and prosperity, at least for a while. Other people remember the same promises from the mining industry in the previous century when the minerals were taken with little benefit to the locals, who were left with little profit but large environmental disasters that were never cleaned up. They would rather see the Salar de Uyuni kept as a Bolivian geological national treasure. It's a common tension concerning the use of lands everywhere, and frankly, one that's only going to get more challenging as time goes on and human populations and industrialization continue to increase.

It's time for my top five, and I have to start, of course, with the region I just mentioned to the south, the Salar de Atacama, in Chile. It's very much akin to the Salar De Uyuni, a little bit farther south, a little bit higher. It's up along the Altiplano, just like Uyuni, and it's smaller. It's about a third the size of the Salar de Uyuni. However, it's also not nearly as smooth as Uyuni because in many places now it no longer floods, and it's permanently dry. In fact, if you look at images of it you'll often see a very rough texture to the salt. This area contains 27 percent of the world's known lithium, but provides about a third of the world's annual supply. And I'm going to talk a little bit more about this in the Atacama Desert, which is the driest place in the world, at the end of the next lecture.

Next, let me take you to the Bonneville Salt Flats, in Utah. It's the largest of many salt flats that are west of the Great Salt Lake, in Salt Lake City. Both the Salt Lake and the Bonneville Flats are the remnants of the once-huge Lake Bonneville, which at its peak, about 20,000- to 30,000-years ago, was about the size of Lake Michigan, only much deeper. It's hard to imagine Utah as being so wet, but at the time that the Ice Age was at its peak and things were frozen to the north, Utah, which is hot and dry now, was wet and moist, low evaporation rates and high rainfall. You can still see some of the ancient shorelines of the former Lake Bonneville, way high up on the sides of the mountains there. It gives you a sense of how much water there was filling in this whole region.

It seems as if Lake Bonneville actually has been a recurrent feature of the cycles of Ice Ages. It seems to have filled up and then dried away at least 25 different times over the past three-million years; that's the time that the large cycle of ice ages began on Earth. So it is possible that Lake Bonneville will fill up again the next time we have a severe Ice Age. That is, if we have one, of course, if we haven't developed geoengineering to the point by then that we can keep global climates from ever changing again, and a lot of people are working on that.

Most people know the Bonneville Salt Flats as the place where so many car racing speed records have been set. And this is because the Bonneville Salt Flats, like Uyuni, are remarkably flat. So you can drive for 10 miles and now worry about hitting any kind of a speed bump. Many people would also recognize the Bonneville Salt Flats as the setting for large numbers of movies, *Independence Day*, the last of the *Pirates of the Caribbean* movies, and others.

Next, let me take you to Australia, for Lake Eyre. It's both the lowest point in Australia, about 15 meters below sea level, and the largest lake in Australia. The latter is only true when it rains, which frankly is not very often there, in the huge desert of the Lake Eyre Basin in South Australia. Lake Eyre is largely a salt pan with some small, salty lakes, but every now and then over the course of a century there's a huge set of winter rains, and the lake thoroughly fills in. The last time was back in 1976.

And last, let me go to Lake Makgadikgadi, the Makgadikgadi Salt Pan, in Botswana. It's a large salt pan in the middle of the dry savanna of northeastern Botswana. It's also one of the largest salt flats in the world. And it's all that remains of the formerly enormous Lake Makgadikgadi, which once covered a huge, vast area, but dried up several thousand years ago.

I wanted to end with this location, because it provides a nice bridge to the next lecture. Lake Makgadikgadi is at the edge of the Kalahari Desert and its Okavango Delta, and these are adjacent to the severe Namib Desert, and these are the sites that we're going to be visiting in the next lecture.

Namib/Kalahari Deserts—Sand Mountains
Lecture 31

Along the west coast of Africa is one of the world's most inhospitable places: the Namib Desert. There are no volcanoes here or acid lakes; it's just incredibly dry and has been so for more than 50 million years. Still, this region has its own unique beauty. We see colors and shapes here that can't be found anywhere else on the planet. Just over a ridge of mountains from the Namib is the Kalahari Desert, which has a completely different character and much more plentiful life. In this lecture, we'll continue our theme of dry and arid places with a visit to these two fascinating deserts.

"The Land God Made in Anger"
- The Bushmen of the Namibian interior have called the region of the Namib Desert "the Land God Made in Anger." It is one of the driest places on Earth, which is unusual given that it rims an ocean. It receives less than 1 centimeter of rain a year. Deserts are often defined as regions that receive less than 25 centimeters of rain a year.

- Hot deserts have a different appearance than cold deserts. Sand dunes are common in hot deserts, although much more common is a surface called the desert pavement, a hard, dry, packed surface of large rocks and cobbles. This kind of surface forms by different processes, particularly the strong winds that are often found in deserts. The winds blow away lighter dust and small sand particles, leaving the rocks behind.

- The infrequent rains in a desert chemically weather away the rock, dissolving some of the minerals and leaving behind small particles that the wind then blows away. From this process comes the sand for the giant sand dunes of the Namib Desert, which are larger than anywhere else in the world. The sand is blown across the surface and accumulates into dunes.

- The desert pavement can develop by a process of freezing and thawing or wetting and drying of the ground, which causes the ground to expand and contract.
  - This strange process is not completely understood. If the ground is constantly frozen and thawed, large rocks underneath will work their way up to the surface.

  - Freezing and thawing is, obviously, more common in cold deserts, such as Antarctica or the Gobi Desert, but it also takes place in high regions of dry deserts.

  - The freezing and thawing change the volume of the soil. The soil expands when it freezes, but when it thaws, it seems as if smaller rocks are wedged downward, leaving the rocks a little bit higher each time the process takes place.

  - If you vibrate a set of objects of different sizes, over time in certain cases, the larger objects will rise to the surface. Something similar to this "Brazil nut phenomenon" may take place in deserts.

- Even hot deserts, such as the Kalahari, can experience significant temperature swings, with freezing at night. Temperatures in the winter in the Kalahari are often below freezing; the reason for this is simply the lack of water.
  - Water vapor in the atmosphere has a tremendous moderating effect on temperatures. It is actually the strongest greenhouse gas, essentially keeping our atmosphere warm, and it forms clouds.

  - Clouds block incoming sunlight during the day, making the temperature cooler on warm days, but the water vapor absorbs energy that radiates back off of Earth's surface at nighttime, keeping the atmosphere warm.

  - In the desert, with no water vapor in the air, the sun heats the surface during the day, but the heat escapes quickly at night.

- Deserts are generally some of the least inhabited places in the world because of the lack of water, but remarkably, some people live in the Arabian Desert, the Sahara, and other deserts.
  o There is also a growing modern interest in desert regions, at least partially because of their mineral resources.

  o Deserts have many useful resources that form as evaporates, such as sodium nitrate, which is used for fertilizer and in gunpowder; gypsum, which is used for construction; and the salts, such as lithium, that are washed into playas.

A Coastal Desert?
- The coastal location of the Namib Desert seems puzzling. How could this dry region exist right next to so much water?

- The West Coast of the United States is very green, but once you travel up and over the coastal mountains, you reach desert. The reason for this change is that the winds blow in a different direction.

- In the area of the Namib, the prevailing wind blows east to west, which is the opposite of the western United States. As moist air from the Indian Ocean rises up over the Drakensberg Mountains of South Africa, along the east coast, it cools; it loses its water into water droplets that rain out. The air is dry when it crosses the Namib escarpment, and as it drops and warms even further, it absorbs any available moisture, making the ground even drier. For this reason, the area right along the coast is drier than even a little bit inland.

Features of the Namib
- The Sossusvlei region of the Namib is a sea of sand that has a rich ochre color. The dunes here rise more than 1000 feet, 300 feet taller than the next largest sand dunes in the world—in Arabia.
  o The older a sand dune is, the brighter its color. The color itself is the result of two factors: a slow oxidation of minerals that contain iron and tiny fragments of garnets, which make the sand sparkle.

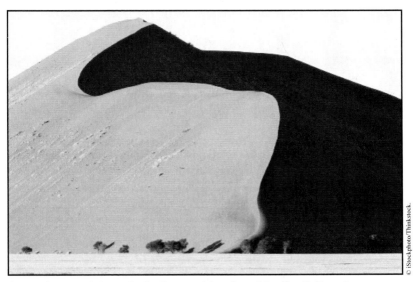

Some of the sand dunes in the Sossusvlei region of the Namib Desert are more than 1000 feet tall; in other areas, they might qualify as mountains.

     o   The dunes refract spectacular colors as the light changes in the desert, moving from bright orange through red to a deeper mauve color over the course of the day.

- The giant Fish River Canyon in southern Namibia is similar to the Grand Canyon in Arizona. Clearly, at one time in the past, a good deal of water was present here. Beautiful purple, pink, and gray rock layers stretch along a 100-mile course. The canyon walls sometimes drop by almost 2000 feet out of the flat, dry plateau. In some places, the canyon is almost 30 kilometers across.

- Along the coast, the Namib can experience thick, blinding fog. When the dry, hot desert air meets the moist, cold air generated by the Benguela Current, the dry air pushes the moist air down. As it falls and warms, the moist air causes thick banks of fog. This fog is the only moisture that some parts of the desert ever receive, and life has evolved to adapt to it.

Features of the Kalahari

- The Kalahari Desert is much more vegetated than the Namib, and large numbers of mammals live here, including meerkats, lions, jackals, buffalo, and people.

- Technically, much of the Kalahari is not a desert but a steppe, a semiarid region. We don't find giant sand dunes here; much of the land is low, flat, scrubby, dry bush.

- The most interesting aspect of the Kalahari is in the northern region, where the Okavango River empties into the desert and disappears.
  - In January, heavy rains in Angola flow southward through the Okavango River, which begins to swell. The water slowly works its way southward, finally reaching down into the Okavango Delta after about four months.

  - The delta then becomes, briefly, one of the largest river deltas in the world, 250 kilometers across by 150 kilometers long. The topographical variation across this delta is only about 6 feet.

  - As a result of the flatness of this region, anything on the ground that sticks up, such as a clump of trees, can start to accumulate silt from the incoming water. More vegetation develops, and small desert islands start to build up.

  - The flood in the Kalahari is rejuvenating for desert life, but even during the flood, most of the water evaporates. Only enough of it seeps into the ground to keep the trees alive and to support life until the next year's flood.

Top Deserts

- The Arabian Desert covers most of the Arabian Peninsula. Though it's much smaller than the Sahara, it is still more than 2 million square kilometers. The Arabian Desert has vast oceans of sand, with dunes rising more than 250 meters. The sands here are mostly quartz with small amounts of potassium feldspar, giving them a slight orange color.

- o Satellite images show evidence of the camel tracks of ancient caravans in certain sections of the Arabian Desert. Archaeologists have found the remains of lost cities here that were once a part of the frankincense trade.

- o Before 5000 years ago, monsoon rains fell here, and the deserts were green. Evidence, such as hand flints and other tools, has been found of Paleolithic humans living in what is now a wasteland of sand.

- The Gobi Desert is in Mongolia and part of China. This is an elevated, cold, dry land that's in the rain shadow behind the Tibetan Plateau. Much of the Gobi contains steppe regions that support diverse ecosystems. Because this region is so high in elevation and so dry, it's susceptible to significant temperature changes, sometimes of more than 90°F in a single day.

- The Great Victoria Desert is the largest desert in Australia, about 0.5 million square kilometers. Located in the south-central area of the country, this desert supports a small population of indigenous Australians, though it's unable to support any agriculture.

- The Atacama Desert, along the west coast of South America, is the exact analog to the Namib Desert. It sits on the west side of the continent with air blowing from the east; by the time the air drops down over the Atacama, not only it is devoid of water vapor, but it absorbs any water it comes in contact with. The Atacama is the driest place on Earth. Much of it receives less than 1 millimeter of rain a year.

Suggested Reading

Johnson, *The Ultimate Desert Handbook*.

Martin, *The Deserts of Africa*.

1. Along the West Coast of the United States, the situation is reversed from the Namib Desert: Lush vegetation is found from the coast up the sides of the coastal mountains, and dry desert area exists east of the coastal mountains. What causes this reversal from the conditions of the Namib Desert?

2. How has life evolved to adapt to the situation at the Okavango Delta, where there is a good deal of water for a brief period and arid conditions the rest of the time?

Namib/Kalahari Deserts—Sand Mountains
Lecture 31—Transcript

Hello. My name is Michael Wysession, and welcome to Lecture 31 of our course on the Geologic Wonders of the World. In the last lecture, we visited the flattest place on the planet, the remarkable Salar de Uyuni, the Salt Flats in Bolivia. In this lecture, I will continue my theme of dry and arid places and visit two of the world's most fascinating deserts, the Namib and Kalahari Deserts in southern Africa.

Along the west coast of Africa is a place, the Namib Desert, that is one of the world's most inhospitable. There are no volcanoes, there are no acid lakes; it's just incredibly dry and has been for over 50-million years. I'll also show you, though, this region has its own unique beauty. You will see colors and shapes here that you just won't find anywhere else around the planet. The shoreline of the Namib Desert has long been called the Skeleton Coast. If you go there, there are more than 1,000 shipwrecks scattered up and down the coast. Thick fogs and sharp rocks make it very easy to have a shipwreck. And if you do get shipwrecked and manage to survive and make it to shore, you're really not any better off. There's not a drop of freshwater to be had. And because of the constant heavy surf, large waves, it's also almost impossible to get back off the beach once a human-powered boat would land there. In fact, the Bushmen of the Namibian interior have called this region The Land God Made in Anger, and Portuguese sailors called it The Gates of Hell. And actually, in terms of skeletons here, on the Skeleton Coast, there are a lot of skeletons of whales that still remain from the early days of whaling.

The Namib Desert is one of the driest places on Earth, which is particularly unusual given that it rims the ocean. It's surrounded by water. It gets less than a centimeter of rain a year, however. In fact, the western part gets even less, less than half a centimeter a year. If you're stuck there, there's no way to survive. And as a result, the area is totally uninhabited.

Just over an escarpment, a ridge of mountains, from the Namib is another desert; it's actually one of the largest in the world, the Kalahari. But it's totally different in character. And I will talk about the Kalahari and its difference between it and the Namib a little bit later in the lecture. We've already visited the world's largest desert—that's the desert down in Antarctica. We've also visited some very high, cold deserts, like the Gobi Desert, in Asia.

The exact definition for a desert can vary, but a common definition is that a desert gets a small amount of rainfall, less than 25 centimeters of rain per year. That's about 10 inches. At less than one centimeter a year, the Namib is way at the low end of this. Some deserts are huge. I mean, the Sahara is almost 10-million square kilometers; it's about the size of the United States, including Alaska. But many of them can be very small. You do get desert microclimates as well. Most deserts, as I've mentioned before, are found where the dry, descending air of the atmospheric Hadley cells come down; that's roughly 30-degrees north or south, away from the equator. There are also some deserts, like the Gobi and Turkestan Deserts, however, that are rain shadows, and these happen when air rises over a mountain range and loses its moisture. Essentially, anywhere that you have air forced to go up, where it gets cold, it can no longer hold water as a vapor form, it converts into a liquid, and it rains or snows out.

Hot deserts end up having a very different appearance than cold deserts. Sand dunes are very common in hot deserts, though actually much less than you might think. There are places in the world where there are seas of sand that will just stretch for hundreds of miles, like an endless ocean of repeating tan waves. But they only turn out to be 20 percent or so of hot deserts. A lot more common is a surface called the desert pavement, and it's a very hard, dry packed surface of large rocks and cobbles. And this kind of surface forms by different processes. A common one is the strong winds that you often find in desert areas. And the winds will blow away lighter dust and small sand particles leaving the rocks behind. It's actually a very slow process. And it actually occurs, largely, because of rain, which is infrequent in deserts, but does happen occasionally. The rain falls, it chemically weathers away the rock, dissolves away some of the minerals leaving small particles behind that the wind then blows away. This is really important because this is where you get the sand for the giant sand dunes of the Namib Desert. And the sand dunes in the Namib are larger than anywhere else in the world. The light dust gets blown away. In fact, in the lecture on the Blue Hole in Belize I talked about how the dust from the Sahara actually can get blown all the way across the Atlantic, and you can measure it in places like the secluded bottom of the Blue Hole there.

The sand is too heavy to get blown away, however, so it gets blown across the surface and can accumulate into a dune. If your desert is really old, like the Namib is—50 million years—then you've had a lot of weathering, mostly from nearby mountains of the escarpment, and therefore, a lot of sand, and that's how you get the world's largest sand dunes.

You can also develop this desert pavement by a process of freezing and thawing the ground, or also wetting and drying it, anything that will cause the ground to expand and contract. And this is a strange process that's really not very well understood. If you constantly freeze and thaw the ground, large rocks underneath will actually work their way up to the surface. They'll come right up out of the ground. Freezing and thawing is obviously more common in cold deserts, places like Antarctica or the Gobi Desert, but you also find this in very high regions of dry deserts. The freezing and thawing change the volume of the soil, and the soil ends up expanding when it freezes, but then when it thaws, when it falls back down, it seems as if the smaller rocks are maybe able to wedge their way down leaving the rocks a little bit higher each time in the process.

There's a mathematical enigma called the Brazil-nut phenomenon. If you take a set of objects of different sizes and shake them or vibrate them, over time, in certain cases, the larger objects, like a Brazil nut compared to smaller nuts, will end up rising to the surface. And it seems like something very similar happens in the case of deserts.

Even in hot deserts, like the Kalahari, there can be huge temperature swings with freezing at night. In fact, the winter in the Kalahari is often commonly below freezing, and the reason for this is simply the lack of water. When you have water vapor in the atmosphere, it has a tremendous moderating effect on the temperatures. This happens in two ways. Water vapor is actually the strongest greenhouse gas, essentially keeping our atmosphere warm, and it also forms clouds. The clouds block incoming sunlight during the day, and that makes it less hot during warm days, but the water vapor absorbs energy that radiates back off of Earth's surface at nighttime and that keeps the atmosphere warm, so it's less cold during cold nights. In the desert with no water vapor in the air, the sun heats the surface greatly during the day, but the heat escapes quickly at night.

How about wetting and drying? I said you don't get a lot of water in the desert, but no rain is rare. You still do get storms, and so you can have this expansion of the ground when water sinks into it and contraction when it dries out again. In fact, actually, one of the leading causes of death in deserts is from flooding, partly because people don't expect it, but also because the desert pavement is so hard-packed that water will often runoff quickly into streams and not soak into the ground very well.

Deserts are generally some of the least inhabited places in the world because of water, but remarkably, there are people in Africa who live in them. For instance, in the Arabian Desert, in Saudi Arabia and also in parts of Egypt and Libya, you have the Arabic peoples, the Bedouins. And then you have the Berbers, like the Tuareg, in central and western Sahara in countries like Mali, Niger, and Algeria. These are traditionally nomadic people relying on caravans of camels for trade, moving wherever they can find oases or green areas.

There is also; however, a modern growing interest in desert regions. There are more people moving into them for a variety of reasons, a large one is mineral resources. Deserts have a lot of useful resources that form as evaporates, for instance sodium nitrate, which is used for fertilizer and used in gun powder; gypsum, which is used for construction, or the salts that are washed into playas. For instance, we saw lithium in the last lecture. You also have lots of sunlight, and it's good for solar energy. You have lots of sunlight in very open areas with no vegetation; it's a good combination, so there are places like the Mojave Desert, in California, where you have large numbers of solar-power projects popping up.

I have to say it was hard for me to pick a single desert to focus on for this particular lecture. I knew I wanted to pick a desert. The Sahara is the largest, and that would've been an easy choice. The Rub al Khali, the southern third of the Arabian Peninsula, has the largest single Sand Sea, and then there's the Atacama Desert, which is the world's driest. The average rain over the whole region is about a millimeter a year. There're actually some weather stations there they have never received any rain at all, areas with no rain during their habitation since 1570. There are mountains there that are cold, that should have glaciers on them, but there's no snow to make ice.

The Namib is the oldest, and the region has the tallest sand dunes in the world, which I mentioned before, and they are a striking red color. And the reason they're red is actually very fascinating. I also find it amazing that you could have a region that is so dry right next to so much water. Why does the Namib exist? Why do we even have a desert here? After all, if you look at the west coast of the United States, just farther up the coast of the Pacific, you find that the U.S. is very green along the coast, places like Los Angeles, but once you go up and over the coastal mountains, you're in deserts. Go from Los Angeles over the mountains and you're in the Mojave Desert. The reason is the winds blow a different direction.

Here, the prevailing wind blows east to west, which is the opposite of the western United States. These are called the southeast trade winds, and that's because the Namib Desert is closer to equator than west coast of the U.S. It would be more comparable to the climate of the southern Baja peninsula. As moist air from the Indian Ocean rises up over the Drakensberg Mountains of South Africa, along the east coast; it cools; it loses its water vapor into water droplets that rain out; it's dry when it crosses the Namib Escarpment; and then as it drops and warms even further, it absorbs any available moisture that's there, so it makes the ground even drier. In fact, that's the reason why it's drier right along the coast than even a little bit inland.

Though Namib is incredibly dry throughout, there's still a lot of variation when you visit. As I mentioned, the largest sand dunes are here, the particular region, the Sossusvlei region. And this sea of sand has a rich ochre color. The dunes, as I said, are huge. They rise over 1,000 feet. These would qualify as mountains in some areas, but just one after the other of these mountains of sand. This is 300-feet taller than the next largest sand dunes anywhere in the world. That would actually be in Arabia. It's interesting, the older the sand dune, the brighter the color. And this comes from two factors, from a slow oxidation of minerals that contain iron, and also from tiny fragments of garnets. So the sand is sparkling here. It has this rich color because of the presence of microscopic garnets. Why are the garnets there? Remember these sand dunes are ancient. They're millions of years old. And most other minerals have long since crumbled and weathered away so what you have left are the minerals that are very resistant to weathering, and garnet is one of these.

These dunes end up as refracting spectacular colors, as a result, with the changing light, and they turn from sort of a bright orange color, through reds, to sort of a deeper mauve color over the course of the day. There are also some fascinating regions topographically there. There's a Grand Canyon there that's called the Giant Fish River Canyon in southern Namibia, very similar to the Grand Canyon, in Arizona. Clearly, at one time in the past, there was a lot of water here. Here there are rock layers of beautiful colored rocks, purples, pinks, and grays, that stretch along about 100-mile course of a canyon. The canyon walls sometimes drop by almost 2,000 feet out of the flat, dry plateau. In some cases the canyon is almost 30-kilometers across. There's a legend, according to the Bushmen that live in the area, the many twists and turns of the canyon were carved by a giant mythical serpent in an attempt to escape being captured.

Right along the coast, there's a very bizarre phenomenon here at the Namib. There can be thick, blinding fog. What happens is you have this very dry desert air that's very hot. And it meets the cold, moist air, the cold Benguela Current there in the ocean; it's running up along the coast. And the dry air goes over the moist air and pushes it down. And as it falls and warms, it ends up causing clouds; it causes thick banks of fog that condense. And that fog is the only moisture that some parts of the desert ever get. And it's remarkable, life has actually evolved to adapt to it. The only moisture that some parts of the desert ever get, and it's remarkable, life has actually evolved to adapt to it. I mean, incredible, even though the desert is remarkably dry, and the total biomass here is certainly low compared to most any other place in the world, the difficult conditions cause a high degree of biodiversity because life has had to adapt in unique ways to survive these incredibly harsh conditions. For instance, there are species of beetles here have strange protrusions from their body because they act as nucleation points for condensation from the fog. In other words, water droplets actually form on their bodies, and this is how they survive. There are plants that do the same. For instance, mammals usually maintain a constant body temperature, unless you're fighting an infection or something and you become feverish. The body temperatures of mammals here can change to adapt to the heat. There's sort of a deer-like oryx called a gemsbok, and its body temperature goes up naturally to about 104°F in the heat of the day.

As a contrast to the Namib though, if you go across the Namib Escarpment, you get into the broad area of the Kalahari, and here life is a lot more plentiful. Even if you haven't been here, you probably have a sense of what this look like if you've ever seen movies like *The Gods Must be Crazy* or even the animated movie *The Lion King*, to give you some sense of what it looks like. It's a lot more vegetated. And there are large numbers of mammals that live here. The strange meerkats that stand up vertically, lions, jackals, buffalo—and people. The Bushmen of the Kalahari have lived here in essentially an unchanged manner for more than 20,000 years. They don't drink water. There isn't any to be had. They end up getting almost all their water needs from plant roots and plants like desert melons that grow under the ground.

Technically, much of the Kalahari is not a real desert. In other words, there's enough rainfall that we give it a different ecological name. We call it a steppe. This is a semi-arid region, though there are parts of the Kalahari that are true deserts with very low rainfall, but you don't find the giant sand dunes here. It's sort of low, flat, very scrubby, dry brush. The most interesting aspect of the Kalahari, however, is in the northern region, and this is where the Okavango River empties into the desert and disappears. It's a remarkable process. It happens every year. It starts in January when heavy rains in Angola flow southward through the Okavango River, which had been dry, and then begins to swell. And the water slowly works its way southward, really slowly. It takes up to four months for the water to finally reach down here into the Okavango delta. The delta, which had been dry, then becomes a huge wetlands. It actually becomes, briefly, one of the largest river deltas in the world, 250-kilometers across by 150 kilometers, but really flat. I mean, the whole topographical variation across this whole delta is only about six feet, about two meters. Remember, we saw something similar in Bolivia with the Salar de Uyuni, and also in Utah, with the Bonneville Salt Flats, where the repeating wetting and drying of the salt made the regions incredibly flat. Something similar has happened here.

The Kalahari is actually the dried remains of an ancient, giant lake, Lake Makgadigadi. I mentioned this briefly at the end of the last lecture. And in fact, you can see the remains of the Makgadigadi salt pans right here on this image. It's this white salt flat here down in the corner. As a result of this region being incredibly flat, if you have anything on the ground that sticks up, a single clump of trees, it can actually start to accumulate silt from this incoming water, and more vegetation will develop behind it, and you can build a small island. And the desert area is dotted with these small islands all over. Actually, trees often start on termite mounds, which are very common here. During flood times there's actually only one large island. It's called Chief's Island because it used to be the sole hunting grounds of the local chief there. And that island becomes a refuge to huge number of animals at the very peak of the flooding.

I should add that for much of the world, "flood" has a negative connotation, but not here. Here it's rejuvenating, it's life-giving. It's what the whole region survives on: the water from this one hard time of the year, this one part of the year, it has to last the whole rest of the year. Before the arrival of the flood, animals have to be very creative in finding water. Either they migrate elsewhere, or animals like elephants will actually dig down into the ground to find the top of the water table and get anything, even mud, to drink. But, even during the flood, most of the water ends up evaporating. It's a delta to nowhere, the water just dissipates away. Enough of it seeps into the ground to keep the trees alive, and to support life until the next year's flood.

It's time for my top five. The largest two deserts in the world, I've already mentioned—Antarctica, which I devoted a whole lecture to, and the Sahara Desert, which I'm going to talk about in the next lecture. So first, let me talk about the Arabian Desert, which covers most of the Arabian Peninsula. Though it's much smaller than the Sahara, this is still a vast desert, more than two million square kilometers. I said previously that normally no more than about a fifth of deserts involve sand dunes. That's not the case here. The Arabian Desert has vast oceans of sand. The Rub' al-Khali in the south is the world's largest single sea of sand. It covers the whole lower third of Saudi Arabia, as well as most of Yemen, Qatar, and the United Arab Emirates. Sand dunes can routinely be more than 250 meters, not as tall as Namib, but still remarkably high.

This sea of sand is connected by a corridor of sand that runs north, called the ad-Dahna Desert, and that connects the Rub' al-Khali with another vast sea of sand in the north, the An-Nafud Desert. Even from satellite photos you can see that the sand seas are just enormous, and they have a slight orange color to them. The reason for the color here is slightly different than Namib, however. The sands are mostly quartz, but it's small amounts of potassium feldspar, the same mineral that can give granite its orange color. That's what gives the sand dunes here their distinctive reddish-tan color.

The Rub' al-Khali is also known as the Empty Quarter, and it really looks that way. There are very few plants and animals, and nobody lives there. But interestingly, satellite images can actually show evidence of the camel tracks of ancient caravans, caravans that repeatedly crossed the Empty Quarter 2,000 years ago. And this was part of a big trade network for frankincense, the aromatic resin from the Boswellia tree that grows in this region in places like Yemen. In fact, the remains have actually been now found of lost cities in the desert that were once part of this frankincense trade, cities like Ubar, or Iram. But the area became increasingly arid, and the caravans stopped by about the year 300.

Going back even farther in time, there was a time before 5,000 years ago when monsoon rains did fall here in the Arabian Desert. I'm going to talk about this period of time a little bit more in the next lecture. The deserts here were green, and there is Paleolithic evidence, hand flints and other tools, of humans living here in what is now just a wasteland of sand. Interestingly, one group of people who do go into the Rub al-Khali is scientists looking for meteorites. Because of the extreme dryness here, rocks last an enormously long time without weathering. And if you find a rock out here that isn't sand, there's nowhere else it came from. It's probably a meteorite that fell from space.

Next, let me highlight the Gobi Desert, which I've mentioned before. It's in Mongolia and part of China. This is an elevated, cold, dry land that's in the rain shadow behind the Tibetan Plateau. Much of the Gobi contains semi-arid regions called steppes. They're very dry, but they still support diverse ecosystems, and one of the most famous animals that live there is the double-humped Bactrian camel. The region is probably best known from its history for being an important part of the Mongol Empire, and several very important cities along the trade route of the Silk Road were here. Because this region is so high in elevation and it's so dry, it's susceptible to enormous temperature changes, sometimes more than 90°F in a single day, though I have to say, I was surprised to find this, but the record for this is actually in Montana, in the United States. Yes, temperature changes both dropping by 100°F or rising by 100°F or more in a single day have been recorded in Montana. The Gobi Desert has been steadily increasing in size due to the rapid desertification here. And this is creating a significant problem. China is actually trying many efforts to stop this. In fact, there's a plan to build an enormous amount of trees here called the Green Wall of China, but we'll see if it's able to stop this march of the desert.

Next, let's go to Australia for the Great Victoria Desert. It's the largest desert in Australia, which is a country that's pretty dry to begin with. It's about a half-million square kilometers, located in the south-central area of the country. This desert supports a small population of indigenous Australians, though it's unable to support any agriculture. The desert here is probably best known for being the site of many of the British nuclear bomb tests.

And last, let me go to the Atacama Desert, along the west coast of South America, along the countries of Chile, Peru, Bolivia, and Argentina. We visited the Atacama Salt Flat in the last lecture, high up on the plateau. But the Atacama Desert stretches from that region high up in the mountains down westward all the way to the coast. And the Atacama is the exact analogue to the Namib Desert. It sits on the west side of the continent with air blowing from the East, and by the time it drops down over the Atacama, it is not only devoid of water vapor, but as it drops, it warms and it absorbs water that it comes in contact with. The Atacama is the driest place on Earth. Much of it receives less than a millimeter a year as I've already mentioned.

The tall mountains are often entirely bare, very similar to the dry valleys in Antarctica because no snow falls there. Because of its dryness and the high elevation, the highest regions of the Atacama Desert are also some of the best places in the world for very unusual scientific activity, astronomy. A large number of telescopes of astronomical observatories are located here in the Atacama Desert, including a new internationally funded radio telescope, ALMA, which started working in the year 2011. Actually, the year 2011 was also the year of a very unusual occurrence. There was a freak change in air patterns that occurred very briefly, and an Antarctic cold front broke over the rain shadow and dumped over a meter of snow on the dry plateau of the Atacama. Many people got stranded. They had never seen so much snow. And that spring when some of the snow melted off, there was an infrequent but absolutely spectacular sight, a massive blooming of wildflowers in the Atacama Desert.

One last thing about the Atacama, it has a very strange geologic enigma. There are some valleys there where there are large numbers of very large boulders that have been sitting for millions of years down in the bottom of this valley, and they have smoothed sides. And geologists have puzzled about this for awhile. Was it somehow ice in the past that had worn them smooth? A group of geologists think that they've finally figured this out. The rocks have been smoothed by millions of years of earthquakes that have jostled the rocks against each other. The shaking from repeated earthquakes not only shakes the boulders loose from the surrounding hills and brings them down to the valley, but it causes them to bang against each other. In fact, there were some geologists there during a magnitude five earthquake, and they heard the sounds of the rocks grinding against each other. And they calculated that if the rocks have been there two-million years, and that earthquakes of a magnitude five or larger occur every four months, that would mean 50,000 to 100,000 hours of jostling against each other, and that would do it.

In the next lecture, I'm going to talk about one of the most unusual features of deserts, the existence of desert oases, and this will take us to the Siwa Oasis in western Egypt.

Siwa Oasis—Paradise amidst Desolation
Lecture 32

The Sahara Desert is remarkably dry; there's almost no green here. But even in this setting, we find the Siwa Oasis, a well-watered island in a giant sea of sand. The Siwa Oasis sits in a broad depression that is bordered on the north by a set of cliffs at the edge of the Qattara Depression. It's bordered on the south by the enormous dunes of the Great Sand Sea. For ancient caravans, Siwa was the last stop before crossing the large desert into what is now Libya. The springs here are plentiful enough to support several permanent salty lakes, whose seemingly magical presence has spawned many myths about the area.

The Sahara Desert
- The Sahara Desert is enormous; at 9.5 million square kilometers, it is almost as large as the continental United States and Alaska (9.8 million square kilometers). Only the Antarctic Desert is larger.

- The Sahara sits below the top of a Northern Hemisphere Hadley cell; the cool, dry air falls and absorbs available moisture out of the ground.

- The land here is extremely varied geographically. Only about 20 percent of the Sahara is sand; most of the rest of it is desert pavement, called hamada. Mountain ranges pop up in various places, including the Atlas Mountains, which border the Sahara on the northwest side and rise up to 4 kilometers in places.

- The Sahara also has a variety of unusual smaller features, such as the famous Richat Structure in Mauritania, a 50-kilometer-wide "bull's eye." This structure is actually a dome that has been eroded so that what we see now are different layers of rock exposed in circles on the flat surface.

- Cities have existed in the Sahara, but they have been few and far between. Timbuktu, in Mali, was once a major center of the caravan trade, but its importance has steadily declined as the southern Sahara has become increasingly desertified. Essentially, over time, the Sahara has been pushing its border southward.

- The Sahara is divided into three major geographical regions.
  o The Western Sahara starts from the border with the Atlantic Ocean. It encompasses the central mountains in southern Algeria, called the Ahaggar Mountains, and the tall Aïr Mountains in Niger.

  o The Ténéré Desert is a dry desert between Niger and Chad. The Tibesti Mountains, also in Chad, are a set of continental intraplate volcanoes, very similar to Yellowstone. This area sits over a deep mantle hotspot.

  o The region in the far east is known as the Libyan Desert. This region, about 1000 kilometers square, is the most arid, but it contains the Siwa Oasis.

The Oasis
- The Siwa Oasis sits next to an impassable area called the Qattara Depression, up to 60 meters below sea level in some places. The oasis has more than 1000 springs; most of them are too salty to drink from, but a few hundred provide fresh water. The springs support several permanent salty lakes spread over a wide area. The largest of these is Lake Siwa, covering about 30 square kilometers.

- Because the water of the oasis is generally so salty, few types of plants grow here. The date palm has adapted to survive here and provides much of the sustenance of the people. Roof beams, furniture, mats, baskets, and wine are all made from date palms. Olive trees also survive well in the salty soils here.

- The oasis contains about 3000 small mountains and hills, most of which exist because they have a tough capstone at the top.

Human Habitation of the Oasis

- The Berbers have inhabited the Siwa Oasis for at least 12,000 years. At that time, Egypt may have been even drier than it is today.

- From about 9000 to 5000 years ago, northeastern Africa benefited from a wet, moist climate. At that time, it was called the Wet Sahara or Green Sahara. Egypt had a monsoon climate with strong rains for part of the year. The land was green, and people traveled easily from the central to the northern parts of Africa. Now, the Sahara largely cuts off travel; the only corridor is along the Nile.

- Neolithic cave drawings that suggest the presence of large amounts of water have been found in a region south of Siwa called the Wadi Sura.

- Siwa was an independent Berber oasis for thousands of years, but at some point, it was conquered by the dynastic Egyptians, probably Ramses III, and became part of the Egyptian Empire. The caves in some of the hills were used as tombs for wealthy people.

© iStockphoto/Thinkstock.

Siwa traditionally traded dates and olives with other communities; as a result, there are probably more caravan tracks leading out of Siwa than any other oasis.

- o The Mountain of the Dead, Jebel al-Mawta, is the tomb of a particular merchant named Si-Amun, meaning "man of Amun." Amun was an important Egyptian god who had a temple in Siwa. A famous oracle lived in a nearby village.

- o When the Greeks settled in Libya, they heard of this wise oracle and elevated the Siwa Oasis to a place of great honor. Both Cleopatra and Alexander the Great are known to have visited the oracle.

- The Siwa Oasis was occupied later by the Romans, who built many structures that can still be seen throughout the oasis.

- From about 700 onward, Siwa became Christian but was finally conquered by Islamic attackers around 1150.

- Currently, about 23,000 people live on the oasis. The population is Islamic and speaks Arabic but also still speaks the original Berber language and retains Berber culture.

Sources of Water

- The Sahara and other deserts are occasionally interrupted by small regions of water and green, but these regions don't come directly from rain. The water comes from a layer of rock underground called an aquifer. An aquifer can be any type of rock; it's often sandstone, which is both permeable and porous. It has pore space that can hold water, and the water can flow through it easily.

- Water reaches the surface in a number of different ways. When the aquifer comes into contact with the surface, the result is a standing lake that represents the top of the water table. Faults from earthquakes may also cut across the aquifer and allow water to bubble up and reach the surface.

- Often, water is pushed by pressure from the aquifer extending upward, forming a mountain. Rain falls and fills in the aquifer, which is then pushed up and may cause an oasis. The water often enters the aquifer far from where the oasis is, having traveled hundreds or even thousands of kilometers underground.

- Beneath Siwa is a layer of sandstone, called the Nubian Sandstone, that is about 2.5 kilometers thick. Estimates are that this sandstone contains 50,000 cubic kilometers of water.

  o As we've seen several times in this course, layers of limestone and sandstone—the typical sediments of sedimentary rock—formed in Egypt when the ocean flooded the continent and deposited sediments.

  o These layers were initially flat, but in Egypt, they began to be tilted upward in the south by the Afar hotspot. This hotspot has elevated a region at the bottom of the Red Sea.

  o By 35 million years ago, a large river system called the Gilf River drained much of Egypt into the Tethys Sea at the exact location where the Siwa Oasis is now. In fact, Siwa was the location of the river delta.

  o By 25 million years ago, an early Nile was forming, but it ran in the other direction—south, emptying somewhere into the desert.

  o Over time, the Gilf River began to shrink, and the coast moved northward as sediments were repeatedly deposited by the rivers and as sea levels dropped. By 10 million years ago, the tilting of Egypt had increased to the point that the Nile River moved northward and drained toward the Mediterranean, and the Gilf River system was entirely drying up.

- By looking at the chemical composition of materials in the water, scientists have determined that the water being pulled up at the Siwa Oasis was deposited underground more than 20 million years ago. In other words, it sank into the ground when Siwa was topped by a major river system for millions of years. It's essentially fossil water.

- Siwa has a limited future, as do all oases in the Sahara. The current heavy draw on the water is making the soils so salty that even the date palms are starting to die. Groundwater is often needed most in dry areas, but this water found its way into the ground during a time of much wetter climates; it is not a renewable resource during our lifetimes.

Top Oases

- The Chebika Oasis is also in the Sahara, in Tunisia. It sits at the north end of a large sand sea called the Grand Erg Oriental. This area is where the giant sand sea meets the eastern extension of the Atlas Mountains. Two thousand years ago, the Chebika was a Roman outpost; it has been occupied by the Berbers since that time.

- The Huacachina Oasis in Peru is a pretty, round lake that sits in the middle of giant sand dunes at the northern end of the Atacama Desert. This region has become a tourist site; the draw here is sand-boarding down the sides of the enormous sand dunes.

- The Ubari Oasis is located in the western desert of Libya, at the edge of the giant Ubari Sand Sea. This region is extremely dry, sometimes going decades without rain. Ubari sits in a broad, wide, and extremely flat depression, but the area used to be the location of a giant lake during wetter climates, Lake Megafezzan. The ancient lake water charged up an underground aquifer that is now pumped for fresh water.

- In the central Sahara, in Algeria, is the Tuat region, a string of small oases to the south of the sand seas of the Grand Erg Occidental and to the east of the Erg Chech. These oases stretch out over a distance of about 160 kilometers and are remarkably fertile, yet not a single drop of water usually falls here. The water comes from an aquifer that spans more than 1 million square kilometers and is situated only a couple of meters below the surface.

Sampsell, *A Traveler's Guide to the Geology of Egypt*.

Vivian, *The Western Desert of Egypt*.

Questions to Consider

1. Why are the Siwa Depression and the larger Qattara Depression to the north below sea level? (Hint: Why doesn't this happen more often in other parts of the world?)

2. The date palm tree has evolved to extract fresh water out of salty water. What are the implications of this adaptation for agriculture and soil quality?

Siwa Oasis—Paradise amidst Desolation
Lecture 32—Transcript

Hello. My name is Michael Wysession, and welcome to Lecture 32 of our course on the Geologic Wonders of the World. In the last lecture, I looked at the interesting contrasts of the Namib and Kalahari Deserts, next to each other in southern Africa. In this lecture, I will head up to the largest desert in the world, the Sahara, and focus on one of the most unusual aspects of deserts, desert oases.

First, I just want you to appreciate how remarkably dry the Sahara is. There's almost no green here. There's plenty of green down here at the equator in the Congo, but look at how the Sahara stretches across from the Atlantic all the way across the Arabian Desert and the Arabian Peninsula and into the Indian Ocean. If we zoom in even further, into the Libyan Desert, which covers Libya and western Egypt, you can see we're now even in the driest part of the Sahara. And the remarkable thing is, it's in this setting here, if we zoom in even further, that we find the water-filled Siwa Oasis. This is an island of water in a giant sea of sand. It's truly a geologic wonder.

Let me take a moment to talk about the Sahara, and I want to just say a quick word about this particular figure. In this figure, the green here shows elevation. I don't want you to think that this is lush here; this is incredibly dry land, but it's very low, and in some places it's below sea level, and that shows up as very dark green here. The Sahara is enormous, it's 9.5-million square kilometers, and to give you some comparison, the United States including Alaska is 9.8-million square kilometers. So this is as large as the entire United States, one desert.

The word "Sahara" comes from the Arabic word for desert: *Sahara*. And only the Antarctic Desert, which of course is a very different type of desert, is larger. The Sahara exists because of the global circulation of the Hadley cells; I've talked about this before. The Sahara sits below the top of this northern hemisphere Hadley cell. The cool, dry air falls and absorbs available moisture right out of the ground. But the land is also extremely varied geographically. Only about 20 percent of the Sahara is actually sand; I mentioned that in the last lecture. Now, there are places, in fact, these orange areas here, these are sand seas; these are places where you get your camels crossing seas of sand in large caravans. But most of this is actually a desert pavement, and I talked about that also in the last lecture. The word here for that is a hamada.

If you look across the whole extent here you can see that there are not only dessert, sort of sand-sea areas, there are also some mountain ranges that pop up in various places. The largest, by far, are the Atlas Mountains, and these end up playing a very important role. In fact, I'm going to come back to this at the very end of the lecture. This is in Morocco, Algeria, and Tunisia. It borders the Sahara on the northwest side, and it rises to up to four kilometers in places. The Atlas Mountains are very old. They began more than 300-million years ago during the collision with North America that helped form the supercontinent Pangaea, at the same time making the Appalachian Mountains. Most of the current height of the Atlas Mountains; however, is due to the collision between Africa and Europe, and that started about 60-million years ago.

The Sahara contains a variety of unusual smaller features as well; one particularly famous one is the Richat Structure in Mauritania. This is a 50-kilometer-wide bull's eye, at least seen from space, that is a dome that got eroded so that, essentially, what you see now are circles that are all the different layers of rock all exposed at the flat surface; this is the far western end of the Sahara. This feature is also called the Eye of the Sahara, and when seen from space, at least, with the way that the sand sort of flows around it, it really looks remarkably like an eye.

Over history, there have been cities that have existed in the Sahara, but very few and far between. One of the most famous is Timbuktu, in Mali; it's at the very southern edge of the Sahara. At one time, it was a major center of caravan trade for things like salt, gold, and ivory, and slaves too, starting back in the 1100s. But its importance has steadily declined as the southern Sahara has become increasingly desertified. Essentially, over time, the Sahara has been pushing its border southward.

The native inhabitants of much of North Africa, from western Egypt all the way over to the west, have been the Berbers. And cave paintings from these people show evidence of them living here going back at least 12,000 years. They were assimilated into the Islamic empire in the 11th century, but they still maintain their own identity. And there has been travel and trade, long caravans that have crossed the desert between settlements for a long time. One particular group of the Berbers, the Tuaregs, is noted for their very nomadic lifestyles. And they've crossed the desert with salt caravans for centuries. In fact, some of them still do. Even today, there are Tuareg caravans that will have over 10,000 camels stretched out in a line for 25 kilometers that will cross the Sahara over a three-week period, going from places like Timbuktu, down in Mali, all the way up to the Mediterranean.

The Sahara is divided into a couple of major geographical regions. There's a part we call the Western Sahara, starting from the border with the Atlantic Ocean. There are some central mountains here in southern Algeria called the Ahaggar Mountains. There's also an area of tall mountains here, the Aïr Mountains. This is a region of desert mountains and very high plateaus, about a mile high, in Niger, with striking granite outcrops and some ancient old volcanoes. You also have a very large desert called the Ténéré Desert; it's a dry desert between Niger and Chad. There're the Tibesti Mountains, also in Chad; it's actually a set of continental intraplate volcanoes very similar to Yellowstone. It also sits over a deep mantle hotspot just like Yellowstone. And in fact, there is one particular volcano here, Emi Koussi, that is 80 kilometers wide. It's the tallest mountain within the Sahara, not including the Atlas Mountains. It reaches an elevation of 3.5 kilometers.

And finally, there is the region in the Far East, what's known as the Libyan Desert. And this is the most arid region; it contains Libya and western Egypt. It's about 1,000 kilometers by 1,000 kilometers.

It's in here where the Siwa Oasis is located, in the middle of a huge, dry, and barren area, with almost no rainfall. But there it is, water, springs, lakes. It's really a remarkable occurrence. It's very hard to get to. It's very remotely located, and it sits right by a really impassable area called the Qattara Depression. So caravan routes had to either go north through Alexandria and then down towards Siwa or travel down to Baharia and then go west, and Siwa was the last stop before you then cross the large desert into what is now Libya. There are more than 1,000 different springs in the Siwa Oasis.

It's a remarkable thing in the midst of this broad desert to find so much water. Most of the springs are too salty to drink from, but there are still a few hundred of them that provide fresh water. Siwa sits in a broad depression that is bordered on the north by a set of cliffs at the edge of the Qattara Depression. And it's bordered on the south by the enormous dunes of the Great Sand Sea. It's that stretch 500-kilometers down to the south.

The depression in Siwa is so low that it's up to 60 meters below sea level in places. The springs here are plentiful enough that even in the midst of this dry desert they support several permanent salty lakes over a wide area of the region. The largest, Lake Siwa, or Birket Siwa, as you would say it locally, covers an area of about 30 square kilometers. The presence of these lakes has created a lot of myth and legends over time. Arabs considered these lakes to be magic, in fact, supposedly on one of the islands in Lake Siwa is buried the saber and seal of the Prophet Mohammed. Though, in another version it's the ring, sword, and crown of King Solomon that are buried here. Because the water is generally so salty, very few types of plants will grow here. However, there are some plants that have adapted to these salty conditions. And one in particular, the date palm, has adapted to survive here, and there are over 200,000 date palm trees here, and they provide much of the sustenance of the people, all parts of the tree are used, so roof beams, furniture, mats, baskets, are all made from the date palms. The heart of the palm is a delicacy to eat, but removing it usually kills the tree, so it's actually very rarely harvested.

Wine is made from the dates. It's traditionally been used in all of the Berber festivals. It's illegal under Islamic law, so it's currently made in secret. There are also over 25,000 olive trees in the oasis; an olive tree is another plant that will survive well in the salty soils. And because currently olives fetch a much higher price than dates, they actually earn more than the date crop. Siwa traditionally traded these commodities with other communities, and there are probably more caravan tracks leading out of Siwa than any other oasis, though some of them are so narrow that a 4 X 4 truck can't make it. I mean, these are for camels.

Because the water is so salty, the mud that is used to make the bricks of all the buildings here is filled with a huge amount of salt. And this is usually not a problem, except that a few times per century Siwa will get a large rain storm, and when it does, the salt just dissolves. There was one particular enormous storm in 1928, and the ancient town of Shali, which actually was founded back around 1200, was essentially destroyed. It was damaged so badly that people entirely abandoned it. But the remains of the town are still there to be seen.

The oasis contains about 3,000 small mountains and hills, most of which exist because they contain a tough capstone at the top. The Berbers have inhabited the Siwa Oasis for at least 12,000 years. And at that time, Egypt may have been even drier than today. But from about 9,000- to 5,000-years ago, northeastern Africa benefitted from a wet, moist climate. At this time it was called the Wet Sahara or Green Sahara. There was a shift in air circulation patterns, and Egypt got a monsoon climate with strong rains for part of the year. Egypt was green, and people travelled easily from the central to the northern parts of Africa, now the Sahara largely cuts them off. The only corridor is actually along the Nile.

There are famous caves in a region south of Siwa called the Wadi Sura, where there are Neolithic cave drawings that suggest large amounts of water here; one in particular called the Cave of Swimmers inspired a similar story in the book *The English Patient*. Siwa was an independent Berber Oasis for thousands of years, but at some point, it was conquered by the dynastic Egyptians, probably Ramses III, about 3,000 years ago, and it became part of the Egyptian Empire. They began using it for tombs of wealthy and important people, using the caves in some of the hills. One of the best known of these is the mountain of the dead, Jebel al-Mawta, which is the tomb of a particular merchant named Si-Amun. The name Si-Amun literally means man of Amun, Amun being the important Egyptian god, though the writing in some of the pictures of him and his family suggest he might actually have been Greek. An important Temple to the god Amun was then built here in Siwa soon after, and there began to reside, at about that same time, a very famous oracle in a temple nearby in the village of Agurmi. When the Greeks settled in Libya they heard of this wise oracle at the Temple, and they elevated Siwa Oasis to a place of great honor because of it.

Soon, one by one, all the great leaders of their times came to Siwa to visit the Oracle, supposedly not always happy with what they were told. Cleopatra came here often and is known to have visited largely to bathe in the hot springs here. In fact, there is a hot spring here just south of the temples that's named after her. The most famous visitor of all, however, was Alexander the Great, who came here in 331 before the Common Era. And he was told that he was a god and the rightful leader of the entire empire. He was very happy with what he was told. The Siwa Oasis was occupied later by the Romans as well, who built many structures that you can still find throughout the oasis. In fact, there are half a dozen Roman temples here and also some remains of some of their ancient olive oil presses.

It seems that later on that Siwa became Christian at some point and fended off Islamic attackers, that was from about 700 onward, and was finally conquered and became Islam in 1150. At that time, there were only about 40 people or so who lived here. This was not a big outpost. Currently there are about 23,000. It's currently Islamic. The people speak Arabic, but they also still speak their original Berber language and really retain their Berber characteristics. They haven't fully assimilated into the culture. They were also attempted to be pulled into the nation of Egypt in 1819 by the Egyptian leader Muhammad Ali, Siwa, as well as other oases. It took 20 years for him to do it, and he eventually succeeded, but Siwa has always retained a sense of independence. Unfortunately, Siwa was the site of a lot of activity and played important roles in battles during both World War I and World War II, and there's a lot of damage that still remains there from these battles. Unfortunately, islands traditionally play very important roles in military strategies, and in a very real sense, Siwa is an island, only it's geographically inverted. It's an island of water within a sea of sand.

So the big geologic question here is, why is there even water here? How is it that there are 1,000 springs of water here in the middle of the desert? The Sahara and other deserts are occasionally interrupted by small regions of water and green. Where does this come from? It doesn't come from above, from rain, at least, not directly. It turns out it comes from a layer of rock underground that we call an aquifer. The aquifer can be any type of rock. It's often sandstone that is both permeable and porous. It has a lot of pore space that can hold water, and the water can flow through it very easily. The water comes to the surface by one of several different ways. It can happen when that water-rich layer—that aquifer—actually comes into contact with the surface, and so you can get a standing lake there that actually represents the top of that water table there. You can also have geologic structures, like faults, from earthquakes that will cut across that aquifer and allow water to bubble up along it and come up to the surface.

Why would the water move up to the surface, though? Often it gets pushed by pressure from that aquifer extending upward, such as into a mountain. So for example, in this diagram you see that the aquifer actually extends up into a mountainous region, rain will fall in there, fill in the aquifer, and push water up in places where a fault might cause an oasis. The water will often enter the aquifer far from where the oasis is and can travel hundreds, or even thousands, of kilometers underground, coming up at various places in the middle of the desert.

In the case of Siwa, there is a layer of sandstone, called the Nubian Sandstone, that is both porous and permeable. Beneath Siwa it's about 2.5-kilometers thick. It's an enormously thick layer of rock. And estimates are that this sandstone contains 50,000 cubic kilometers of water. To give you some sense of how much water that is, that's equal to about 600 years of Nile River water flowing. That's an enormous amount of water.

The water is scarce in this region because there's not a lot of rainfall. So the next question is, how did so much water get down into the Nubian Sandstone layer? Where did this water come from? Well, you have to look at Siwa's past geologic history. It wasn't always so dry. Again, this is a theme that's come up several times in this course; it's often a mistake to look at geologic history and expect things to be the same in the past as the way they are now.

Layers of limestone and sandstone, the typical sediments of sedimentary rock, formed in Egypt just like other places around the world, at past times when the ocean flooded the continent and deposited sediments. These layers were initially flat, but here in Egypt they began to be tilted upward in the south, and that was associated with something we've seen previously. The Afar hotspot that's causing Africa to break up into three pieces. It's elevated that whole region there at the bottom of the Red Sea. By 35-million years ago, there was a very large river system called the Gilf River that drained much of Egypt. But it's not where the Nile River is now. In fact, it emptied into, then, the Tethys Sea, this was before the Mediterranean even existed, at the exact location where the Siwa Oasis is now. Back then the coast was farther south than it is currently.

So not only did a large river run across where Siwa is now, but it was the location of the river delta. There was a huge amount of standing water there. By 25-million years ago, an early Nile was just forming, but it ran the other direction. It ran south, emptying somewhere into the desert. We're not sure where. There very well could have been an inland delta just like the current Okavango that empties into the Kalahari Desert. Over time, the Gilf River began to shrink, and the coast moved northward as sediments were repeatedly deposited by the rivers and as the sea levels dropped. By 10-million years ago, the tilting of Egypt had increased to the point that the Nile River was now moving northward and draining towards the Mediterranean, and the Gilf River system was entirely drying up.

So, where did all that water of today's Siwa Oasis come from? You can actually use radiometric dating to determine its age. By looking at the chemical composition of the materials in the water, scientists have used radiometric dating to find that the water being pulled up at Siwa Oasis was put underground more than 20-million years ago. In other words, it sank into the ground when Siwa was topped by a major river system for millions of years. This is not renewable water. It formed during a much warmer and wetter period. It's essentially fossil water.

Though the lectures I'm giving are on distinct geologic wonders in different geographic locations, they still can be connected in often very surprising ways. And here's a connection with something we've talked about previously. In the lecture on the Rock of Gibraltar I mentioned that when the Mediterranean closed at the Straits of Gibraltar 6- to 5-million years ago, the Nile River here in Egypt, suddenly dropped off kilometers downward at the delta. This became a huge canyon that cut back into Africa through the desert for hundreds of miles. Eventually the Mediterranean flooded again, the sea rose, and the deep Nile canyon eventually filled with sediments. But that was very significant in shaping the whole dynamics of the region in Egypt back at that time.

The Siwa has a very limited future, as do all oases in the Sahara. The current heavy draw on the water, more than 20,000 people, is making the soils so salty that even the date palms are starting to die. It's too salty for them as well. Groundwater is often needed most in dry areas, but this water was put in the ground during a time of much wetter climates, so it's not a renewable resource during our lifetimes, and so this is an example of one of these geologic wonders that simply may not be there for long.

It's time for my top five. First, let me go to another oasis in the Sahara, the Chebika Oasis, in Tunisia. It sits at the north end of one of these large seas of sand called the Grand Erg Oriental. This is where the giant sand sea meets the eastern extension of the Atlas Mountains. Out of the brown, dry land, is nestled this beautiful, lush green oasis that's fed by a spring that gurgles out of a narrow gorge in the mountains. Two thousand years ago it had been a strong Roman outpost, and it's been occupied by the Berbers ever since then. I picked this because it's very likely that if you see pictures of this you will recognize it, that you are familiar with many aspects of it. This is where they filmed many of the scenes from the first *Star Wars* movie of the home of young Luke Skywalker. And supposedly, the name for the character Chewbacca actually comes from this name Chebika, of the oasis. Parts of the film *The English Patient* were also filmed here.

Next I want to go to Peru to look at the Huacachina Oasis. And this is one of the most striking desert oases. It's a pretty, round lake that sits in the middle of giant sand dunes that tower up above it on all sides at the northern end of the Atacama Desert. This region has become a large tourist site, and the big attraction here is sandboarding down the sides of these enormous sand dunes.

Next, let me take you to Libya for the Ubari Oasis. This is located in the western desert of Libya, at the edge of the giant Ubari Sand Sea. Just to the south of the sand sea is a broad, dry plateau. The whole region is extremely dry, sometimes going decades without any rain. Ubari is the capital of a large region, the Fezzan Region. And it sits in a broad, wide, and extremely flat depression. However, this whole region used to be the location of a giant lake during wetter climates, called Lake Megafezzan. I think you're probably coming to expect this, a very dry, flat area probably means it was a lake bed at some point in the past. Sand dunes now cover most of this former lake bed, but the ancient lake water charged up an aquifer that sits underground, and it's this aquifer that the Ubari lakes tap into. High evaporation rates here make these particular lakes too salty to drink, but local peoples live here by digging wells into the ground and pumping fresh water up out of the aquifer. Evidence that this region used to be a large lake comes not only from geology, but from archaeology. There are rock carvings and paintings from people here that show wetland conditions, and animals like crocodiles and hippopotami.

Last, let me go back to the central Sahara to the Tuat region, which is in central Algeria, it's this region right in here, where there's a string of small oases to the south of the sand seas of the Grand Erg Occidental and to the east of the Erg Chech. These oases stretch out over a distance of about 160 kilometers, and they're remarkably fertile. They contain over 800,000 date palm trees. And yet, there's not a single drop of water that usually falls here. Where do they get their water from? They get their water from a broad aquifer that, is in this region, only a couple of meters below the surface. In fact, you get a clue by looking at this topographic map and seeing the green there, which means its low elevation. The aquifer underneath spans more than a million square kilometers, but usually isn't very close to the surface. But where it is here, it's able to feed these large numbers of date palms. Where does the water come from? The water comes from the Atlas Mountains up here in the north. It enters into that aquifer and flows southward under the vast deserts for hundreds of kilometers, poking up every now and then as an oasis.

In the next lecture, I'm going to take a big step in a very different direction, and I'm going to go both toward the North and South Poles, and I'm going to look at the phenomenon of the aurora, the northern and southern lights.

Auroras—Light Shows on the Edge of Space
Lecture 33

So far in this course, we've looked at wonders that are tied to the geosphere—the land and the water and ice that are on it. But of course, the atmosphere also contains wonders: clouds in amazing shapes; severe weather, such as tornadoes and hurricanes; and fascinating light effects associated with weather, such as rainbows. In this lecture, we'll talk about a phenomenon of space weather: the Aurora Borealis, or northern lights. To witness the auroras is a truly remarkable experience; they form a dancing, shimmering curtain of green and pink fire in the sky. To explain this phenomenon, we'll look at the workings of Earth's core and the Sun and even some quantum mechanical behavior of atoms themselves.

The Earth's Magnetic Field

- The Aurora Borealis is most likely to be seen in northern Canada, Alaska, Scandinavia, and other places at very high latitudes. An auroral zone that is a few hundred kilometers wide tends to run in an east-west band around the north magnetic pole. A similar zone runs around the southern magnetic pole for the southern lights.

- Earth's magnetic field looks roughly like the dipolar field of a bar magnet. Field lines run from the North Pole to the South Pole. In terms of magnetism, the Earth's South Pole is the North Pole, and the field lines run all the way up to the northern latitudes.

- The field is much more complex, however, than a bar magnet. Inside the Earth is liquid iron at a temperature of more than 5000°C. This iron is constantly convecting and churning, just like the mantle but much faster because the viscosity of the liquid iron is low; it probably has a similar thickness to honey. It's not entirely clear what drives the convection, though there are probably three factors at work.

o   As the heat from the outer core passes into the mantle above, the iron becomes a little colder and sinks, helping to drive the convection.

o   Heat is also probably generated by the radioactive decay of certain isotopes, such as potassium 40.

o   Further, the inner core tends to crystallize more pure iron and nickel, leaving a chemically lighter, more buoyant fluid. This, too, may help drive the convection.

o   These three factors, however, are not sufficient. It seems that the Coriolis effect, caused by Earth's rotation, is also important. Because of the Earth's rotation, the convecting iron becomes spiraling columns that are parallel to the axis of the Earth and are lined up surrounding the inner core.

o   The locations and shapes of these spiraling columns tend to shift over time. As a result, the locations of the magnetic north and south poles changes, as well.

The Solar Wind
*   The northern lights themselves aren't in any one location. At certain times, they extend in a wider band and come down to lower latitudes. The times of active auroras on Earth are times of increased solar activity, which produces the solar wind, a stream of ionized particles that blasts through the solar system away from the surface of the Sun.
    o   The Sun is 99.85 percent of the mass of our solar system. It contains a mixture of all the elements, but it's dominated by hydrogen and helium. Nuclear fusion in the core powers a layered structure inside the Sun. Away from the core is a radiative zone, which then powers a convecting layer; the top of that layer is called the photosphere. At the top of the photosphere, the temperature is about 5700°C.

- Hydrogen and helium exist in a special state called plasma, a condition so hot that the electrons are stripped off the nuclei of the atoms. It's essentially an incredibly high-temperature soup of atomic particles.

- The outer layers of the Sun, the corona, are much hotter, even though they are much less dense. High-temperature ionized particles are thrown off the layers of the Sun at great speeds.

- During times of increased solar activity, the Sun may experience a coronal mass ejection, in which hydrogen is thrown off the surface of the Sun. Some of these ejections create giant magnetic loops that leave the Sun and return, causing a much stronger solar wind.

- The solar wind doesn't arrive at all locations on Earth's surface. The Earth's magnetic field is warped by the incoming solar wind, creating a shape called the magnetosphere. The boundary between the magnetosphere and the incoming solar wind is the magnetosheath.
  - The magnetosheath presents a significant barrier to the solar wind and protects our atmosphere. If we didn't have a magnetic field, the solar wind would strip away our atmosphere over time.

  - The high-energy particles of the solar wind are extremely damaging to living tissue and cause problems for radio telecommunications.

  - When the particles of the solar wind reach the Earth, they tend to follow Earth's magnetic field lines, which are concentrated closer to the poles.

- Interestingly, the ionized particles of the solar wind can't punch through the Earth's magnetosphere. They actually travel far past Earth and then double back when the magnetic field lines become so deformed that they snap. This process is called magnetic reconnection. The magnetic field lines get stretched, and when they stretch too far, they suddenly snap back to a new shape. At that point, large numbers of solar wind particles come to the Earth in shimmering bands that circle the northern and southern poles.

The Colors of the Auroras

- The auroras occur high in the thermosphere, more than 50 miles above the Earth, where there are very few atoms; the thermosphere is close to a vacuum. The particles there have very high energy from the sunlight constantly hitting them.

- Earth's atmosphere is primarily made of two materials, nitrogen and oxygen. Like all atoms, the electrons of these materials can exist at discrete energy levels, called quantum energy levels. These electrons are at their lowest energy state, but they can be knocked into a higher energy state by any source of added energy, such as interactions with the solar wind particles.

- The electrons don't stay at higher energy levels for long, however; they drop back down quickly to their lowest energy levels. Because the energy has to go somewhere—energy is always conserved in any interaction—it goes into photons, light.

- Because the quantum levels are discrete amounts of energy, they correspond to discrete, specific frequencies of the light emitted. When the electrons of oxygen atoms return to their lowest energy levels—the ground state—they tend to release a green or brownish-red light, depending on the amount of energy absorbed. For nitrogen atoms, the light tends to be blue or red.

- Oxygen is unusual in terms of its return to the ground state. It can take up to 3/4 of a second for green light to be emitted and then jump to the lower energy level and up to 2 minutes to emit red light.
  - If there are any collisions with other atoms or molecules in the atmosphere during that time, the collision will absorb the added energy and prevent the emission of light, and we won't get an aurora. But because the very top of the atmosphere is so close to a vacuum, such collisions are infrequent—

infrequent enough to allow the 2 minutes needed for oxygen to emit red light.

o   The collisions become more frequent further down in the atmosphere, so that red emissions don't have time to occur, and the oxygen atoms primarily release green light. Eventually, the atmosphere becomes dense enough that collisions between atoms happen frequently, and even green light emissions are prevented.

o   This explains why different auroras release different colors. At high altitude, oxygen red dominates, then oxygen green and nitrogen blue or red, and finally, nitrogen blue or red.

Flipping the Magnetic Field
- Auroras don't usually occur in the continental 48 states, but there are times when auroras are centered over the United States. The last time this occurred was about 780,000 years ago.

- For reasons that are still not fully understood, Earth's magnetic field randomly reverses itself. This reversal takes about 1000 years, and in the process, the magnetic north pole wanders down to the south.

- When the magnetic field reverses, the total strength of the dipole field drops by about 90 percent. That means that the Earth's magnetosphere is much weaker, and many more solar particles reach Earth during this time.

- These reversals usually happen every few 100,000 years, which means we are overdue for one now. Over the past century, the strength of the Earth's geomagnetic field has dropped by 10 percent. It's not inconceivable that in 200 years, we could see large auroral displays overhead in the middle of the United States.

Top Atmospheric Phenomena
- Sun dogs represent an interesting refraction occurrence that happens as a result of the presence of hexagonal ice crystals in high, cold

Processes that take place inside the Sun, the Earth's core, and atoms themselves contribute to the auroras—the greatest light shows on our planet.

cirrus clouds. As we know, rainbows form from refraction through water droplets. With sun dogs, the light from the Sun is refracted by ice crystals, usually at an angle of about 22 degrees from the Sun. If the ice crystals are randomly aligned through the atmosphere, the appearance is a stunning circular halo of light around the Sun.

- A variety of phenomena can cause a green flash, an optical effect that can be observed at the last moment of a sunset or the first moment of a sunrise. Because of the refraction of sunlight, the very top of the setting Sun actually has a faint green rim; it's present all the time, but it's usually too small to see directly. Under certain conditions, the green light will get bent around the Earth's surface and appear as a sudden green flash.

- A Fata Morgana is a mirage that seems to show land up in the air or above the horizon. This kind of mirage can be seen when a temperature inversion—a layer of warm air on top of cold air—

occurs in the atmosphere. This warm air causes light rays to be bent more than the curvature of the Earth. One result is that islands that are actually below the horizon become visible. Light from the ocean surface may also be bent so much that it appears as if land is floating in the air.

- Under just the right conditions—just after sunset or before sunrise, during the spring or fall—it's possible to see sunlight reflected off microscopic dust particles floating in the solar system. This phenomenon is known as zodiacal light. The particles appear as a weak, triangle-shaped cone of diffused light, extending a little way above the horizon. This dust is largely the remains of comets, which slowly drifts into the inner solar system.

Suggested Reading

Davis, *Aurora Watcher's Handbook*.

Hall, Pederson, and Bryson, *Northern Lights*.

Questions to Consider

1. Why don't we see auroras in the part of the atmosphere that is close to the ground?

2. Every few 100,000 years, Earth's magnetic field reverses. When this happens, the magnetic field drops to about 10 percent of its current strength and the poles wander across the Earth, the magnetic north pole moving to be near the South Pole, and the magnetic south pole moving to be near the North Pole. What do you think auroras would be like during this time?

Auroras—Light Shows on the Edge of Space
Lecture 33—Transcript

Hello. My name is Michael Wysession, and welcome to Lecture 33 of our course on the Geologic Wonders of the World. In the last lecture I looked at desert oases and focused on places in the Sahara, like the Siwa Oasis, where green vegetation amazingly appears in the middle of desolation. In this lecture, I'm also going to talk about green colors that wondrously appear where you don't expect them, but this time close to the North and South Poles, and not by looking at anything on the ground, but by looking up, up at the aurora.

So far, in this course, I've stayed away from atmospheric phenomena, and I've interpreted geologic wonders to deal with the geosphere, that's the land and the water and ice that are on it. But there are also plenty of fascinating and beautiful things in the atmosphere.

To begin with, you have clouds in all their amazingly different shapes. There's also severe weather, things like tornadoes and hurricanes. There're also fascinating light effects associated with weather. For example, one of the most common, but one of the most beautiful, is a rainbow. It can be seen anywhere, usually after a storm when you have direct Sunlight, but still a lot of water drops in the air. You probably know how rainbows form. Sunlight goes into the raindrops, it refracts in, reflects off of the back side of these little circular raindrops, and then refracts back out. And the reason you see different colors is the different colors are bent at different angles; they're refracted at different angles. So you have to look at different angles in order to see those different colors coming from the Sun. It's actually very fun to see rainbows from an airplane, because you get to see that they're not arcs, but they're really circles, and there're no pots of gold there. Sometimes you can even see double rainbows. In this case, light bounces twice inside of all the little raindrops. And the second rainbow, actually, has a reverse color spectrum, red to blue, instead of blue to red.

But in this lecture, I want to talk about a very different kind of weather phenomenon, space weather, the aurora. My main interest in talking about auroras is because of the remarkable story of how something like this even comes to exist. Auroras are known in the United States as northern lights. The technical name is Aurora Borealis. Aurora was the Roman goddess of dawn and boreas is the Greek name for north wind. But these are also observed at very southern latitudes as well. They go by a different name, aurora australis, the southern lights.

I've had the fortune of witnessing northern lights once in my life. And it was a truly remarkable experience. It was in middle school, I think, and I was in New Hampshire in the summer time, and I was driving back home with my family, and we were driving up over a ridge. And the trees fell away, and in the sky was just this amazing dancing, shimmering curtain of green and pink fire. It was enormous. It spread high up into the sky, and we just stood there transfixed in the cold. None of us had ever seen anything like this.

You can get a small idea of what this looks like if you look at an animation of this. This is a sped-up video from Jan Mayen Island. We saw that in the lecture on Iceland in the North Atlantic, and it's just incredible, this curtain, this shimmering, tall green curtain of fire dancing about over, illuminating the mountains, the whole sky is lit up. It was the same for me. For me, it was the north face of the Presidential Mountains, in New Hampshire. It is just this incredible experience to look up and see this. I remember we eventually got cold and we got back in the car and drove home. I don't think we said anything. There isn't really much you can say after seeing something like this for the first time.

What I had no way of knowing was, in addition to the beautiful spectacle of these, the beautiful complexity of what's actually involved with creating the northern lights. And to explain this, I'm going to need to talk about how the inside of Earth's core works, how the Sun works, and even some quantum mechanical behavior for how atoms themselves work.

As I said, there are some places you can go where you're more likely to witness the aurora, northern Canada, Alaska, Scandinavia, places at very high latitudes. Though even there it still happens rarely. There tends to be an auroral zone that's usually a few hundred kilometers wide, and it runs in a band east/west, but not around the North Pole, the true North Pole, which is based on the axis of rotation, but around the north magnetic pole. And they're not exactly the same thing. This also happens around the southern magnetic pole, for the southern lights.

So what is it that's so important about Earth's magnetic field when it comes to creating auroras? First of all, why does Earth even have a magnetic field? I have to say we don't really know the answer to this, but we have some very good ideas. Earth's magnetic field looks roughly like the dipolar field from a bar magnet. You have field lines that run from the north to South Pole. Actually, in terms of magnetism, the Earth's South Pole is a north pole, and the field lines run all the way up to the northern latitudes.

The field is actually much more complex than this, however, because there isn't a big bar magnet inside the Earth. What we have is fluid motions of a liquid iron outer core; liquid iron that's over 5,000°C. This liquid iron is constantly convecting and churning just like the mantle convects, only a lot faster, because the viscosity of the liquid iron here is really low; it probably has the similar thickness of core syrup or honey. We're not entirely sure what drives the convection, though we think that there're probably three factors here. As the heat from the outer core passes up into the mantle above, that iron becomes a little bit colder, so it sinks, so that helps drive the convection. There's probably heat generated by the radioactive decay of certain isotopes like potassium 40. And also, as the inner core crystallizes out, it tends to crystallize more pure iron, iron and nickel, and it leaves a chemically lighter, more buoyant fluid, and that may help drive the convection.

But that's not sufficient. What we also seem to need is rotation, because you can go to planets, like Venus, that are about the same size as Earth, but are hardly rotating, and they don't have the magnetic field at all. So it seems like the Coriolis effect due to Earth's rotation is important. And what it does is take the convecting iron and turn it into these spiraling columns that are parallel to the axis of the Earth and are lined up surrounding the inner core.

The locations and shapes of these spiraling columns tend to shift and change over time. And as a result, the location of the magnetic north and south poles actually changes as well. The magnetic north pole now is very close to the true pole of the axis of rotation. It's at about 86 degrees north. A hundred years ago, though, it was well down south within Canada at about 70 degrees north. It has been moving steadily, though slowly, northward, and it's on track to go past the North Pole and head over towards Russia. The magnetic south pole is doing something totally different. It's a long ways away from the true South Pole. It had left Antarctica moving northward over the ocean, though now it seems to be stalled at a latitude of 64.4 degrees south. That's 25 degrees away from the true South Pole and currently it's stationary, for now, at least.

But the northern lights themselves aren't stationary. They aren't in any one location; they move around. At certain times, they extend in a wider band and come down to lower latitudes. That's when I saw them in New Hampshire. So there's, clearly, something other than Earth's magnetic field involved. And this is the activity of the Sun; this is what we call space weather. The times of active auroras on Earth are times of increased solar activity producing what we call the solar wind. The solar wind is a stream of ionized particles that blast through the solar system away from the surface of the Sun.

I should say a quick word about the Sun. The Sun is most of our solar system; in fact, it's 99.85% of the mass of our solar system. It contains a mixture of all the elements, but it's dominated by hydrogen and helium, frankly, just like the composition of the universe. Nuclear fusion within the Sun's core, that's the fusing of hydrogen to form helium, powers a layered structure inside the Sun. As you go away from the core, there's a radiative zone, which then powers a convecting layer, the Sun also convects, and the top of that convecting layer is called the photosphere. It isn't a real surface in any sense that we're used to, but it's what you see when you look at the Sun, and the top of that photosphere, the temperature is about 5,700 degrees Celsius.

Hydrogen and helium exist in a special state called a plasma. This is where it's so hot that the electrons are actually stripped off of the nuclei of the atoms. It's essentially an incredibly high temperature soup of atomic particles. But the outer layers of the Sun, the corona, are even much hotter, now this is a little bit strange because they're much less dense; there are fewer atoms, but they are millions of degrees hot. These incredibly high temperature ionized particles, mostly electrons and protons, which is the nucleus of hydrogen, and the nucleus of helium, which is two protons and two neutrons, these get thrown off the layers of the Sun at a variety of giant, great speeds.

One effect that you can see of the solar wind is if you've ever looked at a picture of a comet. Comets tend to have two tails. One of them traces the path that the comet has taken, but the other one points directly away from the Sun. And this is the solar wind hitting the surface of the comet, stripping away the outer layer, exciting the atoms to a high-energy state so that they continue to glow for millions of kilometers as they head off into space. During times of very high solar activity, you get enormous, what are called, coronal mass ejections. This is hydrogen thrown off the surface of the Sun, enormous solar flares. Some of these create giant magnetic loops that leave the Sun and come back, and this causes a much stronger solar wind.

The solar wind reaches Earth, but it doesn't arrive at all locations at Earth's surface. You don't usually see the aurora in the lower 48 states of the United States. Why is this? It's because of Earth's magnetic field. The Earth's magnetic field gets warped and shaped by that incoming solar wind and creates a shape that we call the magnetosphere. The boundary between the magnetosphere and the incoming solar wind is called the magnetosheath, and the magnetic field gets bent backward into a large structure called the magnetotail.

This is really good news for you, because the magnetosheath actually presents a significant barrier to the solar wind and protects our atmosphere from it. It turns, out if we didn't have a magnetic field, the solar wind would strip away our atmosphere over time. These high energy particles are also extremely damaging to living tissue and are a real problem for radio telecommunications as well. Normally, the solar wind gets deflected around Earth, but sometimes during solar storms, some of it is able to reach Earth.

This actually can be a real problem. There's a very famous case where this happened in March of 1989. A large eruption, a solar corona, occurred on March 9. Three-and-a-half days later that blast of solar wind hit the Earth. Satellites got knocked out of communication. It was during the Cold War, and the U.S. government thought that the Russians had jammed their communications. The ionized particles induced huge electrical currents in the power line in places north, like Quebec, and actually overloaded the circuits of the whole Quebec power grid, knocking the region out of power for nine hours.

When the particles of the solar wind do reach the Earth, however, they tend to follow Earth's magnetic field lines down towards Earth's surface, and these are concentrated closer to the poles. I can do a quick demonstration of how the invisible magnetic field lines can actually physically channel particles. What I'm going to do is take this piece of board here, and I'm going to sprinkle something on it here. Something very unusual is going to happen, though, when I start to tap this. You will see that very quickly the particles I dropped, which are iron filings, are lining up in a set of circular lines. What's going on here? I have a bar magnet underneath the board here, and so as I tap this, the iron filings are following the lines of the magnetic field. So you can see how the invisible field lines are actually able to channel physical objects; in this case pieces of iron. And in the case of the solar wind, you have these ionized particles channeled in to either the north or the South Pole. You'll notice there are no iron filings here at the equator. They get channeled in the field that's most concentrated at either pole.

It turns out that I've left off one very important detail. The ionized particles can't actually punch through the Earth's magnetosphere. This isn't what happened. It's actually something much more interesting. They take the back door. They go actually far past Earth and then double back when the magnetic field lines get so deformed that they actually snap. This is a process called magnetic reconnection. The magnetic field lines get stretched, and when they stretch too far they suddenly snap back to a new shape. I can show you an animation of how this works. So here's the Sun, and you can see off the edge this steady stream of particles. This is the solar wind, and it wouldn't actually look like this, but you get a sense from the animation of this material coming off. In the case of a storm, you have high numbers of these particles hitting the magnetosphere, and it actually begins to strip away the magnetic field lines. And if one of these field lines can bend so much out of shape that it actually folds on itself, it can snap, and what you then have is large numbers of these particles coming down in, coming to the Earth in these shimmering bands that circle the northern and southern poles, and these are the auroras.

The magnitude, speed, and direction of those coronal mass ejections are very important; they end up playing a role in what you actually see as the different auroras on Earth. But we're still missing one thing. Why are there colors? And why are the colors of the aurora so varied? This actually requires some understanding of the quantum energy behavior of atoms.

The auroras can occur high up in the atmosphere, way up in the thermosphere, more than 50 miles up, where there are actually very few atoms. It's close to a vacuum there. But the particles have very high energy from the sunlight constantly hitting it. The fact that the conditions here are close to a vacuum turns out to be very important as I'll show in a moment.

Earth's atmosphere is primarily made of two materials, nitrogen and oxygen. And like all atoms, their electrons can exist at different, discrete energy levels. We call these quantum energy levels. Quantum simply means a discrete amount of something. These electrons are usually at their lowest energy state, but they can be knocked into a higher energy state by any source of added energy, such as the interactions with the solar wind particles. They don't stay at the higher energy levels for long, however, they'll drop back down very quickly to their lowest energy levels. But the energy has to go somewhere; energy is always conserved in any interaction, so where does it go? It goes into photons, light. Because the quantum levels are discrete amounts of energy, they correspond to discrete specific frequencies of the light emitted. For oxygen atoms, when their electrons return to their lowest energy levels, what we call the ground state, they tend to release a green or brownish-red light, depending on the amount of energy absorbed. For nitrogen atoms, it tends to be blue or red. Red if the atom returns all the way to its ground state from an excited state, blue if the atom gains an electron after it's been ionized and essentially has a new ground state level.

Oxygen is unusual in terms of its return to the ground state, and this is very important. It can take up to three-quarters of a second for that green light to be emitted and then jump to the lower energy level and up to two minutes to emit red light. The reason this is important is, if there're any collisions with other atoms or molecules in the atmosphere during this time, that collision will absorb this added energy and will prevent the emission of light, you won't get an aurora from it. But because the very top of the atmosphere is so close to a vacuum, these collisions are very infrequent, infrequent enough to allow those two minutes needed for oxygen to emit red light.

The collisions become more frequent as you go down in the atmosphere, so that red emissions don't have time to happen, and the oxygen atoms primarily release green light. Eventually, as you go farther down, the air is dense enough that collisions between atoms happen so frequently that even green light emissions are prevented. That's why there are different colors here. If you look at different examples here of different auroras, they release different colors. At high altitude, oxygen red dominates, then oxygen green and nitrogen blue/red, then finally nitrogen blue or red when collisions prevent oxygen from emitting anything at all. Green is the most common of all the auroras; that's what I saw largely, and that's usually what's observed.

Next common is pink, which is a mixture of light green; and red, followed by pure red; then yellow, which is a mixture of red and green; and lastly, pure blue. This is actually a very simplified description. There are many added complexities. But gives you a sense of what's going on. In fact, I have to say the science behind auroras is all remarkably complex. To really understand it you have to know the churning behavior of a very restless star that we've only begun to understand. You have to know the magnetic field is generated by a magnetogeodynamo that's, frankly, so complex we've only just begun to make reasonable mathematical models of it. And it involves an understanding of atomic quantum mechanics to understand how the colors themselves are actually generated.

I mean, I'm not sure that you will remember all of this when and if you are lucky enough to see an aurora for yourself, in person. Though, this view of the northern lights over North America just as day is beginning to break is something you would only see if you were aboard the International Space Station, which is where this was taken. You certainly don't need to in order to appreciate the stunning beauty of the shimmering lights that are here. But f me, I have to say it greatly deepens my appreciation to know that processes inside the Sun and in Earth's core and processes within the very atoms themselves getting down to the fundamental nature of matter, all of these are needed to put on the greatest light shows on our planet.

Incidentally, I said that auroras don't usually occur in the continental 48 states. As with so much of this course, you can't always go by what you see today in trying to understand what has happened in the past. It turns out there are times when the auroras are centered over the U.S. and really big ones, too. The last time was awhile ago, it was about 780,000 years ago. For reasons that are still not fully understood, Earth's magnetic field randomly flips. In other words, your compass would point south instead of north. This reversal doesn't happen overnight; it takes about 1,000 years. And here's the interesting thing, in the process, the magnetic north pole doesn't just shut down and reappear down south, it actually wanders over centuries, all the way down from the north to the south . However, it doesn't take some random path. It seems to prefer to travel down two different paths. One of them is along the western Pacific edge and the other is right down the Americas. There's more. When the magnetic field reverses, the total strength of the dipole field gets much weaker; it drops by about 90 percent from its normal strength. That means that the Earth's magnetosphere would be much weaker, and a lot more solar particles would reach Earth during this time.

These reversals usually happen every couple 100,000 years or so. It's now been 780,000 years since the last one. We are way overdue. And what's more, over the past century, the strength of the Earth's geomagnetic field has actually dropped by 10 percent. So it's not inconceivable that in a couple of 100 years there could be some whopping big auroral displays right overhead in the middle of the United States.

It time for my top five. I actually have a lot to choose from here, but I'll just pick a couple of examples. First, let me talk about Sun dogs. This is a very interesting refraction occurrence that happens due to the presence of hexagonal ice crystals in high and cold cirrus clouds. Remember, rainbows form from refraction through water droplets. Here, the light from the Sun gets refracted by ice crystals, usually at an angle of about 22 degrees from the Sun. And if the ice crystals are randomly aligned through the atmosphere, the appearance is a stunning circular halo of light all the way around the Sun, at an angle of about 22-degrees away. However, it's common that the crystals get preferentially aligned as they fall down through the atmosphere, and the result is two bright lights, the Sun dogs, on either side of the Sun.

Next, let me talk about a green flash. There are actually a variety of phenomena that can cause a green flash. But it's a fascinating optical effect that often occurs when it is observed at the last moment of a Sunset, or also at the very start of a Sunrise. Because of the refraction of Sunlight, the very top rim of the setting Sun actually contains a very faint green rim. It's there all the time, but it's usually too small to see directly. If you have just the right conditions, this is if the temperature of the air at the surface is just right, the green light will get bent right around Earth's surface and actually appears as a sudden flash of green light, usually lasting just a second or two at most, well, usually. Remember how I said that at the north or South Pole you can have a Sunset that lasts for hours, with the Sun right at the horizon moving horizontally? Remember that video I showed? In 1934, there was a group of explorers on the Ross Ice Shelf in Antarctica, and they witnessed a green flash that occurred on and off for 35 minutes as the Sun slowly moved right at the edge of sinking below the horizon, all the way across the horizon.

Next, let me talk about another phenomenon called a Fata Morgana. It's named after Morgan le Fey, the fictional, magical half-sister of King Arthur. This is a mirage that looks like there is land up in the air or up above the horizon. This kind of mirage occurs when there is something we call a temperature inversion in the atmosphere. Normally as you go from the ground upward, temperature gets increasingly cold. If you have a layer of warm air on top of the cold air, this is what's known as an inversion, and it causes light rays to be bent more than the curvature of the Earth. So one result is that you see things, like maybe islands out at sea, that are actually below the horizon. You shouldn't be able to see them, but the light gets bent up around right at where you look. You can actually see around the edge of the Earth. It can also look like there are islands when you may just be seeing light from the ocean surface that's bent so much it looks like there's land floating up in the air.

This is especially common in very cold regions, and has even given rise to a fictional land in the North Sea, the Crocker Land. There have been several reported sightings of mountains in the Arctic Sea. We know there are no mountains in the Arctic Sea, but ships would sometimes see these objects that look like mountains, and they would sail towards them, but they could never reach them, and would eventually give up. In one expedition in 1906, the Captain Robert Peary saw what he thought were mountains in the distance, and he even named them after a deceased explorer, George Crocker. This appeared on many maps for awhile, but it never existed. It's a totally fictional land; all he saw was a mirage, a Fata Morgana.

Last, let me talk about zodiacal light, and this isn't a mirage. This is a real effect. And though it's very subtle and very hard to see, it's remarkable in its very existence. Under just the right conditions, just after Sunset or before Sunrise, it's best during the spring or fall, you can actually see the dust of space. You can see Sunlight reflected off of microscopic dust particles floating within the solar system. These tiny particles, they're just micrometers in size, will deflect Sunlight enough that they can actually be seen as a weak, triangle-shaped cone of diffused light, extending a little ways up above the horizon. This dust is largely the remains of comets, which slowly are drifting into the inner solar system.

In the next lecture, I'm going to continue the theme of particles arriving on Earth from outer space, but not small particles, this time, large particles, really large—meteoroids and asteroids large enough to gouge out large impact craters on Earth. And I will start with Meteor Crater in Arizona.

Arizona Meteor Crater—Visitors from Outer Space
Lecture 34

I n the last lecture, we saw auroras, spectacular colors that appear in the troposphere as a result of particles of the solar wind bombarding Earth's magnetosphere. In this lecture, we'll look at the arrival on Earth of slightly larger particles: meteoroids that create craters on the surface of our planet. We'll start by visiting Meteor Crater in Arizona. This crater is only about 1.2 kilometers across, but it's 170 meters deep and makes a stunning impression. For scientists, a "meteor" is defined as the streak of light in the sky produced by a meteoroid; a "meteoroid" is the rock that produces the streak; and a "meteorite" is a meteoroid that has hit the Earth.

Description of the Meteoroid

- Meteor Crater formed less than 50,000 years ago. At that time, the climate on the Colorado Plateau was much cooler and damper than it is now. This part of Arizona was open grassland with occasional woodlands and was inhabited by creatures that are now extinct, such as woolly mammoths and giant ground sloths.

- The meteoroid that formed the crater in Arizona was perhaps only 40 meters across and was made of nickel and iron. This size doesn't seem very large, but the energy of a moving object is proportional to the square of its speed, and this meteoroid was moving fast.
  - The formula for kinetic energy is simple: $1/2mv^2$, where m is the mass of an object and v is its speed. The meteoroid that made Meteor Crater was probably traveling at a speed of slightly more than 11 kilometers per second (25,000 miles per hour).

  - We know the speed had to be at least 11 kilometers per second because that's the escape velocity of Earth—the speed an object has to have to escape Earth's gravity, not taking into account air pressure. It's also the speed of an object that falls to Earth from far out in space. Earth's atmosphere significantly slows down smaller meteoroids, but the effect of the atmosphere is much less for larger meteoroids.

- The initial nickel-iron meteoroid that produced Meteor Crater was probably on the order of about 300,000 metric tons. Half of it may have been broken off during its passage through the Earth's atmosphere, making a pancake-shaped cloud of iron fragments. Most of the rest of it would have vaporized when it hit the ground.

- Meteoroid craters are always circular; they don't show any preferential indication of direction. The reason for this is that the intense energy of the impact causes much of the impactor to vaporize and then explode outward with an intense shock wave. That shock wave gradually converts into a seismic wave that propagates out in all directions from the impact across the planet.

- This explains why Meteor Crater could be formed by a relatively small impactor. The 40-meter chunk of iron was compressed, vaporized, and then exploded outward. In fact, pound for pound, the energy released by an impacting meteoroid is about 25 times greater than that released by the same mass of TNT.

Identifying the Crater's Cause

- At one point, there was significant debate about whether or not Meteor Crater was actually caused by a meteor. In 1891, G. K. Gilbert, the brilliant chief geologist for the U.S. Geological Survey, concluded that the crater was the result of a volcanic steam explosion.
  - Gilbert assumed that if it were an impact crater, then the volume of the crater plus the meteoritic material should be present on the rim, which it roughly is. His calculations showed that the volume of the crater and the debris on the rim were roughly equivalent, and he thought that the mass of the hypothetical impactor was missing. What he didn't know is that a huge meteoroid isn't needed to create a large crater.

  - Gilbert also assumed that a large portion of the iron meteorite should be buried under the crater and would generate a large magnetic anomaly, but none was present. Impact physics was poorly understood at the time, and Gilbert was unaware that most of the meteorite vaporized on impact. He argued that the iron meteorite fragments found on the rim were coincidental.

- In 1903, a mining engineer and businessman named Daniel Barringer suggested that the crater had been produced by the impact of a large iron-metallic meteorite. His company, the Standard Iron Company, received a patent signed by Teddy Roosevelt in 1903 for mining the 640 acres around the center of the crater. In 1906, Roosevelt also authorized the establishment of a newly named post office at Meteor, Arizona.
  - o Barringer, like G. K. Gilbert, believed that the bulk of the impactor could still be found under the crater floor. He spent 27 years trying to trying to find the large deposit of meteoritic iron that never existed.

  - o Barringer estimated, incorrectly, from the size of the crater that the meteorite should have had a mass of 100 million tons. The current estimate of 150,000 tons or so for the impactor is less than 0.02 percent of Barringer's estimate.

Meteorite Crater Structures
- Meteorite craters have specific structures, usually an excavated crater with the material (impact ejecta) ejected out on a rim. At the bottom is a combination of rock that has been melted (impact melt) and rock that has been fractured or shattered (breccia). In certain cases, especially for larger craters, material may stick up as a central peak in the middle.

- We have learned about the structure of impact craters by looking at craters on the surface of the Moon, where there is no weathering or erosion. Craters on the Moon remain perfectly preserved, allowing us to see the ejecta blanket and the details of the inner peak in the center of the crater.

A combination of impact melt and breccia at the bottom of a crater is a good indication that it was caused by an impact from outer space.

- Meteor Crater has the same raised rim as craters on the Moon, materials thrown outward, and a significant amount of rubble lying at the center of the crater. The rim is 45 meters above the surrounding plain.

- An added clue that the crater was created by an impact is the upside-down layering of the rock around the rim. In fact, the oldest rock, the Coconino Sandstone, which is about 265 million years old, is now found at the top. The Moenkopi Formation, which is 200 million years old, is near the outer foot of the rim. Inside the crater, however, all the layers are in their expected order.

Behavior of Quartz
- In 1960, a geophysicist named Gene Shoemaker conducted experiments in which he subjected various materials to very high pressures. In the process, he discovered a particular phase of quartz called stishovite.

- A phase diagram shows that raising the temperature of quartz changes its phase. It first becomes tridymite, then cristobalite; if it is heated more, it will melt and become liquid.

- If the quartz is subjected to high pressure, the atoms rearrange to form the mineral coesite. At very high pressures, quartz becomes stishovite, which is found in the rocks at Meteor Crater. The only other place stishovite can be found is deep in the interior of the Earth. Finding it at the surface indicates that the rock has been suddenly and intensely compressed.

Disappearance of Craters
- Three factors explain why craters on Earth don't last long.
  - First of all, the seafloor is 60 percent of Earth's surface, but the oldest seafloor anywhere on the planet is 200 million years old; that's only 4 percent of the age of the Earth. Almost any impact crater that has formed on the ocean seafloor has long since subducted into the mantle at an ocean trench.

  - Further, tectonic collisions on land have deformed the Earth's surface beyond recognition; thus, any feature on the surface is likely to be gone, as well.

  - Most important, of course, erosion due to water, ice, and wind constantly removes and alters the top layers of the rock on land, making it difficult to identify impact craters on Earth.

- As mentioned earlier, the lack of erosion on the Moon allows us to understand the details of the cratering process. Both the surface of the Moon and the surface of Mercury, which is also intensely covered with craters, have been essentially unchanged for billions of years.

Top Impact Craters
- The Vredefort Dome in South Africa is the largest confirmed impact basin in the world, at about 300 kilometers in diameter. The impact here occurred 2 billion years ago, which means that much of the detail has disappeared, but it was large enough that the shape of the circular crater is still clearly visible in the surrounding lands. The object that formed this crater might have been about 10 kilometers across.

- Sudbury Basin in Ontario, Canada, is the second largest confirmed impact basin, at 250 kilometers across. This crater is also extremely old, about 1.8 billion years. It has been deformed by several tectonic events in North America, but it also was big enough to retain characteristics that allow it to be identified.

- Three craters—Manicouagan in Quebec, Saint Martin in Manitoba, and Rochechouart in France—form an interesting triplet. All of them are 214 million years old. If we move North America and Europe back to their positions in Pangaea at that time, they all three align. It seems likely that they were all part of one asteroid that broke up during arrival.

- The Chicxulub Crater in the Yucatan Peninsula in Mexico is certainly the most famous of the impacts and potentially the most important from our perspective as humans. At 170 kilometers in diameter, this crater is the third largest verified impact crater on Earth.
  - o This impact occurred 65 million years ago and would have triggered an environmental catastrophe, ejecting so much debris into the atmosphere that the skies would have gone black and global temperatures would have plummeted. The impact likely played a major role in the extinction of the dinosaurs and many other species. The severity of this impact and of its consequences brings up an interesting point.

  - o Meteoroid impacts are part of a continuous process, similar to the flow of a river. Several tons of cosmic debris reach Earth each day, mostly tiny particles that burn up in the upper atmosphere. Sometimes, this debris is large enough to make it to the ground and survive as rocks, but every few tens of millions of years, a very large meteoroid hits, and the results can be catastrophic.

  - o This fact presents the history of life on our planet from the perspective of a few chance events, any one of which can have great consequences for the course of evolution and the future of life on Earth.

Suggested Reading

Mark, *Meteorite Craters*.

Norton and Chitwood, *Field Guide to Meteors and Meteorites*.

Questions to Consider

1. You buy land in a remote area, and the seller tells you that there was once a meteor impact there. How can you tell if this claim might be true or not?

2. Jupiter acts as a good shepherd, gravitationally diverting out of the solar system most of the large rogue objects that might otherwise one day strike Earth. How do you think the course of evolution of life on Earth would have progressed if large impacts were much more frequent? How about much less frequent?

Arizona Meteor Crater—Visitors from Outer Space
Lecture 34—Transcript

Hello. My name is Michael Wysession, and welcome to Lecture 34 of our course on the Geologic Wonders of the World. In the last lecture I talked about the aurora, spectacular colors up in the troposphere due to particles of the solar wind bombarding Earth's magnetosphere. In this lecture I will continue the theme of extra-terrestrial visitors and I'm going to talk about the arrival of particles of a bigger nature; the impacts of meteoroids that create craters on Earth's surface. And I will start with Meteor Crater, in Arizona.

I have to say, from a planetary perspective, it seems a little strange to me to be highlighting a crater that's only 1.2 kilometers in diameter; that's less than a mile. After all, our closest neighbor in space, the Moon, has over 500,000 craters of a kilometer or more. But imagine the splash it would make if a tree were suddenly found on the Moon. People often take for granted the things that are commonplace to them. And the fact remains that Meteor Crater, on Earth, is a remarkable and bizarre feature.

Meteor Crater is in the middle of a dry region. It's about 43-miles east of Flagstaff, AZ, in the northern Arizona desert, so it really stands out. And this turns out to be a very important aspect, which I'm going to get to shortly. Meteor Crater, for its modest width, again just 1.2 kilometers across, makes a stunning site if you go visit it. It's about 170-meters deep. And if you stand at the rim and look down, you realize it's a really great, big hole in the ground. It took some serious energy to excavate a hole like this. By the way, Meteor Crater will look familiar to you if you ever saw the charming 1984 movie *Starman*, with Jeff Bridges and Karen Allen. This crater was used as the setting for the final scenes of that movie. And actually, you may have seen it on the news or in old newsreels. During the 1960s NASA astronauts went and trained in this crater to prepare for their Apollo missions to the Moon. In fact, the remains of their work is actually still visible along the bottom of the crater. Meteor Crater is often referred to by scientists as the Barringer Crater in honor of Daniel Barringer, who was the first person to suggest that it was produced by a meteoroid impact.

The crater and the surrounding land are now privately owned by the Barringer family through the Barringer Crater Company, and as they advertise it, Meteor Crater is the first proven, best-preserved meteorite crater on earth. I should give a quick word about nomenclature. People often use meteor, meteoroid, and meteorite interchangeably, but they do have distinct meanings. The meteor is the streak that you see across the sky. The meteoroid is the rock that's doing the streaking, and when it hits the ground and you pick it up, that's a meteorite.

The crater here geologically is very young. The Meteor Crater formed less than 50,000 years ago. And at that time, the local climate on the Colorado Plateau there was a lot cooler and damper than it is now. That was during the last Ice Age, but it was at a time of relatively warm global climates, at least for an Ice Age. At that time, this part of Arizona was an open grassland covered with occasional woodlands, inhabited by creatures that are now extinct, like woolly mammoths and giant ground sloths.

If you were to go there and look at the crater, how large would you guess that the meteoroid was that hit it? Well, you might be surprised, but it really wasn't all that big, maybe only 40-meters across, about half a football field. It was a nickel-iron meteoroid, at least based on samples found around the crater. Now, 40 meters doesn't sound very big, but the energy of a moving object is proportional to the square of its speed, and it was moving very fast. The formula for kinetic energy is very simple; it's ½ times the mass of an object, times its speed, squared. And the meteoroid that made Meteor Crater was probably traveling at a speed of just a little more than 11 kilometers per second. We know it had to be at least 11 kilometers a second because that's the escape velocity of Earth. That's the speed that an object has to have if you hurl it directly off the surface of the Earth and have it escape Earth's gravity, not taking into account air pressure. It's also the speed of an object if you leave it far out in space and just let it fall in to the Earth. It's about 25,000 miles per hour. For smaller meteoroids, Earth's atmosphere will significantly slow them down, but for large rocks like this, the effect of Earth's atmosphere is much less. Though the speed of the Barringer impact has actually been a subject of quite a bit of scientific debate. There were some calculations initially suggesting that the meteoroid struck at a speed of maybe twice that, over 20 kilometers a second. More recent research suggests the impact was likely to be just at, or slightly above, Earth's escape velocity. And this can actually be calibrated in a very strange way from one of the few other things that will make a crater of this size; we've already seen this, a nuclear bomb. Remember at the end of the lecture on the Maldive Islands, I talked about the nuclear bomb test called Castle Bravo that was set off on the Bikini Atoll? Remember it blew a hole in the coral reef a couple of kilometers across? At 15 megatons of TNT, it was about the same size in terms of energy released as the impact of the Barringer meteoroid that made Meteor Crater.

The initial nickel-iron meteoroid was probably on the order of about 300,000 metric tons. It's thought that maybe half of it got broken off through its passage through the Earth's atmosphere, making a pancake-shaped cloud of iron fragments. And most of the rest of it would have vaporized when it hit the ground. This actually solves another interesting paradox that has puzzled researchers of meteoroid impacts, and that is, meteors, of course, can hit the surface from all directions, so it's unlikely that they would always come directly from above. Suppose I take a baseball and throw it into a sand box. The sand will splash out in the direction that I throw it. But, that's not what happens with meteoroid impacts. The craters are always circular. They don't show any preferential indication of direction. That's because the intense energy of the impact actually causes much of the impactor to vaporize and then explode outward with an intense shock wave, which then gradually converts into a seismic wave that will propagate out in all directions from the impact across the entire planet.

This is why you don't need a big impactor to make Meteor Crater. The chunk of iron the size of half-of-a-football field is compressed, vaporized, and then explodes outward. In fact, pound for pound, the energy released by an impacting meteoroid is about 25-times greater than that same mass of TNT. Strangely, however, though I just told you that meteorite craters are always circular, Meteor Crater is not perfectly circular. It actually has a slightly squarish shape to it, as you can see. And this is somewhat puzzling, but it's thought that this is likely due to pre-existing jointing within the rock here. And you can see it almost seems as if the two sides here are parallel, and these two sides here are parallel, and it's likely that this represents some pre-existing condition within the rock.

I find it hard to imagine, but there was actually a significant debate about whether or not Meteor Crater was actually from a meteor. The evidence seems so clear to me from what we know now, but that's just how discovery works. Hindsight is golden. Things often look obvious once the hard work is done and they've all been figured out. In 1891, G. K. Gilbert, the brilliant, famous chief geologist for U.S. Geological Survey, investigated the crater here, and he concluded that it was the result of a volcanic steam explosion. I mean, after all, we've seen several volcanoes in this course with craters at their summit, or that form a caldera. He assumed that if it were an impact crater, then the volume of the crater plus the meteoritic material should be present up on the rim, which it roughly is. His calculations showed the volume of the crater and of the debris on the rim were roughly equivalent, and he thought that the mass of the hypothetical impactor was missing. What he didn't know is that you don't need a huge meteoroid to create a large crater. But he also assumed that a large portion of the iron meteorite should be buried deep down under the crater and that this would generate a large magnetic anomaly. And he investigated, and he found no magnetic anomalies.

It's not really his fault. Impact physics was poorly understood at the time, and he was unaware that most of the meteorite vaporized upon impact. G. K. Gilbert argued iron meteorite fragments that were found on the rim were coincidental. And he publicized these conclusions in a series of lectures, in 1895. And the irony of this is, just three years earlier Gilbert was the one to propose that the Moon's craters were caused by impacts and not volcanoes. He got it right on the Moon, but not here at Meteor Crater.

However, a couple of years later in 1903, mining engineer and businessman Daniel Barringer suggested that the crater had been produced by the impact of a large iron-metallic meteorite. And his company, the Standard Iron Company, received a patent signed by Teddy Roosevelt, in 1903, for mining the 640 acres around the center of the crater. In fact, 1906, Roosevelt also authorized the establishment of a newly named post office at Meteor, Arizona.

Barringer, like G. K. Gilbert, believed that the bulk of the impactor could still be found under the crater floor. The poor guy, he spent 27 years trying to find the large deposit of meteoritic iron that never existed. I mean, he even drilled down to a depth of more than 1,300 feet, but of course, no significant deposit was ever found. Barringer estimated, incorrectly, from the size of the crater, that the meteorite should have had a mass of 100-million tons. And the current estimate of 150,000 tons or so for the impactor is less than 0.2 percent of Barringer's estimate. We can look at the evidence now and see that it clearly was an impact, but that's only because we've had the opportunity to look at a lot of other craters around the solar system, so we have a good idea of what happens. Meteorite craters have very particular structures. You tend to see craters of slightly different forms. There can be a simple crater and a complex crater, but what you will often see is an excavated crater with the material ejected out on a rim. We call that the impact ejecta. And down at the very bottom you find a combination of rock that's been melted; we call that the impact melt. And also, rock that's been fractured and shattered; this is a particular type of rock called a breccia. So if you find this combination of melt and breccia together, it's a very good indication that you have a crater from some sort of impact from outer space.

In certain cases, you can, actually, especially for larger craters, you can have material from the middle sticking up as a central peak, and so that's another distinguishing characteristic. For a volcano, you might not always have that kind of a feature. We have learned about the structure of impact craters by looking at craters on places like the Moon. And the nice thing about the surface of the Moon is, because there's been no weathering, no erosion, really no geology for four-billion years, the craters remain perfectly preserved, so we can see all the fine details, the ejecta blanket thrown out, the rays of material spreading outward, the details of that inner peak in the center of the crater. And we see these features at Meteor Crater. There is the same raised rim, the materials thrown outward, there's even a significant amount of rubble, about 240-meters across, lying at the center of the crater. The rim is 45 meters above the surrounding plain, and in addition, there's an added clue here, and that is, the impact created an upside-down layering of the rock layers around the rim. In fact, the oldest rock is now found at the top.

We know the names of these rocks. In fact, you do. I've talked about them already in the lecture on the Grand Canyon. The Coconino Sandstone, which is the oldest, 265-million years old, is right up at the top, and the Moenkopi Formation, which is 200-million years, is near the outer foot of the rim. If you go inside the crater; however, then you find that all of the layers are in their expected, normal order.

It wasn't actually until 1960 that Meteor Crater, and other meteorite craters around the world, for that matter, were finally determined to be the result of impacts from space. And this is due to the work of a geophysicist by the name of Gene Shoemaker who took different materials and squeezed them to very high pressures. And he discovered a particular phase of quartz called stishovite. And we can look at the way quartz behaves using a common tool for geologists that we call a phase diagram. So this is what happens to quartz if you change its temperature on the vertical axis or its pressure on the horizontal axis. We're over here in the lower, left corner here, if you pick up any normal quartz crystal.

If you begin to raise its temperature it will change phase; it will become something called tridymite, eventually cristobalite, and then if you heat it even more, it will melt and become liquid. But if you take that quartz and you squeeze it, the atoms rearrange and you get a new mineral called coesite. And if you go to very high pressures, you get to stishovite. Stishovite is found in the rocks at Meteor Crater. And the only other place you would find this would be way down deep in the interior of the Earth. So if you find stishovite at the surface, it's the smoking gun and it tells you, indeed, that what you have is rock that has been suddenly and intensely compressed.

I mentioned earlier that it was important that Meteor Crater was both very recently formed and that it's located in a very dry area. Why would this be the case? Let me show you why. I'm going to show you another meteorite crater on the surface of the Earth. Here it is. Can you show me where on this map a large impact crater is located? It's really hard to do so. Let me help you. Right here in the mouth of Chesapeake Bay. This is a 35.5-million-year-old impact, one of the largest in North America. How do we know this? You can't tell at the surface anymore because erosion, changing sea levels, the rivers passing through have essentially worn away the surface appearance of it. But researchers have drilled down and found the melt, the breccias, the fractured rock, and the shocked mineral crystals that tell us that, indeed, this is an impact. It would've been a fairly significant one as well.

Craters on the Earth just don't last very long. There are three main reasons for this. First of all, the seafloor is 60 percent of Earth's surface, but remember, the oldest seafloor anywhere on the planet is 200-million years; that's only four percent of the age of the Earth. So most any impact crater that's ever formed on the ocean seafloor has long since subducted down into the mantle at an ocean trench. You also have tectonic collisions on land making mountains, rifting things apart, and these have deformed Earth's surface beyond recognition, so if something sits on the surface for too long, odds are it's gone as well. And most importantly, of course, erosion due to water, ice, and wind is constantly removing and altering the top layers of the rock on land, so when you do get an impact crater on the Earth, you just can't see it very well.

For the Moon, the lack of erosion allows us to understand the details of that cratering process. Again, half a million craters a kilometer or larger are there and other bodies as well; Mercury is intensely covered with craters. This is because the surface of the Moon and the surface of Mercury are essentially unchanged for billions of years. And actually, the number of craters that exist on a planetary surface can be used as an indication of the age of the surface. What you do is you look at the number of impact craters in a certain area; we call that the crater density, and that gives us a sense of the age of the surface. This is especially important if you can't get there and actually pick up a rock and determine its age through radiometric dating. So for instance, the Moon's Highlands, the bright areas when you look up at the Moon in the night sky, these are older than the Maria, the dark, low, basaltic lava plains. The Highlands have a much higher crater density, and that's because they were formed about 4.5-billion years ago. The Maria formed by a set of many different lava flows that covered parts of the Highlands and other areas between three- and four-billion years, so they have fewer craters on them. Venus is another good example. Venus' surface has only about a thousand Meteor Craters, but it has tens of thousands of volcanoes, in fact, including small ones, hundreds of thousands of volcanoes. And this is because its entire surface is occasionally resurfaced by episodes of enormous and catastrophic volcanism, so the surface there just isn't very old.

It's time for my top five, and this is a little bit tricky. What I will talk about here are confirmed impact craters where convincing geologic evidence is available. And there are currently about 130 confirmed impact craters on Earth that are larger than about one kilometer. That's not very many. Because of the effects of erosion, there are a lot more circular-looking structures that are currently debated as to whether they might or might not be impact craters. Some are much larger than the ones I will mention here. For instance, there's one in Antarctica, in the Wilkes Land area, where kilometers of ice might be covering a nearly 500-kilometer-wide impact crater. It shows up on radar imagery; it shows up on gravity maps. But until we can get down through the ice and see if indeed we have shocked mineral crystals there, we just can't tell if it really is an impact.

Now, I already mentioned Chesapeake Bay, which is the largest impact crater in the United States, 90 kilometers in diameter, so let me visit four others. Let me start with the Vredefort Dome, in South Africa. And this is the largest confirmed impact basin in the world. It's about 300 kilometers in diameter. It happened two-billion years ago, so there's not a lot of detail to see now, but it was large enough that the shape of that circular crater is still clearly visible in the surrounding lands. The object that formed that crater, again, probably wasn't very large, at least compared to the crater, but it might have been as large as about 10-kilometers across.

It's very interesting, however, that nearby the crater there are two large areas that contain enormous amounts of igneous rock that erupted at just about the same time. These are two very famous regions, the Witwatersrand basin and the Bushveld Igneous Complex. What's so interesting is that the Witwatersrand contains the world's largest reserves of gold, and the Bushveld contains the world's largest reserves of platinum and other platinum-group metals. It's possible that these volcanic eruptions only occurred because they were triggered by the enormous energy of the impact that made the Vredefort Dome.

Next, let me go to Sudbury Basin, in Ontario, Canada. This is the second largest confirmed impact basin, at 250-kilometers across. And this one is also extremely old, about 1.8-billion years. The crater has since been deformed due to several tectonic events that have happened in North America, but it also was big enough that it's retained enough of its character that it can still be identified. And similar to the case of Vredefort, the impact triggered a large release of magma that filled the basin with extremely metal-rich lavas. This rock has been very profitably mined for nickel, copper, platinum, and gold.

Next we have a very interesting triplet. There are three craters, Manicouagan, in Quebec, that's 100 kilometers; the Saint Martin in Manitoba that's 40 kilometers; and the Rochechouart, which is 23 kilometers, in France. All of them are 214-million years old. If you move North America and Europe back to the positions where they were at that time when they were together forming Pangaea, they all three line up in a single line, so it seems very likely that they were all part of one asteroid that broke up during arrival. That's something we have seen in other places in the solar system as well.

Last, let me go to Chicxulub Crater, in the Yucatan Peninsula, of Mexico. And this is certainly the most famous of the impacts and potentially the most important from our perspective as humans. This is 170-kilometer-diameter crater. It's the third largest verified impact crater on Earth. And as I previously have mentioned in the course, this impact occurred 65-million years ago and would've triggered an environmental catastrophe, ejecting so much debris into the atmosphere that the skies would have gone black and global temperatures would have plummeted. This impact likely played a very major, if not dominant, role in the extinction of the dinosaurs and many other species as well. And the severity of this impact and of its consequences brings up a very interesting point. Meteor impacts pose a little bit of a conundrum from a geophilosophical perspective. We are sometimes not sure quite sure how to think of them. At one end, they are part of a continuous process, kind of like the flow of a river. Several tons of cosmic debris arrive each day on Earth. Most of it consists of tiny, little particles that burn up in the upper atmosphere. Sometimes they are big enough that they make it all the way to the ground and survive as rocks, and these are meteorites. In fact, I have one in my pocket here. This is a piece of a carbonaceous chondrite meteorite. And it's remarkable for me to hold a piece of rock in my hand that is as old as the solar system; this is 4.567-billion years old. This rock, as with most of the rocks of the asteroid belt, where this probably came from, formed at the very start of the solar system and are essentially unchanged since then.

However, every few tens of millions of years, a really big meteoroid hits. The results can be catastrophic. And this is an entirely different way of looking at history. It's no longer a continual process, but a matter of chance. It presents the history of life on our planet from the perspective of a few, random chance events, any one of which can have great consequences for the course of evolution and the future of life on the planet. Remember in the lecture on the Burgess Shale, how I talked about the five big mass-extinction events, times when enormous numbers of species all went extinct at the same time, but, how these were also times when environments were opened up to new species, when new life forms evolved to fill the environmental niches that had previously been occupied by other species. It's a little bit unnerving for me to think of history in this light, subject to the whims of just a handful of potentially catastrophic events. It's like a giant roulette wheel, constantly being spun. Or maybe Russian roulette would be a better analogy. Suppose, 65-million years ago, the asteroid, this object whizzing through space, that helped kill off all the dinosaurs had just barely missed Earth. All it would have needed was the slightest nudge by the slightest collision with some other tiny object somewhere way back along its trajectories. This nudge would have gotten amplified over time of many orbits, so that 65 million years ago it might never have come anywhere near the Earth. With the dinosaurs still dominating Earth's surface, would mammals have ever had the chance to expand and diversify? Could early humans have survived the vicious and efficient hunting methods of velociraptors? Would I be giving this lecture today, with a long tail; long, sharp teeth; and some very long claws at the ends of my fingers? And when will it happen again? Which of the millions of large rocky objects now orbiting the Sun is the one? Which is the one fated to circle around the Sun seemingly countless times until one particular moment, when by dumb, bad luck it finds itself in exactly the same time and place as the Earth? Which is the one that's going to wipe us out, allowing something else to take our place? Assuming we're even around then. Then again, maybe it won't.

We currently track the locations of over 10,000 objects in space that would be possible candidates for just such a catastrophic collision. And there are actually contests going on now trying to figure out the best way to divert a large asteroid that would be otherwise be on the course for a collision with Earth. This sounds like the plot of some bad Hollywood movie, but this is real.

Well, I have just two lectures left. And I still have too many fascinating geologic wonders on Earth that I haven't had a chance to talk about yet. So, I'm going to break my format, and in the next lecture I will briefly visit 10 different places on Earth to show you 10 more fascinating geologic wonders, 30 minutes, 10 places, 3 minutes a wonder.

A Montage of Geologic Mini-Wonders
Lecture 35

W e've almost reached the end of our course, but there are still many wondrous places that we have not seen. This lecture takes a brief look at 10 geologic wonders that don't fit into any neat categories but still deserve mention. These sites are quite varied, but they still span the range of what we might consider geologic wonders. They aren't presented in any particular order, except that toward the end of the list, the explanations for why they occur become a bit more uncertain. As we have said, science is a process, and we still haven't completely explained all the wonders on Earth.

White Cliffs of Dover

- The White Cliffs along England's southeastern coast rise as much as 350 feet from the ocean. They are made of a soft, crumbly, nearly pure white chalk—almost pure calcium carbonate—with occasional black specks of flint.

- The geologic wonder of these beautiful, iconic cliffs is in their formation. They are made almost entirely of the tiny, fossilized skeletons of ancient single-celled ocean creatures, a type of plankton called coccolithophores.

- The presence of the coccolithophores explains why the cliffs are so white. Unlike other limestone, which is often gray or mottled from impurities washed into the ocean from the land, the chalk of these cliffs formed at a time when the sea level was so high that there was no land nearby. Pure plankton skeletons slowly accumulated on the shallow seafloor for millions of years, not contaminated by any other sediment.

Eisriesenwelt Ice Caves

- The Eisriesenwelt Ice Caves, in Austria, are a 40-kilometer-long system of caves in the Alps. These are the largest ice caves anywhere in the world, and they are the result of an unusual pattern of airflow that reverses direction between winter and summer.

- The cave system has two entrances, one at the top of the mountain and one at the bottom. In the wintertime, when the outside air is below freezing, the relatively warm temperature inside the cave causes an updraft through the cave system. This leads to extreme cooling at the bottom of the cave as a result of cold air being sucked in from the outside at the bottom entrance.

- During the summer months, the outside temperature is much warmer than inside, and the opposite flow happens.
  - The relatively cold air inside the cave, usually about 8°C, causes a downward draft; fairly warm outside air gets sucked in at the top opening. But on its way down, this air is cooled so much that it can no longer warm up the hollow areas in the lower sections. As a result, there's a fairly constant temperature right around the freezing point in the area around the lower entrance.

  - Water that seeps down into the cave freezes over when it reaches the bottom, allowing spectacular ice formations to build up over time.

Moeraki Boulders

- The Moeraki Boulders are huge, almost perfectly round rocks than can be up to 1 to 2 meters in diameter. These rocks fall from the cliffs along the east coast of New Zealand, just north of the city of Dunedin.

- These giant, nearly spherical rocks are called cannonball concretions. They form by the growth of minerals within sedimentary rock that cement the sediment together, making it more resistant to weathering.

- In the case of the Moeraki Boulders, these concretions have formed over millions of years inside a layer of mudstone. The mineral calcite has grown outward from points of nucleation, causing the boulders to slowly grow underground. As the shoreline erodes and cuts into the cliff, the boulders become exposed and simply fall and roll down the shore.

Spotted Lake

- Spotted Lake is in Osoyoos in British Columbia, just a mile north of the U.S./Canadian border from central Washington State. Osoyoos is a warm, dry region, and as a result, the Spotted Lake doesn't drain out; it's a closed basin that fills from rains during the winter months. During the summer, when the water evaporates, it leaves a set of smooth and strangely colored oval-shaped pools.

- The pools are extremely alkaline and are filled with high concentrations of sulfate salts, including magnesium sulfate (Epsom salts) and calcium and sodium sulfates. The water also contains large amounts of many other minerals, such as silver and titanium.

- As the water evaporates, the minerals begin to precipitate in individual pools, which then become cut off from one another. Depending on the exact minerals that are precipitating, the pools can appear yellow, white, green, blue, or other colors.

Nieves Penitentes

- In Mendoza, Argentina, at the foot of Mount Aconcagua, we find strange patterns of ice along the sides of the mountain. The ice looks like a giant bed of knives, with sharp peaks placed one after another. These formations are called *nieves penitentes*.

- The clue to how these peaks form is first seen in the orientation of the blades, which face north, toward the Sun. Because it's so cold here, the ice doesn't melt. It sublimates directly into a water vapor phase.

- Once the ice surface initially becomes even slightly pitted, sunlight begins to reflect back and forth in between the pits, which causes melting in between the peaks, while the tops of the peaks remain frozen. The troughs between the peaks continue to melt downward as sunlight gets trapped within them, bouncing back and forth. Eventually, they will melt all the way to the ground.

Tsingy

- An unusual formation of rocks called *tsingy* occurs in the Bemaraha plateau of western Madagascar. Here is a 1500-square-kilometer park that is covered with jagged, bluish limestone peaks.

- Unlike the icy *penitentes*, which are only years old, the *tsingy* form over tens of millions of years. The limestone was once a coral reef in a large Jurassic lagoon. When Africa was flooded, the lagoon was buried by more sediment and slowly turned to rock. The rock became fractured into a large set of parallel joints when Madagascar rifted away from the rest of Africa, about 135 million years ago.

- The resulting joints became channels for water, and when the surface eroded down to the layer of limestone, the water kept percolating downward. Groundwater dissolved away the limestone and made parallel sets of caves. Rainwater percolated down and widened them out until the peaks intersected at sharp ridges.

The name *tsingy* in the local language of the Bemaraha plateau in Madagascar means "place where one cannot walk barefoot."

Salt Glaciers

- Most salt glaciers are found in one part of the world, the Zagros Mountains of Iran. Here, we find more than 160 separate outpourings of salt.

- Water ice is technically a mineral, although it is able to flow—slowly by our standards but very quickly by geologic standards. Salt can also flow relatively quickly over geologic time, and both of these flow within glaciers.

- Because salt is much lighter than other rocks, if there is a layer of salt underground, the pressure of the overlying rocks will push the salt up. In Iran, the salt layers were folded and deformed underground during the current movement of the Arabian Plate north into Asia.

- In certain places, windows to these salt layers are exposed at the surface, and the salt slowly oozes its way out, flowing downhill, just like an ice glacier. The salt erodes slowly because the climate is very dry. Any rain wears away the salt glacier into fascinating pitted and grooved formations.

Blood Falls

- Blood Falls occurs in the Taylor Glacier, which flows onto the ice-covered surface of West Lake Bonney in the Taylor Valley in Antarctica, not far from McMurdo Base. The snow flowing out from the bottom of the Taylor Glacier is a rusty red color that looks like drying blood.

- The color was initially thought to be due to the presence of red algae, but it now seems to be the result of oxidizing iron in the water. Blood Falls is actually a plume of salty water, rich in sulfates and iron, coming from a liquid saltwater lake beneath the glacier.

- It's possible that this saltwater formed by the evaporation of water from a salt pond. It's also possible that this is an ancient pocket of ocean water that got trapped here a few million years ago when sea levels rose and the continents were flooded. The high level of sulfates is expected for ancient seawater, but the iron is a bit of a mystery.

- Perhaps the most interesting part of this geologic wonder is the fact that the reddish saltwater is filled with life, even though it has been trapped under a glacier for at least 2 million years. Salt-loving bacteria may have survived underground during this time, feeding on the sulfates and iron and evolving along their own isolated paths of evolution.

Morning Glory Cloud
- The Morning Glory cloud is a meteorological phenomenon that forms over the Gulf of Carpentaria on the north coast of Australia. This cloud formation can extend for up to 1000 kilometers in a remarkably straight and sharp line. Each year, between September and October, these clouds roll across the gulf and over land.

- The exact cause of this cloud is not known, but one idea is that it's a result of sea breezes. Sea breezes occur because sunshine heats up the surface of the land much faster than the ocean; thus, warm air rises above the land and pulls the cooler sea-surface air in toward the land to take its place.

- From September to October, conditions of the air and water temperatures at night are just right to create an inversion layer over the Gulf of Carpentaria.

Racetrack Playa
- Racetrack Playa, in Death Valley, California, is the site of one of the greatest geologic mysteries on the planet. The playa is a closed basin that becomes a shallow lake during the infrequent rains, but the water quickly evaporates to leave a dry, flat surface the rest of the year. For most of the year, Racetrack Playa is covered with a layer of cracked, dry mud.

- The playa is also dotted with large boulders, called sailing stones, that have tracks that seem to suggest they have been dragged across the surface of the lakebed. Some of these boulders are extremely heavy, yet they seem to drift across the surface, usually in roughly straight lines but sometimes abruptly changing direction.

- The stones have never been observed moving, but scientists have come up with at least two hypotheses to explain the appearance of the tracks. The rocks may slip or be blown across the muddy floor of the lake in the wintertime, or they may sail across the flat on ice floats. Until someone sees the rocks move, the Racetrack Playa will remain a geologic mystery.

Suggested Reading

Bright, ed., *1001 Natural Wonders You Must See Before You Die.*

Brown, Brown, and Findlay, *501 Must-Visit Natural Wonders.*

Questions to Consider

1. How would you say that the *tsingy* of Madagascar and the Matterhorn in the Alps are similar in the manner in which they were formed?

2. What is the strangest thing you have ever seen in nature? Do you feel as if you have a better sense now of what might have caused it?

A Montage of Geologic Mini-Wonders
Lecture 35—Transcript

Hello. My name is Michael Wysession, and welcome to Lecture 35 of our course on the Geologic Wonders of the World. In the last lecture, I talked about Meteor Crater in Arizona and other impact craters on Earth. In this lecture, I want to try something very different. We're almost done with my list of the Geologic Wonders of the World. And there's just one big problem, there are still so many wondrous places that I haven't had a chance to talk about. And this is even with my top-five list at the end of each lecture. Some of the amazing places I haven't talked about don't fit into neat categories, but they still deserve mention.

There's a particular style of theater performing 30 plays in an hour, each lasting two minutes. It's kind of hard to imagine how that would go over, but it works pretty well. Many theater companies have done it. I want to try something similar. I'm going to do 10 Geological Wonders, in 30 minutes, at three minutes a Wonder. Some of these are big; some of them are small. They're very varied, but they still span the range of what I would consider Geologic Wonders. I won't present them in any particular order, except that as we get to the end, the explanations for why these occur become a bit more uncertain. I mean, science is a process; we don't have everything figured out yet. So, time's a-wastin'. Let me start first with number 10, in England, the White Cliffs of Dover.

This is undoubtedly the best known of the wonders I will talk about today, massive cliffs along England's southeastern coast, rising as much as 350 feet from the ocean. Dover is the closest point in England to mainland Europe, and the cliffs are an impressive sight when you take the ferry over from France. I already mentioned them when I talked about the formation of the English Channel at the end of the lecture on the Rock of Gibraltar. They're made of a soft, crumbly, nearly pure white chalk, with just occasional black specks of flint. They're nearly pure calcium carbonate, which is unusual. These are beautiful, iconic cliffs, but the Geologic Wonder is in their formation. They're made almost entirely of the tiny fossilized skeletons of ancient single-celled ocean creatures, a type of plankton called coccolithophores. These things are microscopic, only a few micrometers in size. They're

100-times smaller than the thickness of a human hair, and their skeletons are made of pure calcium carbonate, which is what makes the chalk. These things live at the ocean surface, and when they die, their skeletons fall down to the bottom of the seafloor.

Given how small they are, and the size of the cliffs, there is an unfathomably large number of them, on the order of 100 quadrillion individual coccolithophores per meter of area given the thickness of the chalk, which is about 250 meters. Given their observed density in water and their lifetime, which is on the order of weeks, their skeletons must've been raining down onto the seafloor for millions of years. And this happened way back during the Cretaceous during a very warm period when sea levels were high.

This actually explains why the cliffs are so white and pure. Unlike other limestone, which is often sort of a gray or mottled color, that's from the many impurities washed into the ocean from the land, the chalk of these cliffs formed at a time when the sea level was so high that there was no land nearby. So pure plankton skeletons slowly accumulated on the shallow seafloor for millions of years, not contaminated by any other sediment.

Next, number nine, let's go to Austria for the Eisriesenwelt Ice Caves. These are some of the most stunning mountains anywhere in the world, the European Alps, with sharp-edged mountains and valleys carved out by millions of years of glaciers. But the Geologic Wonder I'm going to talk about here is not located not outside, but inside the mountain. The Eisriesenwelt Ice Caves, in Austria, are a 40-kilometer-long system of caves in the Alps. It's just about 40 kilometers south of Salzburg. This is long, but not so unusually long. Remember Mammoth Caves, hundreds of miles of caves? But while many caves can boast this size, only a few in the world are filled with spectacular ice formations year round.

The ice formations here form through a very peculiar manner. These caves are the largest ice caves anywhere in the world, and they happen because of an unusual pattern of airflow in the cave that actually reverses its direction between winter and summer. The cave acts like a giant chimney. It has two entrances, one at the top of the mountain and one down at the bottom. In the wintertime when the outside air is very cold, below freezing, the relatively warm temperature inside the cave causes an updraft that rises up through the cave system. This leads to extreme cooling at the bottom of the cave as a result of cold air being sucked in from the outside at that bottom entrance. During the summer months, the outside temperature is much warmer than inside and the opposite flow happens. The relatively cold air inside the cave, usually about 8°C or so, causes a downward draft, so the fairly warm outside air gets sucked in at the top opening. However, on its way down, this air gets cooled so much that it can no longer warm up the hollow areas in the lower sections. And as a result, there's a fairly constant temperature right around the freezing point in the area around the lower entrance. And as a result, water that seeps down into the cave and melts occasionally when that warm air comes in, freezes over when it reaches the bottom, and spectacular ice formations will build up over time.

Next, number eight, we'll go to New Zealand for the Moeraki Boulders. New Zealand is an incredibly beautiful country, filled with a wide variety of stunning landscapes. We already saw the majestic cliffs of the southwestern coast in Fiordlands. But for this Geologic Wonder we're going to visit a region along the east coast, just north of the city of Dunedin. It's not so much the coast and its cliffs that are remarkable, but what's falling out of them. As you walk along the coast here, you will see large numbers of boulders, and these huge, perfectly round rocks can be up to one to two meters in diameter. Some even have a pattern of veins on them that kind of look like how you might think giant fossilized dinosaur eggs would look, but they aren't of course.

These giant, spherical, or nearly spherical, rocks are called cannonball concretions. And they form by the growth of minerals within sedimentary rock that cements together the sediment there, making it more resistant to weathering. In this case here, these concretions have formed, sometimes slowly, over millions of years, occurring inside a layer of mudstone. The mineral calcite has grown outward from these points of nucleation, and this causes these boulders to slowly grow underground. As the shoreline erodes and cuts into the cliff, the boulders become exposed, and they simply fall and roll right down the shore.

It turns out that cannonball concretions, though rare, are found around the world. In fact, during one of my deployments of seismometers, this is when I was looking at the deep geologic structure of North America, and I had a line of seismometers from Florida to Alberta, Canada, one of my seismometers was installed at Teddy Roosevelt National Monument, in North Dakota. And getting in and out of the park there, I would drive past a tall cliff with many of these giant, six-foot cannonball concretions sticking right out of the cliff. However, it's unusual to have one show the veins so clearly. These are called septarian concretions, and I actually have some examples of these here.

This is an example of what one of these concretions would look like, and you can see the veins on the outside due to the crystallization, in this case, of calcite within the rock. If you were to cut one of these and polish it, you can see some of these can be extraordinarily beautiful. You have remarkable colors and shapes here. In the case of the Moeraki Boulders, whole veins, first of calcite and then quartz, have crystallized. The quartz, of course, is very resistant to weathering, and it forms the ridges on the outside of the boulder.

There are other places in New Zealand where these cannonball concretions are found. For instance, at the beach in Koutu, on the North Island, some of these concretions are as large as 18 feet in diameter. But the Moeraki beach was described in early colonial reports dating back to the mid-1800s, and interestingly, it seems that there were even more boulders there at the time, and the Moeraki Boulders have become well known as a tourist site.

Next, number seven, we go to British Columbia in Canada for something that is known as the Spotted Lake. Imagine if Dr. Seuss drew a lake in a picture book of his. It might very well look like this lake in Osoyoos, in British Columbia, called the Spotted Lake. It's located just a mile north of the United States/Canada border from central Washington State. Osoyoos is a warm, very dry region that doesn't get much rainfall. As a result, the Spotted Lake doesn't drain out. It's a closed basin, and it fills from rains during the winter months. However, during the summer when the water evaporates, it leaves this set of oval-shaped pools that are so smooth and regular and strangely colored, they look like they've been drawn by some psychedelic artist. The pools are extremely alkaline and they're filled with some of the highest concentrations of salt, sulfate salts, anywhere in the world, magnesium sulfate, which you know as Epsom salts, and also calcium and sodium sulfates.

The water also contains large amounts of many other minerals like silver and titanium. And in fact, the minerals were actually mined during World War I, but the land has since been bought by a local Native American tribe, the First Nations of the Okanagan Valley, and they consider the lake to be a sacred site, largely because of the therapeutic value of the lake's waters with all those Epsom salts in it.

As the water evaporates, the minerals begin to precipitate within the individual pools, which become cut off from one another. And depending on the exact minerals that are precipitating, the pools can appear yellow, white, green, blue, or even other colors, and the colors actually shift and change over the course of a year.

Next, let's go to number six to Argentina for the *nieves penitentes*. The next two Geologic Wonders form a pair. It's an interesting case where two geologic features look very similar, but have totally different causes. Both of these involve large areas of tall, sharp spikes. But in one case, they're pinnacles of ice; this is the cold, dry region of the Andes, not far from the Chile/Argentina border, and the other will be a large region of west-central Madagascar, where dense, sharp spikes of limestone stick up for hundreds of miles.

If you go up into the Andes, in places like Mendoza, Argentina, which is at the foot of Mount Aconcagua, the tallest mountain in South America, you may come across places where the ice along the sides of the mountain takes on a very strange pattern. It looks like a giant bed of icy knives, with sharp peaks, about a person's height or so, placed one after the other. These things are called *penitentes* after the name of the tall, pointed caps of people doing penance for their sins, such as people from the brotherhood of Nazarenos, there.

Up in these regions it's very cold, but the sun shines strongly. Remember the discussion on the Atacama Desert? There's very little snowfall here, so that snow that does fall may end up staying there for a very long time. How do these things form? The clue to how these sharp peaks form is first seen in the orientation of the blades, which face north toward the Sun. Because it's so cold, the ice doesn't melt. It sublimates directly into a water vapor phase. In fact, if we go back to the peaks we can see that the peaks drop all the way down to the ground level. And what happens here is, there's a runaway effect here as the ice is slowly sublimating directly into a water vapor phase. Once the ice surface initially becomes even slightly pitted, sunlight starts reflecting back and forth in between these pits, and that causes melting down in between the peaks while the tops of the peaks remain frozen.

These troughs between the peaks keep on melting down as sunlight gets trapped within them bouncing back and forth. And eventually, they will melt all the way to the ground. Incidentally, this strange geologic wonder was first described by Charles Darwin, in 1839. This is not the first time we've come across him in this course. He made enormous numbers of important geologic discoveries. In 1835, Charles Darwin had to squeeze his way through snow fields covered in these *penitentes* on the way from Santiago de Chile to Mendoza, Argentina.

The pair to this, next, geologic wonder number five, is in Madagascar, and it's an unusual formation of rocks that we call *tsingy*. It occurs in the Bemaraha plateau of western Madagascar. And it's a 1,500 square kilometer park that is covered with jagged, bluish limestone peaks. These spikes are so sharp in places they'll cut you. I mean, the edges are literally sometimes knife sharp, and they can be less than a meter tall or tens of meters tall. They're called *tsingy* in local Malagasy, which means place where one cannot walk barefoot, and you know, no kidding.

Getting there, to begin with, is an adventure. It's a two-day's ride in a four-wheel drive vehicle over nearly nonexistent roads, bumping past majestic baobab trees and avoiding bandits. But once you get there what you see is an incredible site. Unlike, the icy penitentes, which are only years old, the *tsingy* here have formed over tens of millions of years. The limestone was once a coral reef in a large Jurassic lagoon. Back at a time when Africa was flooded. Remember, Madagascar was part of Africa then. It was buried by more sediments and slowly turned to rock. But the rock became fractured into a large set of parallel joints during the time when Madagascar rifted away from the rest of Africa, about 135-million-years ago. These joints became channels for water, and when the surface eroded down to the layer of the limestone, the water kept percolating on downward. Ground water dissolved away the limestone and made these amazingly parallel sets of caves. The rainwater percolated all the way down and widened them out until the peaks intersected at very sharp ridges. These ridges are so sharp they're impossible for humans to navigate through in most places, though, actually, I was surprised to find there's a growing interest in extreme-sport rock climbing here on the *tsingy*. However, there are several places here where species of lemurs that live in the park can be found leaping between the sharp peaks with ease.

Next, number four, we go to Iran for the Salt Glaciers. In this course we've looked at glaciers in many different parts of the world, from Antarctica to Alaska to the Himalayas, even on Kilimanjaro. But it turns out that glaciers aren't always made of ice. They can also be made of salt. By far, most salt glaciers are found in one part of the world, the Zagros Mountains of Iran. Here you will find over 160 separate outpourings of salt. Water ice is technically a mineral, though it is able to flow, and slowly, by our standards, but very fast by geologic standards. Salt can also flow relatively quickly over geologic time and both of these flow within glaciers.

Salt is much lighter than other rocks, so if there is a layer of salt underground, the pressure of the overlying rocks will push the salt up. But we already saw this when we visited the Dead Sea where the 700-foot-tall Mount Sodom, entirely made of salt, has been pushed up by the weight of the lake sediments. In the case of Iran, the salt layers were folded and deformed during underground during the plate collision that is currently going on, with the Arabian Plate moving north into Asia. We've seen that play an important role in several parts of this course.

In certain places, windows to these salt layers are exposed at the surface, and the salt very slowly oozes its way out, flowing downhill just like an ice glacier. The salt erodes slowly because it's very dry there. But if there is any rain there, it wears away the salt glacier into these fascinating sets of pitted and grooved formations.

Next, number three, we will go from Iran to Antarctica to a bizarre formation that we call the Blood Falls. The next Geologic Wonder is an actual ice glacier, but it doesn't look like any other ice glacier in the world. It occurs in the Taylor Glacier, which flows onto the ice-covered surface of West Lake Bonney in the Taylor Valley of the Dry Valleys of the Trans-Antarctic Mountains, not from McMurdo Base. And we saw that in the lecture on Antarctica.

It looks like the Earth is bleeding. The snow flowing out from the bottom of the Taylor Glacier is a rusty, red color that looks very much like drying blood. There is a significant debate as to what's going on here. And by the way, I might point out in the lower left-hand corner there is a tent for scale on this glacier. This was an initially thought to be due to the presence of red algae, but it now seems that the red color here is due to oxidizing iron in the water. The Blood Falls are actually a plume of very salty water, rich in sulfates and iron, which is coming from a liquid saltwater lake that sits beneath the glacier.

The glacier ice, of course, is made of fresh water, but the saltwater sits down at the bottom underneath it. It's possible that this saltwater formed by the evaporation of water from a salt pond, like the saltiest place in the world that we saw, the Don Juan Pond, which actually is just right over a ridge from here. It's also possible that this is an ancient pocket of ocean water that somehow got trapped up here a few million years ago when sea levels rose very high and the continents were flooded. The high level of sulfates is expected for ancient seawater, but all of the iron is a little bit of a mystery. And actually, it might have been leached out of the underlying bedrock by the activity of microbes. And that is perhaps the most interesting part of this geologic wonder; the reddish saltwater is filled with life, even though it has been trapped under a glacier for at least two-million years, cut off from the surface. The salt-loving bacteria, and there have been more than 17 species identified so far, may have survived underground during this time, feeding on the sulfates and iron, evolving along their own isolated paths of evolution. And if this is true, it has significant implications for astrobiology and the search of life elsewhere in the universe. Maybe you don't need dry land and photosynthesis to have life. Maybe some near-frozen saltwater ponds and a few minerals will do. And you know? We have plenty of places in our solar system that meet those requirements.

Next, we go to number two, and here we're going to move from Antarctica to Australia for a very strange feature called the Morning Glory cloud. There's a wide variety of clouds that form in the atmosphere, from wispy cirrus clouds, to lumpy cumulus clouds, to massive anvil-shaped cumulonimbus clouds. I haven't included and of these in the course because, frankly, they aren't predictable. There isn't a single particular place or time that you can go and count on seeing one of these. But that's not the case for one of the strangest phenomena that occur in the atmosphere. It's the Morning Glory cloud, which forms over the Gulf of Carpentaria on the north coast of Australia. Talk about looking like something drawn by an artist.

The Morning Glory clouds can extend for up to 1,000 kilometers in a remarkably straight and sharp line. Each year, between September and October, they roll across the Gulf and over land. Hang gliders and glider planes flock to a town called Burketown there to try to catch the wave at this time and ride that Morning Glory cloud. Towns are few and far between here; it can be more than 300 kilometers to the next town. About 40 percent of the time, the first thing in the morning, the cloud arrives. It can be just one, but it often appears as a set of lines evenly spaced that roll across the land at about 60 kilometers an hour.

They're huge. They start a couple hundred meters above the ground and extend upward for up to two kilometers. They have a very unusual phenomenon. There's a strong updraft in front of the propagating wave, which gives it this rolling motion. These rolling clouds, similar to the Morning Glory cloud, are sometimes seen in other places around the world, but very rarely, and only here are they so plentiful and predictable.

Atmospheric processes are very complicated. This is why weather forecasts are only given as probabilities; you know, there's a 30 percent chance of rain or something. This is because the best you can do sometimes is to analyze atmospheric processes in a probabilistic manner. And the exact cause of this cloud is really not known, but one idea is that it's a result of sea breezes. Sea breezes occur because sunshine heats up the surface of the land much faster than the ocean, so warm air rises up above the land, and it pulls the cooler sea-surface air in toward the land to take its place. This happens over Cape York here, at the north part of Australia. It's a peninsula that extends far to the north of Burketown.

During September to October, conditions of the air and water temperatures at night are just right to create what's called an inversion layer of air over the Gulf of Carpentaria. I mentioned this before; this is a layer of warm air that sits like a stable blanket on top of a layer of colder air below. During the day, air over the Cape York Peninsula warms and rises. At night, this air cools and falls, and then flows west and south, across the Gulf. But the flowing air is trapped underneath that blanket of warm air, that inverted layer. And as it flows away from Cape York, in a set of pulses, it pushes the cool, moist air up and over it. And as the air goes up the front of the wave, it cools, water vapor condenses, and it makes clouds. As the air goes down the back side of the wave, it warms up again, and the cloud turns back into water vapor and disappears. In any case, it looks like something out of a science-fiction movie as these seemingly endless straight lines of clouds barrel across the surface, but only for a very short time.

Time for my last geologic wonder, this is number one here. This is my last entry in this rogue's gallery of geologic wonders, and to do that we're going to go from Australia to California to Death Valley. Death Valley, in southwest California, is a fascinating place for several reasons. It contains the lowest point in North America, 282-feet below sea level, and yet, it's only 85 miles from the tallest point in the 48 states, which is Mount Whitney. It's surrounded by mountains, which makes the hot air circulate like a convection oven, and the record high temperature here, which is 134°F, is only two-degrees less than the world-record high anywhere on Earth, which was recorded in Libya, in 1922, 136°F, so it gets really hot.

But it's one particular location at Death Valley, called Racetrack Playa, that's the site of one of the greatest geologic mysteries on the planet. The playa, like other playas, is a closed basin that becomes a shallow lake during the infrequent rains; we've seen that at other places, but the water quickly evaporates to leave a dry and very flat surface the rest of the year. Some playas are salt flats, like the Salar de Uyuni, which we saw in Bolivia. This one gets covered with a layer of mud that exists as a set of mud cracks for most of the dry year.

Racetrack Playa is also dotted with large boulders that have tracks that seem to suggest they've have been dragged across the surface of the lakebed.

These things are called sailing stones. Some of them are extremely heavy, more than the weight of a person, yet they seem to drift across the surface, usually in roughly straight lines, but sometimes abruptly changing direction. Many people initially thought that this was a hoax, though there have never been any footprints accompanying the stone's movements. Some people even thought it was supernatural.

Starting in 1948, geologists have been investigating these Sailing stones. The stones still have never been observed moving, so there's still a debate as to how this happens, but there are some hypotheses. First, the stones only seem to move in the wintertime, and that provides some interesting clues because you can get occasional rainstorms here in the wintertime between December and March. And when this happens, the muddy floor of the Racetrack Playa briefly becomes very slippery. You can also get extreme winter winds here, sometimes with measured gusts over 90 miles an hour, and they often are strongly concentrated right along the surface.

So even though this gets brutally hot, record-breaking hot in the summertime, it also can be very cold in the winter; it can freeze on occasion in winter. In a seven-year study, some winters one or only a few rocks moved, but 28 of the 30 monitored stones moved at least some distance during that seven-year period. The longest distance moved was by the smallest rock, not surprisingly, a total of 860 feet. But even an 80-pound rock moved. Some scientists proposed that when the playa gets muddy, it's so slippery that the strong gusts of wind can actually start the rocks sliding across the mud.

However, a preferred explanation is that when a winter rain falls and freezes, it forms ice rafts that lock around the rocks. And because the ice floats on top of the water, when the ice sheet starts to break up, the strong winds can blow the ice rafts, and the rocks sticking up act like sails. Their bottoms scrape along the top of the mud, but the ice keeps them floating. Someday someone will actually see them move, and we'll know for sure, but until then, they remain a geologic mystery.

Well, I'm done with this world. I have one lecture left, and in that last lecture, I will look at geologic wonders that are out of this world and look at some of the strange features of other planets in our solar system.

Planetary Wonders—Out of This World
Lecture 36

O ver the past 35 lectures, we have seen mountains, sinkholes, glaciers, canyons, fjords, volcanoes, geysers, caves, crystals in caves, lava lakes, salt lakes, and acid lakes—more than 200 different locations of geologic wonders of many different types in almost 120 different countries. In this final lecture, we'll look at some of the remarkable geologic wonders that have been discovered on other planetary bodies in the solar system. Thanks to the remarkable robotic probes of NASA and other space agencies, we can now take virtual trips into space and explore some of the truly incredible features found there, some similar to features we have on Earth and some unlike anything seen on our planet.

Venus
- As we have seen, in Hawaii, lava can flow for tens of kilometers across the ground, but on Venus, lava flows can extend for many hundreds of kilometers. The lava is basalt, the same material as lava on Earth, but the surface of Venus is so hot—460°C—that the lava flows easily.

- Venus is covered with volcanoes—hundreds of thousands or even millions of volcanoes. We can't determine a number because we can't see the surface. Venus is covered by such thick clouds, made of sulfur dioxide and sulfuric acid aerosols, that light can't penetrate them. However, satellite information on elevation and the surface roughness of the ground enables us to make images of the surface of Venus.

- We've seen some places on Earth where the crust has been fractured into large numbers of parallel sets of faults called joints. On Venus, large expanses of the surface are densely covered with these parallel fractures. Venus's surface also shows evidence of extreme stretching and compression. There is mantle convection here—the rock of the mantle is flowing—but because there are no tectonic plates, the surface doesn't have anywhere to go. It is just repeatedly stretched and cracked and fractured.

- Volcanism is not currently active on Venus, but the planet appears to undergo a process of catastrophic resurfacing every 300 to 500 million years, when the heat in the mantle builds up to a critical level.

Earth's Moon
- A few lectures ago, we saw the largest impact crater on Earth, the Vredefort Dome in South Africa, at 300 kilometers across. The largest crater in the solar system is on the Moon, the South Pole–Aitkin Basin. It is more than 2500 kilometers in diameter and up to 13 kilometers deep.

- This crater was formed at a time of extreme violence in our solar system known as the Late Heavy Bombardment period.
  - o At this time, the planets Jupiter and Saturn drifted into a 2:1 resonant orbit that caused their own elliptical orbits to become eccentric and destabilized the entire solar system.

  - o Neptune and Uranus were flung to the farther parts of the solar system, and many large icy objects were thrown into the inner solar system.

Mars
- Mars is a place of extreme geologic features. It has many similarities to Earth, including deserts and glaciers, polar icecaps, long-term climate change, and enormous volcanoes and canyons.

- As we saw, the Big Island of Hawaii itself is a volcano, 100 kilometers wide and rising 10 kilometers off the seafloor. At Olympus Mons on Mars, which is the largest single volcano in the solar system, we see something almost an order of magnitude larger. The central caldera sits 27 kilometers above the mean surface level; that's three times the elevation of Mount Everest above sea level. The top sits 22 kilometers above the surrounding plains.

- Hawaii is also the location of the largest hotspot on Earth, but because the Pacific Plate on which it sits is moving westward, all the lava is spread out over a long chain of islands and seamounts.

Mars has the largest hotspot in the solar system, a region known as the Tharsis Rise. The area of the Tharsis Rise sits about 7 kilometers above the surrounding plains and is about 30 million square kilometers.

© Digital Vision/Thinkstock.

Mars has numerous extreme geologic features, including the largest volcano, largest hotspot, and largest canyon in the solar system, along with giant sand seas and complex icecaps.

- In earlier lectures, we saw large canyons that cut through the Himalayas; these can be 5 kilometers deep and extend for 240 kilometers. On Mars, we find the largest canyon in the solar system, the Valles Marineris, at about 4000 kilometers long, 200 kilometers across in places, and more than 7 kilometers deep. This canyon may have both tectonic and erosional origins.

- Mars also has deserts and some giant sand seas. One of these giant ergs, the Olympia Undae, covers 0.5 million square kilometers. The dunes here can be as much as 0.5 kilometers apart and rise up to 25 meters above the plain.

- In dry areas on Earth, we sometimes see dust devils, or small whirlwinds. Dust devils constantly zip across the surface of Mars and are responsible for all the dust in the planet's atmosphere. The dust devils have also served as windshield wipers for the solar panels of two Mars rovers that have been operating there since 2004.

- Larger dust storms on Earth can be a significant hazard, but nothing here compares with the dust storms on Mars. A dust storm may begin in one area, and when sunlight hits the dust, it warms that part of the atmosphere. Temperature differences in the atmosphere are what drive winds. The strong winds pick up more dust, and the dust storm grows; after a couple of weeks, it can cover the entire planet. Once the whole planet is dusty, there are no more variations in temperature, the winds die down, and the dust slowly settles.

- Mars also has the most complex icecaps in the solar system. The ground on Mars is filled with ice, similar to permafrost on Earth. Huge glaciers come out of mountains and gullies on Mars and deposit rock at terminal moraines. In many places on the surface of Mars, we see areas that look like flat soil, but these areas are actually ice covered with a layer of dust—glaciers flowing across the surface of Mars.

- The most unusual ice surfaces on Mars are the giant icecaps at the north and south poles. The icecaps here are two compounds: a thick, permanent, water icecap and a thin, variable, carbon dioxide icecap. The solid-water icecaps are huge, larger than Texas, and have repeating layers that seem to be caused by climate swings.

- Mars shows evidence of a period between 4 to 3 billion years ago when a vast amount of water carved away large portions of the land. Some of this water might have come from impacts of ice-rich planetoids during the Late Heavy Bombardment period. It may also have come as water vapor during an extremely active volcanic phase. In any case, the water is long since gone.

Asteroids
- The asteroids are a belt of rocky, icy objects that revolve around the Sun in between the orbits of Mars and Jupiter.

- A small asteroid named Vesta has unusual craters, including three in a row that look like the outline of a snowman. Vesta also has the tallest nonvolcanic mountain anywhere in the solar system, 21 kilometers high, found within a giant impact basin.

- Another asteroid, Kleopatra, is perhaps the strangest-looking object in the solar system. It looks like a giant dog bone, 200 kilometers long, spinning in space. Kleopatra formed from the loose connection of two smaller piles of rock and dust.

The Gas Giants and Their Moons

- If we go farther out into the solar system, we reach the gas giants, Jupiter and Saturn. The recent Cassini satellite mission sent back amazing images of a variety of remarkable geologic features from these planets.

- The northern and southern lights we saw earlier pale in comparison to the auroras found near the poles of Jupiter and Saturn. These auroras can be hundreds of kilometers across, 250 kilometers above the planet. They form by the same mechanism as auroras on Earth.

- The fast rotations of Jupiter and Saturn cause their atmospheres to break up into many separate bands, and where these bands intersect, there are enormous storm systems. The largest of these is the Great Red Spot on Jupiter, a 23,000-kilometer-long hurricane that has been present for at least 180 years.

- Jupiter's moon Io has hundreds of volcanoes erupting at any given time. Io also has the hottest lavas anywhere in the solar system, at more than 1500°C. The volcanism on Io is generated by its resonant orbit with Europa and Ganymede, two other moons of Jupiter.

- Europa has a liquid saltwater ocean, perhaps 150 kilometers thick, covered with a thin sheet of ice. The ice crust of Europa resembles a giant jigsaw puzzle, with pieces breaking up and drifting around over time. The presence of the liquid saltwater ocean makes Europa a likely candidate for life.

- All of the large planets—Jupiter, Saturn, Uranus, and Neptune—have rings, but the rings of Saturn are by far the largest. They look substantial, but they are actually thin layers of small particles of rock and ice.

- At Saturn's south pole is a vortex, the giant eye of a hurricane that is 8000 kilometers across. At the north pole of Saturn, the atmosphere flow takes the shape of a hexagon. Saturn's atmosphere has been modeled by scientists as a particular jet stream of gas moving at different speeds than the surrounding atmosphere, which causes the flow to break up into six separate eddies.

- Saturn's moon Enceladus has ice geysers that eject ice more than 500 kilometers off the surface. These geysers come out of a region of Enceladus where rifting occurs. The microscopic ice particles from the surface of Enceladus are the source of one of Saturn's rings.

- Saturn's moon Titan has perhaps the strangest surface of any of the planetary moons, with hydrocarbon lakes. These lakes are made of liquid methane and ethane, and the largest is 1200 kilometers across.

Life in the Solar System
- We have some evidence for the possibility of life elsewhere in the solar system, but no confirmations yet. For example, methane is emitted from some regions of Mars, and methane on Earth is often created by biologic activity. The saltwater oceans on Europa, Enceladus, and Ganymede might also support life.

- Keep in mind that we have looked only at the planets of one star. There are hundreds of billions of stars in just the Milky Way galaxy and hundreds of billions of galaxies in the universe. As of 2012, NASA scientists had identified more than 2000 planets around other stars that might be at the right distance from the star to support life.

- It might be impossible for us to ever reach those planets and see what geological wonders they have, but perhaps we can someday see pictures of them. Until then, there is no shortage of amazing geologic wonders on our own planet.

Suggested Reading

Hodge, *Higher Than Everest*.

Lang, *The Cambridge Guide to the Solar System*.

Questions to Consider

1. Venus is much more similar to Earth in size than Mars, but Mars is much more likely to possess life. Why is this?

2. How is it that we can find out about Earth's past by visiting the Moon?

Planetary Wonders—Out of This World
Lecture 36—Transcript

Hello. My name is Michael Wysession, and welcome to Lecture 36, the final lecture of our course on the Geologic Wonders of the World. I hope that over the span of the past 35 lectures I've given you the opportunity to gain an increased appreciation for the staggering diversity of geologic wonders, the curiosities, majestic sights, beautiful locations, bizarre structures, fascinating formations. I have to say that my command of the English language has really been put to the test here, coming up with enough different adjectives to describe everything that we have seen in this course.

There have been mountains, sinkholes, glaciers, canyons, fjords, volcanoes, geysers, caves, crystals in caves, lava lakes, salt lakes, acid lakes, over 200 different locations of geologic wonders of so many different types in almost 120 different countries. And yet, I still feel that so many places had to be left out, places that just as easily could have been featured here.

For example, I've come to the end of the course, yet, I never got a chance to talk about two of the most beautiful places that I have ever visited, the southwest coast of Ireland and the western islands of Scotland. As I said at the beginning, what makes a place beautiful to you is just so very subjective. And likewise, I'm sure that there are places that you have been to that you would nominate for this course, and I apologize for not including them.

However, my list of geologic wonders is not set in stone, so to speak, and I would love to see your nominations. For this final lecture, I was trying to figure out how to best summarize the places I have talked about, but in a new way, and I decided to go in a very different direction. I will show you some of the remarkable geologic wonders that have been discovered on other planetary bodies in the solar system. You and I are not in a position to visit any of these locations, though people at places like NASA have not given up the dream of one day getting us there. Maybe your children's children might do it.

However, using the remarkable robotic probes of NASA and other space agencies, we can now take virtual trips to many of these locations. And some of the things we have found are truly incredible.

While discussing these geologic marvels on other planets and their moons, this will also give me the opportunity to briefly return to some of the remarkable places here on Earth. To the first order, you will find that much of the geology we see on Earth, sand dunes and glaciers and volcanoes, occurs elsewhere in the solar system, sometimes commonly in different many places. But they provide some unusual twists, as you will see. And there are some features that are nothing like anything we have seen here on Earth. So let me show you some of the greatest geologic wonders out of this world, and let me start close to the Sun and then move outward across the solar system.

Let me start with Venus. We have seen remarkable lava flows around the Earth in places like Hawaii, where the lava can flow for many tens of kilometers across the ground. On Venus, these lava flows can go for many hundreds of kilometers. It's the same material as lava on Earth, it's basalt. There's just lots of it. And the surface is so hot—it's 460°C—that the lava just flows easily. Venus is covered with volcanoes, hundreds of thousands of them, maybe even millions of volcanoes. It's tough to figure this out because we can't see the surface. There are such thick clouds on Venus, by the way, they're not water, and these clouds are made of sulfur dioxide and sulfuric acid aerosols that light can't penetrate through, but when you combine satellite information, both on elevation and on the surface roughness of the ground, and that's how we can make these images.

The volcanoes here can be hundreds of kilometers wide, but they're actually remarkably flat, and I have to say these stunning images have actually been vertically exaggerated by a factor of over 20, so the lava flows are actually remarkably flat here. I've mentioned many places that have been described as being like hell, and Venus beats them all. On top of everything, sulfuric acid in the atmosphere and hot temperatures, the atmosphere is so thick it's actually crushing. It's equivalent to being a kilometer under water.

We've seen some places on Earth where the crust has been fractured into large numbers of parallel sets of faults that we called joints. On Venus there are whole expanses that are densely covered with these parallel fractures. They take many forms, some are parallel like this, some are curved, they're given names like tesserae, coronae, arachnids, which as you might guess, have a sort of spidery look to them. Venus' surface shows evidence of extreme stretching and compression. There is mantle convection under here. The whole rock of the mantle is flowing, but there are no tectonic plates, so the surface doesn't have anywhere to go, so it just gets repeatedly stretched and cracked and fractured.

Volcanism is not active on Venus right now. However, Venus does appear to undergo a process of catastrophic global resurfacing every 300- to 500-million years or so. This happens when the heat in the mantle builds up to a critical level. And the surface will just continue to get stretched and compressed until that next resurfacing event.

Next, I want to go to our nearest neighbor, the Moon. A few lectures ago, I showed the largest impact crater on Earth, the Vredefort Dome in South Africa, 300-kilometers across. This is peanuts by planetary standards. The largest crater in the solar system is on the Moon, and it's the South Pole-Aitkin Basin. It's eight times larger than the Vredefort Dome. In fact, it's over 2,500 kilometers in diameter and up to 13-kilometers deep. In fact, in some places, it has entirely removed the crust, and the mantle is exposed. Unfortunately, it's on the far side of the moon, so you can't ever see it directly. You need to use NASA images like this one.

This was due to a time of extreme violence in our solar system, known as the Late Heavy Bombardment period. And this is a time when it seems as if the planets Jupiter and Saturn drifted into a 2:1 resonant orbit. And what this resonance means is, for every two orbits that Jupiter does, Saturn makes one. So Jupiter is moving on the inside and Saturn is on the outside here, and that resonance causes their orbits to be stretched out; their elliptical orbits become very eccentric, and that destabilized the whole solar system, and things were flung outward. Neptune and Uranus were initially much closer in; they got flung to the farther parts of the solar system, and all sorts of large, icy objects, sort of Pluto-like objects, got thrown into the inner solar system. So not only is there the South Pole-Aitkin Basin, but the Hellas basin on Mars, which is 2,300-kilometers across. The Caloris Basin on Mercury is 1,600 kilometers. These are all about four-billion years ago. There might have been something similar on the Earth, but geology has since erased whatever might have occurred here.

There might be one impact crater even larger than any of these. This is the north pole sea on Mars, and this is a region that's 10,000-kilometers across. The whole crust is at a much lower elevation than the rest of the planet. In fact, this possible impact basin might also have been the location of a giant ocean at some point. Both of these are still very speculative.

Mars is a place of extreme geologic features. It sets the record for all kinds of things that we've seen on Earth. It has a lot of similarities to Earth. There are deserts, there are glaciers, polar icecaps; it even has long-term climate change, enormous volcanoes and canyons. Let me give you some examples. We visited the big island of Hawaii, and Hawaii itself is a volcano 100-kilometers wide that rises 10 kilometers off the seafloor. That's pretty impressive, right. If we go and look at Olympus Mons on Mars, which is the largest, single volcano in the solar system, we see something almost an order of magnitude larger.

The central caldera here sits 27-kilometers above the mean surface level; that's three times the elevation of Mount Everest above sea level. The top sits 22-kilometers above the surrounding plains here. The caldera complex alone is 85-kilometers long, and 60-kilometers wide, and 3-kilometers deep, in six different craters in there. And the whole volcano is surrounded by a steep escarpment that's up to 6-kilometers tall; that's a four-mile-high cliff. This is really remarkable. And yet, this volcano isn't even the widest volcano on Mars, there is one wider, Alba Patera, which is 1,600 kilometers across. That's just staggering, three-times larger in width than Olympus Mons; however, it's extremely flat. The total height is only about three kilometers. There's actually much less lava there that has flown out than at Olympus Mons.

Hawaii is also the location of the largest hotspot on Earth, which we looked at as well, but because the Pacific Plate that it sits on is moving rapidly westward, all that lava gets spread out over a long chain of islands and seamounds. Mars also has the largest hotspot, and that's a whole region that's shown by red—this is a topography map—that's known as the Tharsis Rise, or the Tharsis Bulge. It contains Olympus Mons, that's the small, little white-colored volcano in the upper left there, and several other large volcanoes. There's a trio there that are known as the Tharsis Mountains, and that's Arsia, Pavonis, and Ascraeus.

The whole area of the Tharsis Rise sits about seven-kilometers above the surrounding plains. It's up to 30 million square kilometers; that's a quarter of the total surface of Mars, so Mars is really lopsided with this big lump of rock that has stuck out on one side there. It's likely the result of a giant hotspot, but because Mars doesn't have plates, all the volcanism all occurs in just one area. It doesn't get spread out.

On Earth, we looked at giant canyons, and the largest of the canyons are the ones that cut through the Himalayas. They can be five-kilometers deep and extend for 240 kilometers. On Mars, we see the largest canyon in the solar system. That's this feature here, the Valles Marineris. This is about 4,000-kilometers long, 200-kilometers across in places, and over seven-kilometers deep. In fact, it stretches one-quarter of the way around Mars' equator. It would stretch across the entire United States, from New York to Los Angeles. We're not entirely sure how it forms; we think it has both tectonic and erosional origins. We think that it was initially formed during the bulging that made the Tharsis Rise, but because you often have clouds and rain as air goes up mountains, air flowing from the east here would go up the side of the Tharsis Rise. The rain would come out and this valley was carved out to a much greater level by rain flowing through. In fact, you can even see channels working their way all the way to that region of low elevation of the north pole sea on Mars.

Mars also has deserts, and it has some giant sand seas, and these are much farther to the north. One of the largest of these, the Olympia Undae is one of these giant ergs, these sand seas. It covers half a million square kilometers. It's the same size as Rub' al-Khali Desert in the Arabian Desert. The dunes here can be as much as a half a kilometer apart and rise up to 25 meters above the plain.

Also in dry areas of the Earth, you sometimes find an unusual feature called a Dust Devil, and this is a sort of a small mini-vortex. It king of looks like a toy tornado. On the surface of Mars, these things are constantly zipping across the surface, responsible for all of the dust in the atmosphere. For example, if you look at this time lapse picture taken, you can see some of these dust devils zipping across. It sucks the dust up and actually pumps it up into the atmosphere. That's why Mars' atmosphere has a pink color. They have also turned out to be the most fortunate geologic wonders as far the exploration of Mars has been concerned.

There are two Mars Rovers that have been operating on Mars since 2004, Spirit and Opportunity. It was initially expected that the rovers would stop working after just a few months, when the Martian dust would have settled and covered over their solar panels. These dust devils keep zipping across them, and they act like windshield wiper blades. They keep clearing off the solar panels, and the rovers were able to operate for years.

I talked about large dust storms in the Sahara and how sometimes dust storms could be so great that the dust could actually blow all the way over to the Americas. This is also not uncommon. You also get enormous dust storms in the Gobi desert in Mongolia and China that lift up enough dust in the atmosphere that it travels around the globe. You can measure it falling in the middle of the continental United States. Dust storms on Earth are a huge hazard in many different places, and you can find a lot of parts of the world that are devastated by these storms. They even shut down airports in Houston. But nothing on Earth compares with dust storms on Mars. These are the largest dust storms in the solar system. They cover the whole planet. What happens is a dust storm begins in one area and it heats the atmosphere, sunlight hits the dust, and that warms that part of the atmosphere. When you have temperature differences in the atmosphere that's what drives winds. So the strong winds pick up more dust, and the dust storm grows and grows, and after a couple of weeks it can cover the entire planet with dust. Once the whole planet is dusty, there are no more variations in temperature, and the winds die down and the dust slowly settles away. But this whole process can last for more than a month.

Mars also has the most complex icecaps in the solar system. Mars has a lot of ice. To begin with, the ground is filled with ice, like permafrost on Earth. And there are also huge glaciers all over that come down out of mountains and gullies, and these deposit rock at terminal moraines. We can see a lot of these places now around the surface where areas that look like they were flat soil, we now realize are ice covered with a layer of dust. So we don't see the ice, but if you could remove the dust, this is what you would actually see.

These are glaciers of ice flowing down across the surface of Mars. And we find these all over.

The most unusual ice surface on Mars is actually the giant icecaps at the north and south poles. And these take a variety of different features. The icecaps here two compounds. There's a thick, permanent water icecap and a thin, variable, carbon dioxide icecap, which is shown here. Carbon dioxide ice, you know as dry ice. These things are seasonal; they move back and forth between the two permanent icecaps, pole to pole, winter to summer, and back to winter again. About a quarter of the mass of the total atmosphere of Mars, which is mostly carbon dioxide, freezes out at the north pole during the winter there. And then it goes back into atmosphere during spring, and then freezes out at the south pole during the north pole summer, and this repeats over a Martian year.

The solid-water icecaps, and this is a computer generation of this, are fascinating. They're huge; this is larger than the size of Texas, and it has all of these repeating multiple layers that seem to be due to climate swings. Mars' axis of rotation is tilted 25 degrees, very similar to Earth, and that gives it seasons. But over time, that axis tilt changes from 0 degrees to more than 45 degrees, so there are huge, long-term changes in the strength of the seasons, and that causes this layering. But there are also these large canyons that are cut up into the ice glacier, and we have no understanding of why this occurs. A very similar thing happens at the south pole.

I showed you some of the results of catastrophic floods on Earth, such as the flooding of the Black Sea 7,500 years ago. And Mars shows evidence of a period, between four- to three-billion years ago when a vast amount of water carved away large portions of the land. And evidence is still seen all over the surface. For instance, these are strange features called teardrop mesas. You can see this one here is stretching behind a crater that's often a nucleation point for these. But it's clear that a vast amount of water flowed across in this direction, shaping away the ground, carving it away, and leaving these funny shapes.

You also get evidence of enormous outwash of water. This is a giant stream delta, kind of like the Okavango Delta, the delta to nowhere. This water came down, and it's just dumped here on the surface and, of course, it's all dry now. There was a lot of water for a very short period of time, and it might be that some of this water came from these Late Heavy Bombardment period impacts, ice-rich planetoids actually bringing water to the planet. Or it could be water vapor coming out of volcanoes like Olympus Mons during an extremely active volcanic phase. In any case, this happened a long time ago, and the water is long since gone.

Incidentally, on old surfaces, like Mars, you see all kinds of craters, and I think that the most unusual crater is something called the Pierced Crater. So this is an impactor that split in two just as it landed, making a double crater, and in fact, you can see the wings on either side where material got ejected out from the collision. The second place in my mind for unusual craters goes to a small asteroid named Vesta. It's called the Snowman craters. It's three craters in a row that look just like the outline of a snowman.

The asteroids are a belt of rocky, icy objects that revolve around the Sun, in between the orbits of Mars and Jupiter and Vesta, one of these asteroids also has the tallest non-volcanic mountain anywhere in the solar system. It's 21-kilometers high. It's about the same height as Olympus Mons on Mars. It's found within a giant impact basin. And you know, Vesta itself is only a little more than 500 kilometers in diameter, probably formed during the impact process as the central crater peak following that impact.

But actually, I give another asteroid, Kleopatra, the award for the most strange-looking object in the solar system. It looks like a giant dog bone 200-kilometers long spinning in space. This is a set of time-lapsed images, and you can see it rotating. It's a rubble heap. It formed from the loose connection of two smaller piles of rock and dust. And the best hypothesis is that when these two came, they hit each other obliquely and they still are spinning around each other, but the weak gravity keeps them from pulling together into a single, spherical object, and they just stay in this dog-bone shape, spinning over every five and a half hours. We got a very good look at what these strange rubble-heap asteroids look like when the Japanese Hyabusa probe landed on the asteroid Itokawa in 2005. And it also seems to be a binary asteroid, but it's remarkable to see these things up close. They really look like just a loose a conglomeration of crushed rock and dust.

If we go farther out into the solar system, we get to the gas giants, Jupiter and Saturn. And the recent Cassini satellite mission has sent back amazing images of a variety of remarkable geologic features. Two lectures ago I showed you the auroras, the northern and southern lights. These pale in comparison to the enormous auroras found near the poles of Jupiter and Saturn. These things can be hundreds of kilometers across, 250-kilometers above the planet. But they form by the same mechanism as auroras on Earth. They also have strange magnetic flux tubes that actually connect them with their moons; these little white areas there. Before the auroras here, these magnetic tubes contain particles that have erupted from the surface of its moon Io, and the other moons. And they flow down the flux tube to the surface of Jupiter here, adding to the colors of the aurora.

Earth gets some enormous typhoons and hurricanes, such as the ones I talked about devastating The Ganges Delta. But for storms, nothing compares to the atmospheres of Jupiter and Saturn. Their fast rotation—Jupiter rotates once every 10 hours, for Saturn it's 10.5 hours—causes the atmospheres to break up into many separate, different bands, and where these bands intersect there are enormous storm systems. The granddaddy of all of these, however, is the Great Red Spot. This is a 23,000-kilometer-long hurricane that's been there for at least 180 years. So it's not only the largest, it's the longest hurricane.

Venus might have the most volcanoes on it of any planetary object, but the title of most volcanic place in the universe is Jupiter's moon Io. Io has hundreds of volcanoes erupting at any given time, like the little eruption we see on the edge there. Some of them are basaltic lava; some of them are liquid sulfur. Io also has the hottest lavas anywhere in the solar system, over 1.500°C. The source for this is actually the tidal forces from Jupiter. It turns out that Io and two other large moons of Jupiter are trapped in a resonant orbit. Io, Europa, and Ganymede are locked in a 4:2:1 resonant orbit. So in other words, Io revolves around Jupiter four times for every two revolutions of Europa, or every one revolution of Ganymede. That stretches all of their orbits out to being very eccentric in their elliptical shape and keeps them warm internally. It generates the volcanism on Io. It also keeps Europa warm enough that it actually has a liquid saltwater ocean, maybe 150-kilometers thick, covered with a thin sheet of ice on top.

The ice crust of Europa is the most interesting surface in the solar system. Pieces seem to break up and drift around over time. It looks like a giant jigsaw puzzle. The liquid saltwater ocean means that it's a likely candidate for life, even if it might only be single-celled.

Sharing the same orbit as Jupiter are asteroids with the most unusual orbits called Greeks and Trojans. Each of these sets of objects is clustered together at unusually gravitationally stable locations that we call Lagrange Points. They're located 60 degrees ahead of Jupiter and 60 degrees behind Jupiter. These two groups of asteroids will continuously orbit the Sun in the same orbit as Jupiter, but they will never mingle with each other. It turns out that all of the large planets, Jupiter, Saturn, Uranus, and Neptune have rings, but the rings of Saturn are by far the largest.

To begin with, they look substantial but they're really very sparse, very thin layers of small particles of rock and ice. Saturn not only has the largest rings, though, they're much larger than we ever thought. In this picture with Cassini, taking a picture of the Sun right behind Saturn, you can see that the rings actually extend to great distances, a whole new ring was discovered in 2009, the Phoebe ring, just inside the orbit of Saturn's moon Phoebe. And it extends 200-times out beyond the radius of Saturn.

The Polar Regions on Earth are unusual with their icecaps, but for unusual features at the poles, nothing compares to Saturn. To begin with, at the south pole is a vortex—it's a giant eye of a hurricane. You can peer right down into the hurricane. This thing is 8,000-kilometers across—that's two-thirds the size of Earth. And it's ringed by towering clouds; the winds travel clockwise at speeds of more than 500 kilometers an hour.

Another strange feature is up at the north pole of Saturn. Here, the atmosphere flow takes the shape of a hexagon. This was a huge puzzle for scientists until some people modeled it as a particular jet stream of gas moving at different speeds than the surrounding atmosphere, and this causes the flow to break up into six separate little eddies, little swirls. If the differences in speed were different, this could have been an octagon, or a decagon, or some other shape.

Saturn also has some geologically fascinating moons. We looked previously at geysers on Earth, like at Yellowstone, some of which eject water almost 100 meters; that's a football field high. Saturn's moon, Enceladus, has ice geysers that eject ice more than 500 kilometers off the surface. The energy also comes from tides; Enceladus is in a 2:1 orbital resonance with the other moon Dione. In other words, Enceladus revolves two times around Saturn for each revolution of Dione. These geysers come out of the region at the far left of Enceladus where we actually find rifting occurring. It's the only other place in the solar system with active rifting. And it seems like warmer water from underneath is coming to the surface and then ejecting out. By the way, it's these tiny, microscopic ice particles ejected from Enceladus' surface that are the source of one of Saturn's rings, the enormous E ring.

However, it may be another one of Saturn's moons, Titan, its largest moon, that has the strangest surface of any of the planetary moons, and this is the last feature I will show you. These are the hydrocarbon lakes on Titan. These lakes are made of liquid methane and ethane. There are a couple of places on Earth where liquid hydrocarbons bubble up to the surface and exist as small lakes. The best known of these are the La Brea Tar Pits in Los Angeles. The largest are the La Brea Pitch Lake in Trinidad. Actually, it was discovered by Sir Walter Raleigh. But the hydrocarbon lakes on Titan are huge, and there are many of them. The largest, Kraken Mare, named after the mythical sea monster, the Kraken, is 1,200-kilometers across. That's much larger than all of the Great Lakes combined. In fact, it contains many hundreds times the total oil and natural gas reserves on Earth. Liquid methane and ethane rain out of the cold atmosphere of Titan. And this liquid flows through networks of stream channels into the hydrocarbon lakes. By the way, it's the only other place in the solar system other than Earth where we see active steams occurring.

Then we get to the topic of life. I would like to be able to say that there is some other place in the solar system where we will find life. We have a few possible candidates, but no confirmations yet. There's methane coming out of regions of Mars, methane on Earth is often created by biologic activity. There're saltwater oceans on the moons of Europa and Enceladus and Ganymede. NASA probes will continue to look for life, and when and if life on another planet is found, maybe in your lifetime, it will be the greatest scientific discovery of this century, or maybe ever.

It's fun to look at all the strange features within our solar system. In only a half hour I've really just scratched the surface here. There's so much more, but remember, these are the planets of just one star. There are hundreds of billions of stars in just our Milky Way galaxy alone. And there are hundreds of billions of galaxies in the universe, and that's a lot of stars and a lot of planets. We can't even conceive at this point of the other kinds of geologic features that might possibly exist on these planets, but we're trying.

The Kepler satellite has a telescope that is focused on one spot of the sky, near the constellation Cygnus. It's looking at 145,000 stars to try to identify any planets they might have. As of the year 2013, NASA scientists had identified over 2,000 planets around other stars that might be at the right distance from the star to be able to support life. We call that the habitable zone. Over 200 of these candidates are roughly Earth-sized. It would be a long time before we could send a probe to one of these and hear back, many thousands of years, at best. But humans have been around for over 200,000 years, so what's a few more. It wasn't so long ago that Homo sapiens had other intelligent species, like the Neanderthals, as neighbors. Maybe it will happen again.

It might be impossible for us to ever get to those planets and see what geologic wonders their planets have, but maybe they will send us pictures, and they'll tell us. Until then, there's no shortage of amazing geologic wonders down here on our own planet.

I urge you to get out and see them. I've tried my best here with words and pictures to describe some of the many different features of the Earth. But I hope you get a chance to get out, travel, and visit as many of them as you can. Thank you, goodbye.

Earth's Tectonic Plates

Pangaea

Bibliography

Arrieta, R. T. *From the Atacama to Makalu: A Journey to Extreme Environments on Earth and Beyond*. Panama City, FL: Coqui Press, 1997.

Besser, B. *Wyoming Road Trip by the Mile Marker*. Golden, CO: NightBlaze Books, 2010.

Bright, M., ed. *1001 Natural Wonders You Must See before You Die*. Chicago: Quintessence, 2009.

Brown, D., J. Brown, and A. Findlay. *501 Must-Visit Natural Wonders*. London: Bounty Books, 2009.

Chapple, J. *Yellowstone Treasures: The Traveler's Companion to the National Park*. Menlo Park, CA: Granite Peak Publications, 2009.

Chronic, H. *Roadside Geology of Utah*. Missoula, MT: Mountain Press Publishing Company, 1990.

Chronic, H., and L. M. Chronic. *Pages of Stone: Geology of the Grand Canyon and Plateau Country National Parks and Monuments*. Seattle, WA: Mountaineers Books, 2004.

Condie, K. C. *Plate Tectonics*. Oxford: Butterworth-Heinemann, 1997.

Conway-Morris, S. *The Crucible of Creation: The Burgess Shale and the Rise of Animals*. Oxford: Oxford University Press, 2000.

Cousteau, J.-Y. *Three Adventures: Galapagos, Titicaca, the Blue Holes*. Garden City, NJ: Doubleday, 1973.

Davidson, O. G. *The Enchanted Braid: Coming to Terms with Nature on the Coral Reef*. New York: Wiley, 1998.

Davis, N. *Aurora Watcher's Handbook*. Fairbanks, AK: University of Alaska Press, 1992.

Davis, W. *One River: Explorations and Discoveries in the Amazon Rain Forest*. New York: Simon and Schuster, 1997.

De Roy, T. *Galapagos: Islands Born of Fire*. Princeton: Princeton University Press, 2010.

De Roy, T., and M. Jones. *New Zealand: A Natural History*. Buffalo, NY: Firefly Books, 2006.

Dobbs, D. *Reef Madness: Charles Darwin, Alexander Agassiz, and the Meaning of Coral*. New York: Pantheon, 2005.

Fletcher, S. *Bottled Lightning: Superbatteries, Electric Cars, and the New Lithium Economy*. New York: Hill and Wang, 2011.

Francis, P., and C. Oppenheimer. *Volcanoes*. New York: Oxford University Press, 2003.

Friedrich, W. L. *Santorini: Volcano, Natural History, Mythology*. Aarhus, Denmark: Aarhus University Press, 2009.

Gould, S. J. *Wonderful Life*. New York: W. W. Norton and Company, 1990.

Gregory, K. *The Earth's Land Surface: Landforms and Processes in Geomorphology*. Los Angeles: Sage Publications Ltd., 2010.

Grubbs, B. *Grand Canyon Guide: Your Complete Guide to the Grand Canyon*. Flagstaff, AZ: Bright Angel Press, 2011.

Gunderson, M. *Devils Tower: Stories in Stone*. Glendo, WY: High Plains Press, 1988.

Hall, C., D. Pederson, and G. Bryson. *Northern Lights: The Science, Myth, and Wonder of Aurora Borealis*. Seattle: Sasquatch Books, 2001.

Hambrey, M. *Glaciers*. Cambridge: Cambridge University Press, 2004.

Haviv, I. *Trekking and Canyoning in the Jordanian Dead Sea Rift*. Hinckley, UK: Cordee Memory Map, 2000.

Hazlett, R. W., and D. W. Hyndman. *Roadside Geology of Hawai'i*. Missoula, MT: Mountain Press Publishing Company, 2003.

Hemming, J. *Tree of Rivers: The Story of the Amazon*. New York: Thames and Hudson, 2009.

Hodge, Paul. *Higher Than Everest: An Adventurer's Guide to the Solar System*. Cambridge: Cambridge University Press, 2001.

Johnson, D. *The Geology of Australia*. Cambridge: Cambridge University Press, 2009.

Johnson, M. *The Ultimate Desert Handbook: A Manual for Desert Hikers, Campers and Travelers*. Camden, ME: Ragged Mountain Press, 2003.

Johnson, R. G. *Secrets of the Ice Ages: The Role of the Mediterranean Sea in Climate Change*. Minnetonka, MN: Glenjay Pub., 2002.

Kaiser, J. *Grand Canyon: The Complete Guide: Grand Canyon National Park*. Destination Press, 2011.

Kerle, A. *Uluru: Kata Tjuta and Watarrka National Parks*. Sydney: University of New South Wales Press, 1995.

Krakauer, J., and D. Roberts. *Iceland: Land of the Sagas*. New York: Villard, 1998.

Lang, Kenneth R. *The Cambridge Guide to the Solar System*. Cambridge: Cambridge University Press, 2003.

Leslie, S. *Bay of Fundy: A Natural Portrait*. Toronto: Key Porter Books, 2007.

Bibliography

Lewis, G. *Waterfalls: Natural Wonders*. United Kingdom: Vine House Distribution, 2009.

Lillie, R. J. *Parks and Plates: The Geology of Our National Parks, Monuments, and Seashores*. New York: W. W. Norton & Company, 2005.

Lockwood, J. P., and R. W. Hazlett. *Volcanoes: Global Perspectives*. Hoboken, NJ: Wiley-Blackwell, 2010.

Mackley, G. *In Extreme Danger: Chasing and Filming Natural Disasters and Catastrophic Weather across the Globe*. Wellington, New Zealand: Awa Press, 2007.

Mark, K. *Meteorite Craters*. Tucson: University of Arizona Press, 1995.

Martin, M. *The Deserts of Africa*. New York: Random House, 2000.

McGonigal, D. *Antarctica: Secrets of the Southern Continent*. Buffalo, NY: Firefly Books, 2008.

McNassor, C. *Los Angeles's La Brea Tar Pits and Hancock Park*. Charleston, SC: Arcadia Publishing, 2011.

Molloy, J. *A FalconGuide to Mammoth Cave National Park: A Guide to Exploring the Caves, Trails, Roads, and Rivers*. Guilford, CT: Falcon Guide, 2006.

Myers, J. *Wondrous Cold: An Antarctic Journey*. Washington DC: Smithsonian Books, 2006.

Neev, D., and K. O. Emery. *The Destruction of Sodom, Gomorrah, and Jericho: Geological, Climatological, and Archaeological Background*. New York: Oxford University Press, 1995.

Norton, O. R., and L. Chitwood. *Field Guide to Meteors and Meteorites*. London: Springer, 2008.

O'Meara, D., and A. Manning. *Volcano: A Visual Guide*. Richmond Hill, Ontario: Firefly Books, 2008.

Oppenheimer, C. *Eruptions That Shook the World*. Cambridge: Cambridge University Press, 2011.

Oreskes, N. *Plate Tectonics: An Insider's History of the Modern Theory of the Earth*. Boulder, CO: Westview Press, 2003.

Palin, M. *Himalaya*. London: Phoenix Press, 2005.

Palmer, A. N. *Cave Geology*. Dayton, OH: Cave Books, 2007.

———. *Geological Guide to Mammoth Cave National Park*. Dayton, OH: Cave Books, 1979.

Palmerlee, D., S. Bao, G. Clark, C. McCarthy, A. Symington, and L. Vidgen. *Lonely Planet Argentina*. Oakland, CA: Lonely Planet, 2008.

Patrick, B., and N. Peat. *Wild Fiordland: Discovering the Natural History of a World Heritage Area*. Dunedin, New Zealand: University of Otago Press, 2006.

Pavitt, N. *Africa's Great Rift Valley*. New York: Harry N. Abrams, 2001.

Pilkey, O. H., and R. Young. *The Rising Sea*. Washington DC: Shearwater, 2009.

Rosi, M., P. Papale, L. Lupi, and M. Stoppato. *Volcanoes*. Buffalo, NY: Firefly Books, 2003.

Ryan, W., and W. Pitman. *Noah's Flood: The New Scientific Discoveries about the Event That Changed History*. New York: Simon & Schuster, 2000.

Sampsell, B. *A Traveler's Guide to the Geology of Egypt*. Cairo, Egypt: The American University in Cairo Press, 2003.

Scarth, A., and J.-C. Tanguy. *Volcanoes of Europe*. Oxford: Oxford University Press, 2001.

Sharp, R. P. *Living Ice: Understanding Glaciers and Glaciation*. Cambridge: Cambridge University Press, 1991.

Smith, R. B., and L. J. Siegel. *Windows into the Earth: The Geologic Story of Yellowstone and Grand Teton National Parks*. Oxford: Oxford University Press, 2000.

Stoneley, R. *Introduction to Petroleum Exploration for Non-Geologists*. Oxford: Oxford University Press, 1995.

Thordarson, T., and A. Hoskuldsson. *Iceland (Classic Geology in Europe)*. Edinburgh, UK: Dunedin Academic Press Ltd., 2002.

Thurston, H., and S. Homer. *Tidal Life: A Natural History of the Bay of Fundy*. Halifax, Nova Scotia: Nimbus Publishing, 1998.

Trojanow, I. *Along the Ganges*. London: Haus Publishing, 2011.

Veni, G., H. DuChene, N. C. Crawford, C. G. Groves, G. N. Huppert, E. H. Kastning, R. Olson, and B. J. Wheeler. *Living with Karst: A Fragile Foundation*. Alexandria, VA: American Geological Institute, 2001.

Vivian, C. *The Western Desert of Egypt*. Cairo, Egypt: The American University in Cairo Press, 2000.

Waltham, T. *Great Caves of the World*. Buffalo, NY: Firefly Books, 2008.

Wohl, E. *A World of Rivers: Environmental Change on Ten of the World's Great Rivers*. Chicago: University of Chicago Press, 2010.

Zurick, D. *Illustrated Atlas of the Himalaya*. Lexington: University Press of Kentucky, 2006.

Notes